N.G. Howe holds a PhD in history from the University of Nottingham. He has taught at the University of Winchester, University of Nottingham and Bath Spa University. His research focuses on the political history of the eighteenth and nineteenth centuries in Britain, especially their representation in caricature.

Statesmen in Caricature

The Great Rivalry of Fox and Pitt the Younger in the Age of the Political Cartoon

N.G. Howe

I.B. TAURIS

LONDON • NEW YORK • OXFORD • NEW DELHI • SYDNEY

I.B. TAURIS
Bloomsbury Publishing Plc
50 Bedford Square, London, WC1B 3DP, UK
1385 Broadway, New York, NY 10018, USA

BLOOMSBURY, I.B. TAURIS and the I.B. Tauris logo
are trademarks of Bloomsbury Publishing Plc

First published in Great Britain 2019
Paperback edition first published 2021

Copyright © N.G. Howe, 2019

A catalogue record for this book is available from the British Library.

A catalog record for this book is available from the Library of Congress.

ISBN: HB: 978-1-7883-1364-3
PB: 978-0-7556-2713-4
ePDF: 978-1-7867-3671-0
eBook: 978-1-7867-2665-0

Series: International Library of Political Studies, volume 56

Typeset by Integra Software Services Pvt. Ltd.

To find out more about our authors and books visit
www.bloomsbury.com and sign up for our newsletters.

In Memorium of Jonathan Peter Howe (22 August 1946–23 April 2017)
With everlasting love to my wife, Sharron.

Contents

List of Plates

Black and White Plates

1. James Gillray, *The Presentation – or – the Wise Men's Offering*, hand-coloured etching, 9 January 1796, 248 mm × 348 mm (NPG D12553) © National Portrait Gallery.

2. James Gillray, *Very Slippy-Weather*, hand-coloured etching, 10 February 1808, 260 mm × 204 mm (NPG D13700) © National Portrait Gallery.

3. Anon., *The Young Politician*, hand-coloured etching, 1771, 253 mm × 206 mm (LWL 771.00.00.07) © Courtesy of The Lewis Walpole Library, Yale University.

4. James Gillray, *Changing Places; – Alias; Fox Stinking the Badger Out of His Nest*, hand-coloured etching, 22 March 1782, 250 mm × 358 mm (NPG D12982) © National Portrait Gallery.

5. G.M. Woodward, *Reynard the Fox*, N.D., hand-coloured drawing, 285 mm × 224 mm (D5459/1/55) © Derbyshire County Record Office.

6. G.M. Woodward, *The Black Man of the People* (reverse), N.D., c. 1784, hand-coloured drawing (D5459/1/36) © Derbyshire County Record Office.

7. Isaac Cruikshank, *A Right Honourable alias A Sans Culotte*, hand-coloured etching, 20 December 1792, 375 mm × 323 mm (LWL 792.12.20.01.1+) © Courtesy of The Lewis Walpole Library, Yale University.

8. James Gillray, *Guy Vaux Discovered in His Attempt to Destroy the King and House of Lords – His Companions Attempting to Escape – NB – His Associates Were All Afterwards Executed*, hand-coloured etching, 14 May 1791, 354 mm × 500 mm (NPG D13072) © National Portrait Gallery.

9. James Gillray, *The Republican Attack*, hand-coloured etching, 1 November 1795, 250 mm × 352 mm (NPG D12543) © National Portrait Gallery.

10. James Gillray, *Jove in His Chair*, hand-coloured etching, 11 September 1782, 252 mm × 348 mm (NPG D12315) © National Portrait Gallery.

11. James Gillray, *Aside He Turn'd for Envy, yet with Jealous Leer Maligne, Eyed Them Askance*, etching, 12 December 1782, 211 mm × 249 mm (NPG D12302) © National Portrait Gallery.

Colour Plates

Acknowledgements

There are so many people who contribute to the birth of a book; specifically, I would like to thank the staff in the Department of Prints and Drawings at the British Museum, particularly Sheila O'Connell, for their help and patience over a number of visits to the study room and also to Andrew Peppit at the Chatsworth House Archive. Further thanks go to the staff at the University of Nottingham's Hallward Library and the University of Nottingham's Manuscripts and Special Collections, Keele University Library, British Library, National Portrait Gallery, Victoria and Albert Museum, Sheffield Archives (with acknowledgement to the Head of Leisure Services, Sheffield City Council and also to the fact 'that the Wentworth Woodhouse Muniments have been accepted in lieu of Inheritance Tax by HM Government and allocated to Sheffield City Council'), London Metropolitan Archives and Derbyshire Record Office. I am also indebted to the National Portrait Gallery, London; Derbyshire County Archives; Lewis Walpole Library, Yale University; Yale Centre for British Art and Getty for permission to include images of prints and drawings in their collections. Publication has been made possible by a grant from the Scouloudi Foundation in association with the Institute for Historical Research.

The advice and support I have received from the following people have, in short, been invaluable: Fintan Cullen, W.A. Speck, P.D.G. Thomas, H.T. Dickinson, Frank O'Gorman, Charles Watkins, Martyn J. Powell, Johanna Archbold, Richard A. Gaunt, Sheryllynne Haggerty, Gabriel Neher, Penny Pritchard, David Wilson and Carrie Stone. I am also indebted to the help I received from members of the PhD. Community in the School of History, you know who you are. Any mistakes which remain are of course my own.

And finally, I would like to thank my dear wife, Sharron, and son Jeremiah for their forbearance, patience, assistance with bibliography, support and love as I finally completed the task of writing and re-editing. Without their understanding and assistance, this book would never have been started let alone completed.

Introduction

The mid-eighteenth century witnessed an important phase in the development of the peculiarly English art form of caricature.[1] The period *c*. 1770 to *c*. 1780 saw a changing of the guard, with many of the old artists such as William Hogarth and Matthew Darly ceasing production and being replaced by a new generation of increasingly professional artists, which included the likes of James Gillray, Thomas Rowlandson and Isaac Cruikshank. This change of personnel coincided with change in style with a movement away from the old method of emblematic representations and text-laden images towards the sharper accentuation of the 'victim's' personal features.[2] E.E.C. Nicholson has, however, disputed this established view of a 'linear model of "development" … arguing [instead] for the tenacity of "emblematic" characteristics of both an iconographic and structural kind'.[3]

These changes had far-reaching consequences for the ways in which caricatures could be utilized, including increasing its potential as visual propaganda. Meanwhile, J.H. Plumb has argued that the lack of literary censorship in England, and the freedoms which that engendered, created a space for biting political satire, which was unique in Europe at the time. Observing that these prints, at times obscene or pornographic and invariably irreverent, were always biting in their social and political comment, they were exploited to great effect by a whole host of both professional and amateur artists, including Gillray, Bunbury, Rowlandson and Cruikshank.[4] Undoubtedly, freedom from censorship and a reluctance to prosecute both aided the development and success of caricature, with the relative freedom of the press in England also contributing to a wider knowledge of current affairs. In light of this, Hannah Barker has suggested that in London, even those towards the bottom of the social scale would have had some sort of contact with the press.[5] This in turn would have aided the 'reader's' understanding of the prints, as they would likely have heard of the stories being depicted. Shearer West has also commented on the fact that the prevalence of caricature helped reinforce the image of Britain as a land of freedom and libertarianism.[6]

Accordingly, many historians and art historians have dubbed the period following this transition as the 'Golden Age' of English satirical print. The stylistic changes became most apparent around 1780, while historians are broadly agreed that the 'Golden Age' ended around 1820,[7] eleven years after Gillray's last plate and nine years after the death of Isaac Cruikshank and the passing of the Regency Act, which helped to usher in a new age. Todd Porterfield has recently extended the 'Golden Age' to cover the period from 1750 to the 1830s.[8] This book will, however, take the 'Golden Age' to refer to the period *c*.1780 to 1820 and will examine how caricaturists represented individuals during this period, in particular Charles James Fox (1749–1806) and William Pitt the Younger (1759–1806), both of whose active political careers coincided neatly with the 'Golden Age' of English caricature. Fox had his first taste of office as a Junior Lord of the Admiralty (1770–2) before two brief spells as foreign secretary in 1783 and 1806. Meanwhile, Pitt the Younger became Chancellor of the Exchequer in 1782 until the fall of Lord Shelburne's administration in 1783 and was twice First Lord of the Treasury from 1783–1801 to 1804–6. With Fox and Pitt consistently finding themselves on opposite sides of the House of Commons over the course of their careers, much of which was spent at the head of a portion of the Whig Party, their careers and rivalry provide an ideal lens through which to study politicians and political leaders in caricature. Indeed, Michael J. Turner has identified the late eighteenth century as a 'time when the press was expanding rapidly, and when demand for information about public men and affairs reached unprecedented levels, journalists and caricaturists enjoyed a heyday'.[9] It is, therefore, unsurprising that Charles James Fox heads Nicholas K. Robinson's list of most caricatured individuals for the period 1778 to 1797, featuring in a staggering 821 prints. His nemesis, William Pitt the Younger, came next with 457 prints and George III not far behind on 441.[10] The fact that the top two places were occupied by the leading government and opposition figures in the House of Commons is striking and gives credence to the idea that the period saw the emergence of a modern-style party leader, in terms of their visual representation, and as such was a significant development in caricaturing the individual.

Charles James Fox

Charles James Fox was one of the most able and colourful politicians of his generation. His dissolute and rakish lifestyle was a gift to the caricaturists, as were his distinctive physical features. In spite of his long stay in opposition, Fox emerged from the late eighteenth century as the most popular subject for satirical prints.

Charles James Fox was the second surviving son of Henry Fox, later first Baron Holland. Shortly after Charles's birth, his father demonstrated his perceptiveness, writing to his brother, Stephen Fox-Strangways, first Earl of Ilchester, with his usual candour, 'It's incredible how like a monkey he looked before he was dressed.'[11] This reference to his looking like a monkey is interesting, especially since caricaturists made great play of his hirsuteness, and he was also often portrayed in animal form in satirical prints.

Fox received a classical education attending Monsieur Pampellone's school at Wandsworth, followed by Eton and Oxford before embarking upon his Grand Tour. During his time at Eton he was to make some lifelong friends, including Frederick Howard, fifth Earl of Carlisle, and William Fitzwilliam, second Earl Fitzwilliam, both of whom were to play prominent roles in his political career, while his cousins – William Fitzgerald, the future second Duke of Leinster, and Henry Thomas Fox-Strangways, the future second Earl of Ilchester – were also contemporaries at Eton.

He first entered Parliament for Midhurst, Sussex, in 1768, prior to his coming of age, before transferring to Malmesbury in 1774 and Westminster in 1780. He was to remain Member of Parliament (MP) for Westminster until his death in 1806, save for a brief period (April 1784 to March 1785) when he represented Tain Burghs, following the scrutiny of the 1784 Westminster Poll. In spite of being one of the most gifted orators of his generation,[12] the young Fox was to hold office briefly only on five occasions. Shortly after coming of age, in February 1770, he was appointed to the Admiralty Board by Lord North. His initial ministerial career was short-lived, however, resigning in a fit of pique two years later following plans to introduce the Royal Marriages Act. Fox saw this bill as an attack on his family, owing to the fact that in 1742 his father, while still a commoner, had married Lady Caroline Lennox, a distant relation of George III.[13] In December 1772, North appointed Fox to the Treasury Board; however, the two men fell out over how to deal with the printers.[14] On 24 February 1774, Fox was presented with a note from Lord North stating: 'His majesty has thought proper to order a new commission of the treasury to be made out, in which I do not see your name.'[15] His dismissal from the government marked the start of a transitional period in Fox's career. This period was contributed to by the deaths of his father and mother on 1 and 24 July 1774, respectively, and by that of his elder brother Stephen in November 1774. The death of his father can be seen as particularly significant as it allowed the young Fox to expand his horizons and to forge his own career.[16] In the wake of this release from filial obligations, which had hitherto governed his politics, he was successfully courted by the Rockingham Whigs through Edmund Burke. Fox was to remain in opposition for the remainder of his career, save for three short periods as foreign secretary, during the short-lived Rockingham administration (March to July 1782), the Fox–North Coalition (March to December 1783) and in the 'Ministry of All the Talents' from January 1806 until his death in September 1806.

Throughout his political career, Fox was to remain a controversial figure, with civil and religious liberties as cardinal tenets of his political creed.[17] As a friend of the Prince of Wales, the future George IV, he was blamed by George III for encouraging his eldest son's irresponsible and debauched behaviour, as well as denying the Prince's marriage to Maria Fitzherbert in Parliament and picking up some of the Prince's old mistresses.[18] As a gambler he was unlucky, frequently losing vast sums in games of chance. This poor luck was to follow him into the world of politics with many of his political gambles failing to pay off. J.H. Plumb has argued that Fox, by his loyal friendship to the Prince of Wales, 'gambled away most of his political credit'.[19] In spite of his perceived recklessness, in both his public and private life – never being far from scandal – he achieved a huge personal following and inspired tremendous loyalty in those around him,[20] something which was reflected by his friends' numerous efforts to bail him out of his financial difficulties.

William Pitt the Younger

William Pitt the Younger, in common with Charles James Fox, was a second son and according to his principal biographer, John Ehrman, soon became his father's favourite, sharing many of the same pleasures: riding, farming and landscape gardening.[21] In common with his father, Pitt the Younger was considered a solitary figure in Parliament, striving to be free and independent of faction.[22] So alike were the two men in many ways that following his maiden speech to the House of Commons (26 February 1781), Edmund Burke is reputed to have remarked: 'He is not a chip off the old block: he is the old block itself!'[23] Of Pitt's oratorical talent, it is interesting to note the observance of one of the leading parliamentary orators of the present generation, William Hague, who informs us that Fox and Pitt the Younger had contrasting styles of oratory, with Fox making use of his audience's emotions, returning time and again to his main point, while Pitt made tremendous use of logic, constructing an argument, removing emotion from the equation and leaving his audience with little intellectual room to disagree with his conclusions.[24]

Pitt was a delicate child and was educated at home, in part owing to his health and in part due to his father's contempt for Eton. He went up to Cambridge in 1773, aged just fourteen, and remained there until 1779. Owing to his perilous financial state (his allowance was a mere £300 p.a.), Pitt trained for the Bar and pursued a career as a barrister-at-law. He first entered Parliament at the 1781 Appleby by-election, and his parliamentary career began with an air of expectation, owing to the fact that he was the son of Chatham. His name would have ensured him a warm welcome in the House of Commons and there he was able to count on many of his father's friendships.[25] Pitt, in accordance with his father's followers, took his lead from Lord Shelburne, and it was he who gave Pitt his first taste of office, appointing him Chancellor of the Exchequer in 1782, unusually without becoming leader in the Commons, but he did obtain a seat in Cabinet. This need not, however, have been the case as he was sounded out about taking a junior post in the second Rockingham administration earlier in the year, but he refused on the grounds that he would not accept a subordinate position.[26] Interestingly, it was Rockingham who gave Fox his first major office as foreign secretary, and at this time Fox had marked Pitt down as a rival, writing on 11 May 1782 that in public Pitt was obliging and complimentary, however, and on occasion had taken a line that had alarmed him. This led Fox to believe that Pitt would prove to be a man of the old system, which had been revived under Lord Shelburne and lend him his support.[27]

Things could have played out very differently when Pitt approached Fox on 11 February 1783; Pitt approached Fox asking him on what terms he might consider joining the government. Fox replied the removal of Lord Shelburne, at which point Pitt responded, 'Then we need discuss the matter no further … I did not come here to betray Lord Shelburne.'[28] Pitt remained in office until the administration was defeated over the Peace Preliminaries (following the American War of Independence) in February 1783. Following the fall of Shelburne, Pitt was sounded out about forming an administration in his own right, but politely refused on the grounds that 'nothing less than a moral certainty of a majority in the House of Commons could make him undertake the task'.[29] The Fox–North Coalition came in until its removal following a backstairs intrigue, in December 1783, at which point Pitt finally relented and agreed to form a minority administration, which was reliant upon the confidence of the

Crown not the Commons. This led to his government being dubbed the 'Mince Pie Administration' by the opposition, as they predicted that it would fall by Christmas. Pitt clung onto power and slowly but surely support for the old Fox–North Coalition ebbed away, and Pitt's position became stronger. He remained MP for Appleby until 1784, when he was elected as one of the members for Cambridge University, a constituency he continued to represent until his death.

William Pitt the Younger was a skilled political operator and was quick to see the propaganda potential of satirical prints, which prompted Michael J. Turner to argue that:

> Pitt saw that good publicity and visual representations would bolster his image as patriot and reformer. Printed material had growing influence over the public mind, and for himself and his regime Pitt saw the need to manipulate the media as best he could.[30]

Accordingly, he commissioned caricatures to support his position and undermine his opponents at a number of points, including the 1788 Westminster by-election where Gillray was hired, producing prints in favour of Pitt's candidate, Admiral Hood, following them up a few days later with prints opposing him. This did not prevent Pitt from later recognizing James Gillray's services to the government with a pension in 1797.[31] Gillray was not, however, the first caricaturist to be rewarded by Pitt; he had also rewarded James Sayers with the sinecure of Marshall of the Court of Exchequer, following his support for George III's campaign against the Fox–North Coalition.[32]

In common with Charles James Fox, Pitt the Younger, in addition to being one of the leading parliamentary orators of his generation, was a heavy drinker, something that was picked up on by caricaturists.[33] In spite of being a 'six-bottle man' Pitt was not considered as clubbable as Fox and his associates. Fox and Pitt's heavy drinking should, however, be considered within its eighteenth-century context, where 'three-bottle men were accounted little better than milksops'.[34] Michael J. Turner also noted that 'during the 1790s some negative comment surfaced about Pitt's increasing consumption of alcohol, but characterizations of his main political opponent, the dissolute Fox, were usually more condemnatory'.[35] This contrast between the two men in which Pitt, no matter what he did, always appeared to come out better than Fox was to be a constant theme of their relationship in caricature. Another area of similarity was Pitt and Fox developing their own collections of caricature, with Pitt soon beginning to display caricatures of himself on the walls of Holwood House, which he purchased in 1785, while Fox was also an avid collector, producing volumes to show visitors to St. Ann's Hill.[36]

The period covering the parliamentary careers of Charles James Fox and William Pitt the Younger was not an uneventful one. Pitt's first administration successfully navigated the challenges of Regency Crisis (1788–9) and the French Revolution (1789), resigning in 1801 over George III's refusal to countenance Catholic Emancipation, which Pitt saw as a key partner to Anglo-Irish Union (1801). Pitt's absence from office was not to be long-lived, and he returned in 1804 following a renewal of hostilities after the failure of the Treaty of Amiens (1802–3) to secure a lasting peace. Pitt's health slowly deteriorated and he died in office in January 1806. Pitt's legacy has seen him as a safe pair of hands in times of crisis and an incredibly hard worker, who eschewed much of the clubbable nature of late eighteenth-century sociability. He had an eye for like-minded individuals and developed a circle of keen and talented young acolytes, including George Canning and Robert Jenkinson, who after his death sought to continue the 'Pittite System of Government'.

'Modern party leader'

The term 'modern party leader' is synonymous with the idea of the cult of personality and the two have developed side by side. With this move towards a cult of the personality, caricaturists were quick to seize the opportunity this gave them and their art form in shaping and developing the next generation of political leaders. Accordingly, one might expect to find the 'modern party leader' at the forefront of any visual comment upon political affairs. In labelling Fox and Pitt 'modern party leaders', this book is not suggesting that the followers of Charles James Fox and Pitt the Younger resembled a modern political party. Indeed, in May 1788 a computation of the House of Commons suggested that only fifty-two members were attached to Pitt himself.[37] Party was an anathema to many eighteenth-century politicians, who had a loathing of party and faction. Indeed, both Fox and Pitt would have described themselves politically as Whigs, while the reality of 'party' up until the French Revolution of 1789 was of a loose network, held together by filial loyalties, patronage and electoral interests. This all changed during the 1790s, as the French Revolution polarized opinion and divided the political nation along ideological lines for the first time since the demise of the Jacobite cause.[38] For much of the eighteenth century, patronage, or the promise of political office, often played a part in determining the career politician's allegiance. In the context of this book, the term 'modern party leader' is used to indicate an individual whose political power base was not reliant upon electoral interest or filial piety and was instead predominantly down to their personality.

This book will investigate the role of political caricature in the construction of the image and definition of the 'modern party leader' while exploring more widely how politicians were represented in caricature during the 'Golden Age' of the English satirical print. Many of the necessary technical developments surrounding the production of caricature were taking hold during the early career of Charles James Fox and William Pitt the Younger and by the beginning of their rivalry in 1783–4, much of the necessary groundwork had been laid. The caricaturists were quick to seize the opportunity that developments within their genre and the printing industry more widely had provided them. They produced an abundance of etchings, featuring Pitt and Fox, and this book seeks to consider the part this reporting played not only in fuelling their rivalry but also upon the growing interest in the cult of the personality. The major advantage that caricature held over other media was not only that it was relatively quick to produce but also that it readily distilled events into an accessible visual message making it easy to distinguish the heroes from the villains. Accordingly, having moved away from emblematic representation to depicting an individual's facial features during the 'Golden Age', caricature was ready to feed on the cult of personality and help define the 'modern party leader'.

Fox and Pitt the Younger are the perfect case study for examining the representation of an individual in caricature. They spent much of their career in the limelight and were frequently 'victims' of the caricaturist's etching needle. In the case of Fox, one would be forgiven for presuming that a man who was constantly pilloried in satirical prints for his political views and at times supposed unpatriotic actions would struggle to maintain a following in Parliament. Fox, however, retained his following in Parliament 'not because they [his supporters] necessarily agreed with his views, but because they found his character utterly compelling'.[39]

While Pitt had the government's patronage network to fall back on as well as the secret service fund and his own filial networks and those of his close colleagues, Fox had none of the above at his disposal for much of his career. This has led historians such as Richard E. Willis to argue that Fox's personality was key to an opposition group developing around him, with repeated defeats, in the most part, failing to decrease his support.[40] This ability to command a personal following, without the ability to offer seats or place, is remarkable and marks Fox out as a true party leader, as well as emphasizing the growing importance of the cult of the personality.

Why study caricature?

Political caricature has often been used to illustrate biographies of eighteenth-century politicians and surveys of eighteenth-century politics; however, the analysis of the prints is frequently superficial. The Chadwyck-Healey Series, edited by Michael Duffy in 1986,[41] was the first major series of studies into eighteenth-century satirical prints since the production of the *British Museum Catalogue* and marks the height of the 'first renaissance' in the study of Georgian satirical prints. In his review of the series, Roy Porter considered the state of caricature scholarship lamenting:

> Would there were schools of 'visual history' paralleling 'oral history'! For if historians have become more sensitive to what people said against what they read, we still have a long way to go in 'seeing' what people saw and in interpreting the significance of visual signs.[42]

From this it is clear that he felt that there was a lot more work to be done in moving the study of visual culture from the peripheries of historical enquiry to the centre. However, it was not all doom and gloom; Porter found that much of the scholarship was 'absorbed in internal analysis of iconography and influence, [and that] they [art historians] have commonly forgotten to ask who actually saw these sketches or sculptures, and what impact they had upon their consumers'.[43] Recent historiographical work by E.E.C. Nicholson has attempted to revive interest on emblems, revising the view that their use was in decline during the 'Golden Age' of the English satirical print.[44] Questions of who saw the prints and their impact upon their consumers remain relatively un-mined seams of historical research and have not received much scholarly attention since Nicholson's 1996 *History* article 'Consumers and spectators: The public of the political print in eighteenth-century England'.[45] In this article, Nicholson poses questions such as what was the market for political prints? Who were the spectators? Is this the same for the provinces? At the same time, she examined a much broader time frame, *c.*1760–1832, and called for increased scholarly consideration of the field. Her general thesis was that the market for satirical prints was necessarily limited by the relatively low number of impressions that could be achieved from a plate,[46] although she presented a case for them reaching the provinces.[47] Nicholson also argues that plebeian access was limited due to financial constraints, while also casting doubt on the usefulness of print-shop window scenes in assessing exposure to prints through window displays.[48]

A 'second renaissance' in the study of eighteenth-century satirical prints was centred around the publication of the seminal text by Diana Donald, *The Age of Caricature: Satirical Prints in the Age of George III*, in 1996. This book followed on from Herbert M. Atherton's work on political satire in the age of Hogarth, taking the story up to the 1819 Peterloo Massacre. Unlike Atherton, Donald examined social as well as political prints. This book prompted a renewed interest in Georgian satirical prints with a number of exhibitions being held and books being published during the late 1990s and early 2000s. Tamara Hunt's *Defining John Bull: Political Caricature and National Identity in Late Georgian England*, published in 2003, was the first real engagement by an historian, as opposed to an art historian. Hunt not only examined political caricatures within their proper context – eighteenth-century politics, polite society and art – but also made them the central source and theme. *Defining John Bull* touched the boundary of caricature biography, examining the construction of Britishness through the medium of caricature, skilfully blending in-depth analysis of the prints within her contextual framework. This 'second renaissance' also saw a move towards the study of prominent individuals through the medium of caricature and include biographies of George III, George IV and Edmund Burke. This 'second renaissance' highlighted the validity of this approach and revealed the prominent position of Charles James Fox and William Pitt the Younger within the prints.[49] Roy Porter's suggestion that Fox was a caricaturist's dream come true, affording 'endless Aesopian possibilities for animal physiognomy',[50] gives further emphasis to this point. Also, given the clear contrast between Fox and Pitt the Younger in terms of policies, physiognomy and looks, it is apparent that they provide a useful lens through which to develop and expand our understanding of political caricature during its 'Golden Age'. As such, it is timely for a study analysing the role of caricature within eighteenth-century politics.

John Brewer has commented on the problems facing historians, who attempt to utilize Georgian satirical prints, arguing that the success of eighteenth-century caricature stemmed from its visual vocabulary and convention, which prevents historians from viewing them through eighteenth-century eyes and fully appreciating their meaning to contemporary audiences unless they fully understand the visual conventions of the day.[51] In addition to the ephemeral nature of the material, historians are also confronted with the fact that in all probability many more designs were produced than have survived. E.E.C. Nicholson has suggested that the *British Museum Catalogue of Prints and Drawings (BM Catalogue)* accounts for a mere 10 per cent of known prints in the British Museum collections.[52] Furthermore, no one archive holds samples of all known prints and drawings for the period, although the British Museum collection is one of the most complete.

The multilayered, multifaceted and ephemeral nature of the source should not, however, be an excuse for their being ignored or for poor scholarship of them. Instead, what is required is an interdisciplinary approach and one that seeks to understand the very nature of them, from how, when and by whom they were made and sold to the tropes and devices used by the artists to get their message across.

Artists, printsellers and the world of caricature

Caricaturists

This new wave of writing on satirical prints from the late 1990s onwards included a renewed interest in the caricaturists themselves, with Richard Newton and James Gillray receiving most attention. With the exception of Draper Hill's 1965 biography of Gillray, many of the studies of individual caricaturists have been in the form of a catalogue, with only a brief biographical sketch of the caricaturist by way of introduction.[53] Work on caricaturists and printsellers has been limited by the lack of surviving archival material, highlighted by the fact that most do not have an entry in the National Register of Archives, although this does not rule out the possibility of papers surviving in private hands. Generally, little is known about the early lives of late eighteenth-century caricaturists. This is in part due to the perceived lowliness of the genre within academic art, which did not provoke contemporary biographies of them or inspire nineteenth-century historians to study them. Of the main caricaturists, only Thomas Rowlandson and James Gillray attended the Royal Academy School. Isaac Cruikshank is the only other known caricaturist to have undertaken formal artistic tuition. The numerous biblical, classical and literary references to the work of Homer, Ovid, Milton and Shakespeare point conclusively to the caricaturists enjoying a reasonable level of literacy and education.[54]

In addition to government-funded plates, from time to time, caricaturists, including Isaac Cruikshank and James Gillray, would work up ideas sent to them or their publisher from amateur artists.[55] Save for a few instances, such as Gillray and the 1788 Westminster Election, where there is a record of government reward or patronage, the lack of correspondence makes it impossible to ascertain, in most cases, whether a particular plate was the caricaturists' own design or a commission. On occasions James Gillray does credit outside influences, signing J. Gillray *Fect.*, indicating that he has merely engraved a design sent to him. A good example of this is *The Magnanimous Minister Chastising Prussian-Perfidy*.[56] The design for this print was sent to him via a letter addressed to his publisher, Hannah Humphrey.[57] The letter contains an outline sketch of what the print might look like and some bullet point notes explaining the sketch. The author suggests the title 'The Magnanimous Minister Blowing Hot and Cold'. Gillray appears to have rejected this suggestion and made one or two alterations of his own, mainly to the text. In essence, the print and sketch are the same and they both cite the *Morning Chronicle* on 28 April 1806, in which under 'London News' both the 'Ministry of All the Talents' and Fox received a favourable write-up.[58] In November 1803, 'G.G.S.' wrote to Gillray with a suggestion for a print depicting Fox as a member of the Chertsey Volunteers before going on to state that 'you have done me the honour sometimes to illustrate my ideas'.[59] It is unclear whether this suggestion was etched as there is no record in the *BM Catalogue*.

The lack of surviving papers renders it almost impossible to ascertain the political sympathies of the caricaturists. E.A. Smith and L.H. Cust have suggested that unlike most contemporary caricaturists, Sayers did not side with the opposition against the government.[60] This assertion that Sayers, unlike the other caricaturists, tended to favour the government is not borne out by prints featuring Charles James Fox.[61] Indeed, Fox was attacked, not only in the overwhelming number of prints of him by Sayers but also in those produced by the majority of caricaturists across his career, most of which was spent in opposition. The East India Bill crisis of 1773–4 established Sayers as a caricaturist of note, with his print of Charles James Fox as Carlo Khan becoming one of the enduring images of the crisis. It is also unclear to what extent caricaturists produced work that they believed would sell, regardless of their politics. Robert L. Patten has argued that Cruikshank's politics were shaped by 'his dealers and customers' during the period of the French Revolution when he attacked anyone suspected of harbouring radical tendencies.[62] The French Revolution proved to be an event that not only polarized popular opinion but also had an impact on caricaturists, who had to tread carefully in the face of Pitt the Younger's repressive legislation. It provided a backdrop for numerous memorable prints and brought the character of John Bull to the fore as an emblem for Britons and as the long-suffering partner of Charles James Fox and William Pitt the Younger in numerous prints during the 1790s.

Artistic output

Many caricaturists produced work for numerous publishers over the course of their careers, with some publishing elements of their work themselves. While there were a number of big names within the genre,[63] large numbers of prints were unsigned by the caricaturists and there were a great many occasional and amateur artists producing prints throughout the period.

During the period 1770 to 1806, sixty-five artists are known to have produced caricatures containing a depiction of either Charles James Fox or William Pitt the Younger, along with in excess of 400 unattributed images (see Table 1). Of these sixty-five, only eleven of them produced ten or more images that went into double figures with either politician. One could reasonably conclude, therefore, that these eleven caricaturists were the principal producers of political prints during the period 1770 to 1806. An important caveat to take

Table 1 Political Caricaturists 1770–1806

Artist	Prints of Fox	Prints of Pitt	Artist	Prints of Fox	Prints of Pitt
Adam	1	1	J.H.	1	0
Jean Adam	1	1	William Hanlon	0	1
Anonymous	412	260	Nicholaus Heideloff	1	0
William Austin	2	0	William Holland	1	1
J.B.	0	1	James Hook	2	1
Joshua Kirby Baldrey	3	0	John Kay	1	0
Jean Louis Argaud de Barges	0	1	S. Knight	1	1
J. Barrow	11	2	Louis Lecoeur	0	1
J.S. Barth	1	0	W.M.	1	1
Francesco Bartolozzi	2	0	W. Mansell	2	1
John Bewick	2	1	Richard Newton	21	31
Bland	1	0	John Nixon	2	1
John Boyne	22	1	O'Brien	1	0
James Bretherton	1	0	W. O'Keeffe	2	7

Table 1 (*Continued*)

Artist	Prints of Fox	Prints of Pitt	Artist	Prints of Fox	Prints of Pitt
William Henry Bunbury	2	0	W.G. Phillips	1	0
Frederick George Byron	4	3	J. Porter	1	0
William Paulet Carey	7	1	T. Prattent	1	0
John Cawse	3	6	Johann Heinrich Ramberg	1	0
John Chapman	1	0	Piercy Roberts	4	3
Thomas Colley	10	1	Thomas Rowlandson	62	34
Samuel Collings	11	9	Louis Charles Ruotte the Elder	0	1
J. Cooke	1	0	Paul Sandby	1	1
Richard Cosway	1	0	F. Sansom	1	1
Isaac Cruikshank	78	68	James Sayers	55	8
M. Darley	2	0	John Raphael Smith	1	0
De Mailly	0	1	John Thomas Smith	3	0
William Dent	113	79	George Towneley Stubbs	2	0
Robert Dighton	8	5	G. Sauley	1	0
Frédéric Dubois	0	1	Edward Topham	2	0
Espirit Antione Gibelin	0	1.	George, 1st Marquess Townshend	1	0
James Gillray	257	144	Charles Williams	53	51
(N.) C. Goodnight	2	0	G.M. Woodward	7	1
Eudaimon Grollmann	0	1			

into account, however, is the fact that not only is this assumption arrived at through examining a sample,[64] it also favours caricaturists active across the middle period of the career of Charles James Fox and William Pitt the Younger, *c*.1780 to *c*.1800.

During the late eighteenth century, caricaturists would often work freelance, producing prints for a number of publishers each year. Notable exceptions to this are James Gillray, who worked exclusively for S.W. Fores during the mid-1780s and Hannah Humphreys from September 1791, with the exception of a few prints that he published himself.[65] Richard Newton is another exception, working exclusively for William Holland during his short career, publishing under his own name from Holland's premises while Holland was in prison in 1793 for selling one of Thomas Paine's pamphlets.[66] However, Newton's work, unlike that of other leading political caricaturists, did not become well known in his lifetime, owing to low circulation figures.[67] Isaac Cruikshank became the founder of a dynasty with his sons (Isaac) Robert, Robert and more famously George all becoming caricaturists themselves. Both he and Thomas Rowlandson also built up longstanding relationships with a particular publisher, while caricaturists such as Robert Dighton and William Dent published a number of their own prints as well as submitting work to other publishers.

Printsellers

The historiography of eighteenth-century London printsellers has tended to highlight a few principal publishers, including Matthew and Mary Darly renowned for their 'Macaroni Prints', Carrington Bowles, S.W. Fores, William Holland and the three Humphreys, William, Hannah and George. Again, the lack of surviving papers has limited the amount of biographical work that has been undertaken. Of the principal printsellers, only Fores and William Humphrey have their own entry in the *Oxford Dictionary of National Biography*, while Hannah Humphrey has to make do with a subsection in her brother's entry.[68] The entry for William Humphrey lists a cache of letters in the British Library as its only archival source,[69] while for S.W. Fores, the only archival reference is to aspects of his correspondence with James Gillray, held in New York Public Library. Anthony Griffiths's work on the catalogues of British print publishers *c*.1650 to 1830 reveals that of the publishers who produced caricatures, catalogues survive only for Rudolph Ackermann, Carrington Bowles and James Bretherton, indicating poor survival rates.[70] These catalogues are not in complete runs nor are they exclusively for satirical prints. In addition to publishers carrying single-sheet prints, a number of magazines also published prints, at times reproducing previously published prints and at others prints specifically designed for them. There is great difficulty in ascertaining which category many of these magazine prints fit into as only the prints reproduced in *London und Paris* have a distinct entry in the *BM Catalogue*. Prints in the British Museum collection from some older publications from the 1770s, such as *The Ramblers Magazine* and *Oxford Magazine*, having been removed from their magazines were labelled with the magazine title, but in some cases it is almost impossible to tell if a print came from a magazine. This problem was compounded by the fact that images accompanying magazines were printed separately and either inserted loosely into the magazine or sent to be bound-in prior to sale.[71]

Additional information can at times be gleaned from the 'Law Intelligence' section of newspapers, when artists or publishers had been hauled up in front of the bench. From one such report it appears that S.W. Fores was a stationer in addition to selling satirical prints and that he appeared before William Addington Esq., a public-office magistrate at Bow Street, on 22 January 1796, 'charged with selling and exposing for sale a certain burlesque caricature print, alluding to the introduction of the infant Princess to the Prince of Wales and wherein several political characters [including Fox and Sheridan] are introduced'. Fores was bailed and ordered to answer the charge at the ensuing session.[72] James Gillray also found himself before the sitting magistrate at the Public Office, Bow Street, for his part in the sale of *The Wise Men's Offering* (Plate 1).[73] Gillray was also admitted to bail, but there is no information on where and when he was due to answer the charge.[74]

Political prints were published by a great many individuals during the 'Golden Age' of the English satirical print. A survey of the prints published between 1770 and 1806 containing a representation of Charles James Fox or William Pitt the Younger reveals that around 160 printsellers published some 1,292 prints between them at an average of 8.08 prints per printseller.[75] Of these printsellers, twenty-two published eight or more prints,[76] and sixteen printsellers published ten or more[77] and three – S.W. Fores, Hannah Humphrey and William Holland – publishing over 100. Within this group of above-average publishers, there were three caricaturists who published with other publishers as well as publishing their own work: William Dent, Richard Newton and Robert Dighton. Of the big names in eighteenth-century print publishing, William and Mary Darly, James Bretherton and Rudolph Ackermann are conspicuous by their absence from this list. The absence of the Darlys is not surprising for Matthew Darly is thought to have died in 1778 and his wife in 1781. The absence of Rudolph Ackermann is more of a surprise, since he began publishing in 1797, although his primary focus was social satires. Specialization in social satires also accounts for the absence of James Bretherton, who had a long association with the caricaturist Henry William Bunbury. (Meanwhile, only three printsellers just made the list with J. Cattermoul, Robert Dighton and W. Richardson each publishing eight.)

None of the twenty-two publishers, who published eight or more prints of Fox and Pitt the Younger (separately or together) did so prior to 1778.[78] Meanwhile, only five published over fifty prints of them, none of whom appear to have been publishing political prints prior to 1780 and the start of the 'Golden Age' of English caricature. This suggests that there was a changing of the guard in terms of not only caricaturists but also publishers at this time (the start of the 'Golden Age').[79] S.W. Fores published 273 prints; Hannah Humphrey, 218; and William Holland, 118; their closest rivals at the top, William Humphrey, who published 71 prints, and William Dent, 57; they published their last print of either figure in 1794 and 1793, respectively. These five account for just around 46.4 per cent of all prints of Fox and Pitt. The triumvirate of Fores, Holland and Hannah Humphrey were, by the 1790s, the principal publishers of political prints in London and account for just under 38.4 per cent of prints of Fox and Pitt.

The sale of prints in their shops was not the only way through which publishers facilitated access to prints. S.W. Fores and William Holland had exhibition rooms within their shops to which they charged 1s. entry and allowed the public to view both old and new caricatures in a relaxed environment.[80] Meanwhile, their window displays also enabled passing members of the public access to prints. While there are a number of images recording the print-shop window audience, the caricature exhibition room is not so well documented, with Richard Newton's water colour of William Holland's exhibition room an isolated example.[81] This print (Newton's interior of William Holland's exhibition room) apes the annual exhibition at the Royal Academy on a number of levels. His audience, while attempting to act in a dignified fashion as connoisseurs of art, are clearly ridiculed by the caricaturist, not only in the way he portrays them in a grotesque manner but also by questioning their interest: members of the crowd ogle one another rather than study the prints adorning the walls, in imitation of the general behaviour at the Royal Academy exhibition. Countless caricatures, both social and political, are squeezed onto the walls, again replicating the exhibitions of the Royal Academy. The skills of the caricaturist are clearly displayed in a work of this nature, including recognizable miniatures of larger works.

Shop interiors are better illustrated. The *Interior of Rudolph Ackermann's Repository of Arts*, by an unknown engraver, provides one example and again demonstrates high levels of skill.[82] While not as crowded as Newton's snapshot of Holland's exhibition room, it provides an interesting glimpse into the interior workings front-of-house in an eighteenth-century print-shop, with its patrons ambling around, searching through numerous wall displays and stands, seeking out their desired print. The space devoted to light, in particular the two large skylights, was a common architectural feature. Favourable lighting levels were important in order to show off a shop's wares to optimum effect. The term 'repository' in the title of Mr. Ackermann's shop is striking. While one of its meanings during the period was a shop, it could also indicate where pieces of art and other objects of interest were collected and stored for viewing, or indeed a museum.[83] This suggests that shops like that of Rudolph Ackermann might have been multifunctional, with one purpose being the sale of items of art and other curiosities and a second concurrent function as a private art gallery.

Art played an important role in the lives of the upper classes during the eighteenth century, not only as an obvious means of displaying status but also as a pastime, viewing art in galleries and exhibitions. In addition to wall displays, caricatures would also have been stored loosely in drawers, while some collectors such as Charles James Fox and Sarah Sophia Banks also bound prints into folios, bringing them out for the amusement of their visitors.[84] Sheila O'Connell has also suggested that it was mainly prints purchased by collectors and bound into albums that have survived.[85] This line of argument highlights the ephemeral nature of the genre while also indicating the selective nature of the surviving material, based upon the tastes of a few collectors.

Production

During the mid-eighteenth century, several methods could be used to produce satirical prints, including woodcuts, aquatint, engraving and etching. Woodcuts were the preferred means of production in the early part of the century as they were relatively cheap and quick to produce, with images carved onto wood, inked and then pressed onto paper. By the 1780s, these had fallen out of favour, owing to the crude nature of the designs and the growing mechanization of the printing process. As the century progressed, copper plate etching became the preferred format and was used to great effect by caricaturists such as James Gillray. For this a copper plate would be stopped out with wax or varnish, before having a design engraved using a steel etching needle. The plate would then be placed in nitric acid so that the design was driven deeper into the exposed parts. The plate was then inked and pressed onto damp rag paper, with the resultant print normally measuring around 10 inches by 14 inches.[86] From the 1780s, many of these impressions would be hand-coloured by a team of artists at the printer's establishment. The colour could cover up visible signs of wear on the plate. Richard Godfrey has suggested that the caricaturists would probably have coloured the first impression themselves for use as a template for the publisher's team of colourists.[87] There is a certain irony, therefore, that the later prints in a run, often of inferior quality in terms of the underlying print, would sell for more (upwards of 1s.) than the earlier impressions, which were deemed of sufficient quality for sale without augmentation and sold for around 6d. In plate one of *Consequences of a Successful French Invasion*,[88] James Gillray includes price details along with the usual publication details.

Aquatint was a relatively new technique during the late eighteenth century, having been developed in France during the 1760s. It was not particularly popular among caricaturists as it was not as swift a process as etching and each plate yielded fewer good quality impressions. However, it proved popular among artists such as Thomas Gainsborough and Paul Sandby for reproducing watercolour paintings.[89] It was particularly good at providing tonal effects owing to the nature of the resin ground that was applied to the plate, much in the same way as wax ground in etching, before the design was engraved onto the plate and the plate submerged in acid so that the design was bitten into the bare copper.

While advances were continually being made within the printing process, during the late eighteenth century it was not possible to print both images and block text in one go, so lettering accompanying images needing to be etched onto the plate or printed separately. A good example of this two-part process can be seen in a broadside on Fox's speech in Westminster on 10 December 1781, where the oval portrait of him is slightly raised indicating that it was printed separately.[90] This is further evidenced by the fact that the image, which is an etching, is surrounded by typeset lettering. The engraving was etched by C. Knight and dated 11 December 1781, and it is probable that it was commissioned by the broadside's publisher, J. Debrett.

The fact that caricaturists favoured etching meant that new designs could be produced relatively quickly; however, it did require them to have good eyesight and cognitive skills. Hand-colouring made prints more eye-catching and more saleable; however, the move to hand-coloured prints was not universally embraced with caricaturists such as James Sayers refusing to move with the changing tastes.

Advertising

One might expect newspapers to form a key aspect of the printseller's overall marketing and advertising strategy. However, from evidence available in the British Library Collections (The Burney Collection and Nineteenth Century British Library Newspapers Online) it appears that the majority of adverts were principally for 'social' rather than 'political' prints, many of which were contained within magazines such as the *Rambler's Magazine*.[91] A notable exception to this was an advert placed in the *Morning Chronicle and London Advertiser* on 18 June 1782 by Elizabeth D'Archery, advertising a number of political prints, the majority of which featured Charles James Fox.[92] Caricature shops continued to occasionally advertise political prints on contentious issues such as the Test Act, but these adverts are few and far between.[93] This was unexpected, given the fact that as a percentage of prints in the *BM Catalogue*, political prints accounted for 55 per cent of production during the period 1771 to 1807.[94] The fact that political prints tended to centre on the major political issues of the day can explain the low number of adverts, as the public could be certain that within a few days of an event, prints would be in the shops.

When considering the rate of adverts it should be remembered, however, that publishers would place the same advert in multiple newspapers at the same time and this could skew the figures if newspapers containing a particular advert survived. The majority of political themed prints were, not unsurprisingly, published between November and April, when Parliament tended to be in session.[95] It should be remembered, however, that political prints were published all year round. In terms of advertisements by printsellers, it was only the major publishers who regularly advertised and the majority of these adverts were for social prints. The rate of adverts was fairly constant throughout the year with peaks in September, January and February and a slight dip in October and November. It would seem reasonable to argue that they required little announcement owing to their topicality and the fact that the main market was the politically aware. Additionally, the fact that the selfsame newspaper would have carried political intelligence as a matter of course, their readership would know of the latest political events and scandals and be sure that prints on the topic(s) would be available a few days hence. Therefore, the advertising of political prints might have been deemed an unnecessary expense, whereas for social prints, where the topics might not have made the news, advertising was more of a necessity.

Readership

One of the main areas that historians disagree upon in relation to eighteenth-century satirical prints is how many people would have had access to them. A typical print run was between 500 and 1,500, with it being possible to have a run of 3,000 if a pair of identical plates were used.[96] Recently, however, Vic Gatrell has argued against this paradigm, citing a lack of evidence on print runs, suggesting that the current estimates are not as reliable as one might think as 'no records of print runs survive other than for very occasional prints'.[97] The cost of prints was generally placed at 6d. for a 'plain' or 'uncoloured' print, with the price rising upwards of 1s. for a 'hand-coloured' print. This has led to claims that they were beyond the means of the lower orders.[98] But, while one must take the cost of purchasing prints into account when estimating the readership of satirical prints, care should be taken not to underestimate the casual reader as they passed by the shop, pausing to stare at the prints as part of the crowd. Marcus Wood and Vic Gatrell have suggested that prints had a wider readership than their cost suggests.[99] Nicholson, on the other hand, argues that 'the handful of prints which depict the print-shop window audience ... have been invested with a significance which, arguably they do not merit'.[100] Here Nicholson is clearly suggesting that historians have been far too quick to leap on an image of a crowd around a print-shop window and assume that gazing at the window was the crowd's only means of accessing the prints. In reality, most crowd scenes contain members of the middling sorts, who it is likely would have possessed the means to purchase prints or visit the galleries at the caricature shops of William Holland and S.W. Fores. Other assumptions that are often made include presuming that the scene depicted was a regular occurrence and that everyone in the viewing group was able to read and understand the print. While the latter is probable, owing to the fact that most print-shop window scenes portray middle-class patrons, the former is less easy to support, as the window scene could be a handy piece of advertising and entirely fictitious, or only occurs when the latest print by one of the major caricaturists was due to be published. E.P. Thompson summed up the print-shop window scene exactly in his *Making of the English Working Class*, suggesting that caricature was not art for the illiterate, owing to the amount of text present in speech bubbles, titles and captions; however, they were still able to participate within the culture, gazing at the latest Gillray, Rowlandson or Cruikshank in the print-shop window and deciphering the intricate visual minutiae.[101]

In the ongoing debate as to the importance of the print-shop window as a means of providing the less affluent members of London society with access to satirical prints in mind, it would seem unreasonable to dismiss the crowd scenes as purely apocryphal.[102] Clearly, anyone who passed by a printseller's shop could have had access to topical prints of the moment, whether by gazing at the window or visiting the exhibition room. Looking in at prints from the street was not a purely English occupation. In 1803, Pierre Nolesque Bergeret produced a lithograph of a crowd scene outside a print-shop in Paris.[103] The fact that the shops in these prints are easily identifiable is significant and indicates that, in addition to providing a social commentary, these prints also acted as an advertisement for the print-shop to the reader viewing the print in another setting. In *The Macaroni Print Shop*,[104] the name Darly is visible and 'St. James's Street' is conveniently etched above the shop in *Very Slippy-Weather* (Plate 2)[105] in both instances clearly locating the shop. Meanwhile, *A Real Scene in St. Pauls Church Yard on a Windy Day*[106] achieves this name-dropping in a subtler way by containing the shop's address in the title.

While the market for prints was undoubtedly centred on London, it should be remembered that the Engraver's Copyright Act of 1735 came about in part from a desire by artists such as William Hogarth to protect their prints from being pirated, thus suggesting a market outside of London. The Act is an invaluable tool to the historian of satirical prints as, to be covered by the Act, a publication date and place needed to be included, thus making it easier to date prints accurately. The presence of prints in magazines of the time again indicates that some prints were able to meet a wider audience than that of the middle and upper classes of London. The presence in the British Museum Collection of a print, published in Augsburg,[107] after Isaac Cruikshank's *The Raft in Danger or the Republican Crew Disappointed*[108] is indicative of the fact that these prints did circulate outside of London with some finding their way to the Continent.[109] Mark Bills has argued that there was a long tradition of English prints being sold on the Continent in spite of their continental readers knowing little about the events they depicted.[110] Additionally, Diana Donald provides an example of William Humphrey selling a number of prints by Gillray while on a trip to Holland during the lull in hostilities between Britain and France in 1802.[111] This evidence all points to prints reaching a market beyond London. It is possible that the Augsburg version was influenced by James Gillray's *The Storm Rising; – or – The Republican Flotilla in Danger*,[112] which also features the opposition leaders attempting to winch a French raft to shore. From these three prints it is clear that not only did caricaturists borrow ideas off each other but also copies of prints could be published and sold abroad, and be translated into foreign languages and sold on the international market with little variation.

The subject of 'readership' also raises questions of literacy. This is particularly important, when one remembers that Georgian satirical prints are steeped in biblical, classical and literary references, as well as the fact that political prints tended to reflect current affairs, which would frequently be reported in newspapers. One also needs to consider the varying levels of text between the caricaturists' various offerings. During the eighteenth century, towns and cities enjoyed superior levels of literacy to countryside villages, while England had an estimated literacy rate of 60 per cent by the second half of the century. It would seem reasonable, therefore, to estimate that during the period 1770 to 1806, London enjoyed fairly high levels of literacy and that the majority of people who came into contact with caricatures would have been able to read them.[113] However, the cost of 6d. plain and upwards of 1s. coloured rendered print ownership beyond the reach of the majority of people outside of the upper and middle classes and some artisanal tradesmen and shopkeepers. Readership, while affected by wealth, literacy levels and the cost of prints, cannot be limited to just those who purchased them. Not only would collectors display and show off their collections to guests,[114] but prints could also be viewed when passing print-shop windows and visiting their exhibition rooms, thus ensuring that in common with newspapers the audience for an edition would have outstripped its production considerably.

Key questions that this book will address are how did caricaturists aid the development of the cult of the personality? How did this feed into the creation of the 'modern party leader'? What techniques did the caricaturists employ to represent ideas of party? What techniques did the caricaturists employ when targeting individual politicians? And how important was the relationship and rivalry of Charles James Fox and William Pitt the Younger?

1

Stock Images

Stock images are the principal images used by satirical artists to represent an individual or group. Richard Godfrey has argued that 'for the most important and frequently recurring characters it was important from the beginning to define a prototype that could be used again and again, allowing for instant recognition'.[1] The notion of a 'stock image' dates back to the emergence of graphic satire and in its earliest form tended to be allegorical, consisting of emblems, symbols and visual puns. For instance, John Stuart, third Earl of Bute, was consistently portrayed as a jackboot throughout the mid-eighteenth century, owing to visual punning between his titular name Bute and boot.[2] Likewise, Henry Fox, later first Baron Holland, was consistently represented as a fox sporting a wig;[3] therefore, it was no surprise that when his eldest two children first appeared in print, they were portrayed as fox cubs.[4] This provided a clear link between father and son, effectively dynasticizing the trope. This style of play on words between surnames and emblems was not uncommon and helped the audience identify individuals within the prints, given time and suitable repetition.

Stock images also had the ability of acting as a visual shorthand, with notable examples including the British people being personified through the person of John Bull[5] and the Royal Navy through his cousin, Jack Tar. The emblem of John Bull as the British people sat well alongside Britannia as a visual embodiment of the British nation and her sister Hibernia, who performed the same role for Ireland. Indeed, Gwyn A. Williams has suggested that James Gillray's John Bull became the 'voice of the people'.[6] During the eighteenth century, John Bull was portrayed as a yokel farmer, who was being played and bamboozled by politicians. Through the caricaturist's representation of how a certain policy would affect John Bull, the reader could envisage how the policy might affect them by substituting themselves for John Bull. Miles Taylor has argued that 'John Bull embodied a common and widely used critique of political power in the late eighteenth and early nineteenth centuries'.[7] The fact that the character of John Bull readily lent itself to public empathy enabled artists to reduce the number of individuals required to construct the message and thus render their comment all the more biting.

The aim of this chapter is to examine the evolution and development of the stock images of Charles James Fox and William Pitt the Younger during their careers and to highlight the importance of the 'stock image' when caricaturing individuals in the late eighteenth century. Key questions that this chapter will address are: What is the purpose of stock images? How do they develop over time? Are old versions revisited? The chapter will focus upon the four 'stock images' of Charles James Fox: Fox as a fox, Fox as 'The Man of the People', Fox as a Jacobin and Fox as a traitor; it will also look at the 'stock image' of William Pitt the Younger: Pitt as minister. While there are several prints of Fox as Carlo Khan during the 'East India Bill crisis' and as Oliver Cromwell, they have not been included here as the image of him as Carlo Khan was really a response to his East India policy and as such would be more properly considered within the discussion of that policy, while the image of Fox as Oliver Cromwell is a constituent part of the stock image of him as a traitor.

Fox as a fox

One of Charles James Fox's earliest appearances in caricature came in *The Child; or a Legacy for the House of Commons*, published in 1771.[8] His representation as a fox not only fits with the pre-'Golden Age' method of emblematic representation but also overtly links him to his father and brother, and accordingly acts as a comment upon the filial nature of his early political line. Within this early 'stock image' of Fox as a fox, there are clear references to his passion for gambling and position as a leading figure within macaroni fashion.[9] Many of these early prints of Fox, unlike the later prints from the 1780s, were published by small publishers and within periodical magazines such as *The Town and Country Magazine* and *Oxford Magazine*.[10]

The Young Heir amongst Bad Councellors, or the Lion Betray'd[11] is another early political print containing a depiction of Fox. It is also noteworthy for its association of the young Fox with a number of significant political figures. The central figure is that of George III as the English lion. He is surrounded by several of his senior advisers: John Montagu, fourth Earl of Sandwich; Lord Frederick North; Augustus Henry Fitzroy, third Duke of Grafton; and William Murray, first Earl of Mansfield. Sandwich can be identified by the presence of an anchor on top of his hat, indicating his position as First Lord of the Admiralty, while North is depicted as a dog and his identification is aided by the presence of a compass symbol, N, above his head.[12] He holds a chain attached to the lion's right front paw, indicating his position as First Lord of the Treasury at the same time suggesting that the King should 'be guided by me and go North about'. One of his legs has a spiked point, which pierces the lion's chest, causing him to bleed, while his left leg is in a jackboot, hinting at the influence of John Stuart, third Earl of Bute. Fletcher Norton is also present and is identified through his Speaker's robes and Charles James Fox portrayed as a fox.

Fox appears in the right foreground and is examining the scene through a looking glass. He sports a bagwig, linking in to his fondness for the macaroni style of fashion. His left foot is stuck in a dice box, with a pair of dice next to it and the playing card in his right hand, which reflected his fondness for gambling. Fox is recognizable predominantly due to his portrayal as a fox cub, an echo of his father's representation as a fox and a visual pun on his surname. In May 1771, Fox was already a junior minister, was a member of the Admiralty Board and was already viewed as one of the leading debaters in the House of Commons. His youth and lack of political experience, combined with the junior nature of his office, are reflected within his portrayal as a cub rather than a fully grown fox. Later, as Fox gained in years and experience, he began to be represented as an adult Fox; however, his father's death in July 1774 might have also influenced this change. Indeed, Lord John Russell recorded a comment from Fox's nephew Henry Fox, third Baron Holland, who always thought that it was most fortunate for the interests of both liberty and truth and the comfort, happiness and character of Fox's political career that he had quarrelled with North, prior to the American Question coming to the fore. He went on to suggest that Fox's dismissal from office and subsequent loss of his father provided him with 'an opportunity of exercising an unbiased and impartial judgment on that great question, [that of America] and the important principles involved in it'.[13]

Matthew and Mary Darly developed a reputation during the mid-eighteenth century for publishing prints concerning macaroni fashion. According to the *BM Catalogue*, the Darlys published two prints of Charles James Fox, in human form and as a macaroni.[14] While he is fairly recognizable in *The Macaroni Cauldron*,[15] the figure in *The Original Macaroni*[16] is less obviously Fox, being rather slender. However, the fox's brushes attached to either end of the pole, which he holds, and one at the back of his head, acting as the ponytail on a bagwig, indicate that the figure is intended to be a member of the Fox family. *The Original Macaroni* emphasizes the continued importance of emblems in early prints attempting to represent individuals using human features as a means of rendering them widely recognizable to viewers, particularly when their physical appearance was not widely known. This is key as it is likely that at a time before paparazzi photos in the newspapers, the satirical print was the closest likeness that people who were not directly acquainted with the individual in question might see.

The Young Politician (Plate 3),[17] published in 1771, is another print of Fox in macaroni guise; however, unlike the Darly images, Fox is portrayed as a fox. In contrast to *The Young Heir*, where Fox is portrayed as a cub, in *The Young Politician* he has grown into a young adult; however, there remains a suggestion that Fox has not reached full maturity. There are also hints of his early politics and accusations of Toryism in the fact that the barbers attending to his wig are tearing strips off a copy of the *Magna Charta* [*sic*], which Fox is holding to help style his wig.[18] Again in this print Fox is recognizable by his vulpine features, including a fox's head and brush. Meanwhile, his macaroni fashion is clearly indicated by his floral breeches and the sword and floral jacket resting on the chair in the corner. While Fox's representation as a macaroni places him as a man of fashion, it could also be intimating that he was perceived as a Francophile. The style of his clothing, alongside the array of bottles on the table behind his valet containing 'Bergamont', 'Essence', 'Rouges' in addition to a bag of 'Poudre à la Maréchale' on the floor, also hint at Fox following French fashion. Meanwhile, on the floor, there is an open book, '*A New Essay on Politiks* by C- F- Esq'', and this could be an ironic reference to his defending his father in the House of Commons in 1771 over his involvement in the Massacre of the Pelhamite Innocents.[19]

One print that clearly demonstrated Fox's political maturity is James Gillray's *Changing Places; – Alias; Fox Stinking the Badger Out of His Nest* (Plate 4).[20] Fox stands in the centre of the print, this time as a fully grown fox. Under him is an open money bag, labelled 'Faro Bank', spilling money onto the ground. There are two playing cards next to it, three in front of Fox and one under his front right paw. The cards again refer to his gambling addiction as does the money bag, which also refers to the Faro Bank that Fox established at Brooks's along with his brother-in-law, Richard Fitzpatrick, with the financial aid of Brooks himself, in order to combat their indebtedness.[21] To the left of him is the running figure of Lord North, depicted as a badger, a compass on his head bearing the word 'north' along the length of his snout and a blue garter ribbon tied around his body.

North is fleeing from the smell of Fox breaking wind in the midst of which Gillray has etched the word 'eloquence', a reference to the forcefulness and fluency of Fox's continual attacks upon North in the House of Commons. Immediately behind North stands a broken signpost with a hand holding the top of a halberd on the end of the left-hand arm pointing the way to 'Tower Hill'. North makes off in this direction, a reference to the speculation that Fox and other members of the opposition sought to have him impeached for his disastrous prosecution of the war against the American colonists. The right-hand arm of the signpost droops down and points towards a hole in the middle of the print. The inscription upon this arm reads 'to the Treasury', while the hole it points to is almost certainly the entrance to the set that North has just fled from. In the background, George III can be seen hunting. The fact that Fox is seen to be effectively forcing Lord North from office is significant, as it demonstrates his rise to political maturity and prominence, not only within the ranks of the Rockingham Connection[22] but also in the House of Commons more generally. It should also be remembered that Fox twice served as a junior minister, once at the Admiralty and once at the Treasury in Lord North's administration. There is clear evidence that Gillray saw in Fox a flawed personality, for example, with references to his heavy gambling debts.

This is highlighted not only by the references to his gambling addiction but also by the statue of the two-headed Roman God Janus behind him, the second face of whom is a fox, while his headdress, which could be meant for a dice box, has a pair of dice on top of it. In the middle of the print is a small barrel of 'small beer' and some bars of soap. The bundle is inscribed 'Budget' and is a clear reference to Lord North's budget of 11 March in which he proposed to increase a number of taxes including those on soap, tea, beer and tobacco in order to fund the war in America.[23]

Fox's emergence as a fully fledged party leader is reflected in many of the attacks upon the Fox–North Coalition. Strikingly, the coalition (contemporaneously christened the Fox–North Coalition) derived its name from the secretaries of state rather, as had hitherto been the custom, from that of the First Lord of the Treasury, who in this instance was the third Duke of Portland.[24] The Opposition Whigs held a staunch belief that the principal office of state should be filled by a member of the first rank of society. Accordingly, they required an aristocrat to be their nominal leader should their de facto leader be a member of the House of Commons. One print that highlights Fox's position as the effective leader of the old Rockingham Connection was *Shelb-n Badgered and Foxed.*[25] In this print, one can clearly see Lord North, once again depicted as a badger, wearing a garter ribbon, uniting with Fox, depicted as an adult fox, attacking the incumbent First Lord of the Treasury, Lord Shelburne, and his plans for peace at the end of the American War of Independence.

Lord Shelburne can be seen seated in the middle of the print holding a paper 'Preliminaries'. On his left, Lord North bites the tail of his jacket, while on his right Fox is urinating and defecating against his left leg, clawing at his right with his left front paw and biting the paper he is holding. It is apparent, therefore, that Fox was viewed by the artist as the senior partner in the coalition, in spite of his youth and lack of experience when compared with his coalition partner.

The depiction of both Lord North and Fox is reminiscent of *Changing Places* and demonstrates an attempt by the artist to arrive at a consistent image for Fox and North, which would have made them more recognizable. In the background, behind Lord North, stands some gallows with Britannia pointing towards it saying 'impeach', a reference to the fact that it was anticipated that Lord North would have been impeached by Fox over his American policies had he not joined him. On the left of the print in the background stands a folly in which a statue of Lord Shelburne (depicted for a second time) stands on a plinth holding two documents, one of which is inscribed 'Preliminaries'. A coronet sits on top of the folly, above which is inscribed 'the idol of the Lords' while the roof of the folly is inscribed 'Corruption'. Three peers can be seen kneeling round the base of the statue of Shelburne. The print attacks not only Lord Shelburne's policy of pursuing peace with the American colonists but also the coming together of Charles James Fox and Lord North in opposition to Shelburne's administration. Such formal unified opposition to an administration was alien to the eighteenth-century House of Commons. That said, there was strong opposition to all governments in the early part of the century (1700–15) as well as to Walpole during the 1720s and 1730s, but this opposition was divided between the Tory opposition and Opposition Whigs and the two were not always united. The inscription under the print, however, praises the actions of honourable and right honourable members of the House of Commons who had voted in favour of an address. The Peace Preliminaries had been rejected by the House of Commons on 17 February 1783; however, an address to the King on the Preliminary articles was also debated in the House of Lords and House of Commons on 17 February and it is presumably to these addresses that the print refers.[26]

It might not have been entirely coincidental that after the death of his parents and brother in 1774, Fox's image in caricature began to evolve, taking on human form, with either a Fox's head, brush or both. Later in his career, however, artists would return to portraying Fox as a fox. A late example of this is Charles Williams's *The Lucky Hit or The Crafty Reynard – Once More at Large*,[27] published after the death of William Pitt the Younger.

Fox as 'Man of the People'

The 1770s marked a turning point in the visual representation of individuals in caricature, with a movement away from emblematic representation towards an accentuation of the 'victim's' physical features.[28] The first major change in Charles James Fox's image in caricature coincided with this more general change, taking on a more human form and becoming recognizable via his facial features and build, rather than merely as a fox or with vulpine features. During the early part of the development of this new image, Fox would frequently retain a fox's brush or head. Another method that was used during this transition between the two stock images involved a literary allusion to Ben Jonson's *Volpone* and his character Reynard, King of the Foxes. G.M. Woodward refers to this in his early undated watercolour, entitled *Reynard the Fox*.[29] It is uncertain whether Woodward's image was published, but it is significant as it demonstrates this other method of linking the new image of Fox with the earlier 'stock image'. In the image, Fox is shown wearing a bagwig, resplendent in blue frock coat and buff waistcoat, frilly shirt visible underneath his waistcoat above his bulging belly. The fact that the image is enclosed within a sketched frame is significant and suggests that this was a preparatory work, either for a larger painting or more likely for an engraving. It was not unusual for artists to create preliminary ink and watercolour sketches as designs for plates, which either they or an engraver would work up ready for printing and publication. Indeed, Paul Sandby produced preliminary pen, ink and watercolour over graphite sketches for his London *Cries* series.[30] In spite of the allusion to Ben Jonson's character, Reynard the Fox, in Woodward's image, does not have any obvious vulpine physiognomy. This new image of Fox as 'Man of the People' was, however, to be characterized by his bushy eyebrows, body hair, pronounced bovine jaw and five o'clock shadow. This 'stock image' was to remain the standard image of him in caricature up to the outbreak of revolution in France in 1789,[31] an event that was to turn the world of politics on its head.

During the American War of Independence, Charles James Fox and his friends adopted the blue and buff uniform of the American General George Washington as an unofficial uniform, and this marked them out from the government ministers who would arrive at Court and Parliament in full court dress and later in Windsor uniform.[32] The caricaturists were not slow to pick up on this sartorial move by Fox and his friends, and they began to illustrate him in a blue frock coat and buff waistcoat in the coloured prints of the period.[33] This 'uniform' arguably aided the development of this image and was as much of a gift to the caricaturists as his highly distinguishing physical features, thus making it relatively easy for them to arrive at an image that would soon help to identify him and his followers. By the same token, the two distinct forms of dress made it easy for the artists to pigeonhole people, grouping them with either the Rockinghamite and later Foxite Whigs or the administration, by virtue of the way they clothed their 'victims'. Interestingly, upon his becoming foreign secretary in 1782, the caricaturists continued to depict him in his trademark blue and buff, thus demonstrating the centrality of clothing to the image.[34]

A Spirited Attack[35] is a good early example of the 'Man of the People' trope and was published around 1780. It is unusual among early examples of this portrayal owing to the fact that Fox is not given a fox's head or brush and is instead recognizable from his physical features. While it is a crude likeness, the anonymous artist does well in capturing Fox's bushy eyebrows, shaggy, unkempt hair and pronounced five o'clock shadow. Although he is not as rotund as in later images, he is depicted resplendent in a frock coat and waistcoat, which presumably are intended to imitate the unofficial 'uniform' of the Rockingham Connection. Meanwhile, the ruffles of his shirt can be seen as the last vestiges of his flamboyant early macaroni style of dress. He stands arm raised, fist clenched and mouth open, holding his hat behind him. From the title, it is apparent that he is involved in some kind of joust and while the clenched fist might suggest it is of a pugilistic nature, the fact that he holds his hat behind and is open mouthed indicates that a verbal duel is more likely.

Another print from 1780 that captures Fox's facial features is William Paulet Carey's The State Dunces.[36] Fox is represented again without a fox's head or brush, but still sporting a frock coat and waistcoat with a ruffled shirt. He again has bushy eyebrows; however, his five o'clock shadow is conspicuous by its absence, while his hair is obscured underneath a bagwig. The devastating nature of Fox's oratory in the House of Commons against Lord North is indicated in the print by the fact that he is physically whipping Lord North. Britannia, sitting on the right of the print, indicates that Lord North's American policy was the reason for Fox's attack, stating:

> My Dominion diminish'd my Blood spilt my Treasure exhausted my People burdened with Taxes my Colonies Revolted Deserted by my Allies my Flag insulted and no longer Mistress of the Ocean and shall the abettors go unpunished? Forbid it Justice.

Here, Britannia is a standing emblem for Britain and her empire, explicating what she sees as the failures of recent governments in provoking conflict with the American colonies through their taxation policies, while the resultant war also put a tremendous strain on the nation's finances. Britannia also reflects that the loss of the American colonies damages Britain's prestige, while the war demonstrates that Britain has slipped back and is no longer the world's principal naval power.[37] By seemingly punishing Lord North for his failure, Fox can be adjudged to be meting out the punishment for which Britannia has called. Indeed, as he whips Lord North he states that 'Was I to give as many lashes as he has made blunders in the State I should not be done these three hours. By G-d'.

George III carries his prime minister on his back towards Britannia and exclaims: 'For supporting them in their Design's thus am I obliged to carry them through condign Punishment'. His speech refers to the fact that on a number of occasions during the war, he had refused to accept Lord North's resignation and was thus thoroughly implicated in the loss of the American colonies.[38] Under his feet lies a paper 'Petition of the People', indicating that he was happy for his government to ride roughshod over the will of the people. Fellow Rockinghamites, such as Charles Lennox, third Duke of Richmond, support Fox, with the Duke offering to take over should Fox tire. Lord Sandwich, North's First Lord of the Admiralty, is also in the crowd behind, complaining at the opposition's attacks on him for his failures. The building behind the scene resembles a church and could be intended for St Stephen's, where Parliament met during the eighteenth century and links to the idea of the opposition attempting to hold the government to account with Fox, their leader in the House of Commons, heading their efforts.

Later in his career, this image of Fox was to be linked to his moniker of 'Man of the People' by the caricaturists themselves. An early example of this was Thomas Colley's *Perdito and Perdita – or – the Man and Woman of the People*,[39] published on 17 December 1782. Colley, like the previous artists producing Fox in his 'Man of the People' guise, depicts Fox with unkempt hair, bushy eyebrows and a pronounced five o'clock shadow, again resplendent in frock coat and waistcoat with a ruffled shirt beneath. He holds a hat with C.F. inscribed inside it. He sits in a gig belonging to the actress and courtesan Mary Robinson, whose cipher is visible on the side and front of it. Mary Robinson sits beside Fox driving the gig past St James's Palace. The fact that she is driving Fox is significant and indicates that Mrs Robinson is looking after Fox and not vice versa. The contemporary wit George Selwyn is reputed to have commented 'the connection was perfectly right; the "Man of the People" and no other, should be the cicisbeo[40] to the "Woman of the People"',[41] thus providing another contemporary reference to Fox being known as 'Man of the People'. It should be noted that the phrase 'Woman of the People' was contemporary slang for a prostitute.[42]

Mary Robinson was often referred to as Perdita, after her portrayal of the character in William Shakespeare's *The Winter's Tale*. At the top of the print, Colley has inscribed a quote, supposedly from Fox, 'I have now not fifty ducats in the World & yet I am in love.' This quote highlights not only Fox's money problems but also the fact that he was in no position, financially, to keep a courtesan, especially not one of the fame of Mrs Robinson, who was in former times the mistress of George, Prince of Wales.[43] Following the end of the Prince's relationship, Fox was instrumental in retrieving some of the Prince of Wales' letters to her and a bond for £20,000, which the Prince had given her during their relationship. Fox's biographer, I.M. Davis, has argued that Fox was as 'eloquent in private as in Parliament', citing Fox's success in persuading Mary Robinson to part with both the letters and bond as evidence while also intimating that Fox 'took advantage of the necessary meetings to negotiate himself into her bed'.[44]

Another print to link this image of Fox with the moniker of 'Man of the People' was G.M. Woodward's *The Black Man of the People*.[45] Again, it is an undated preliminary ink and watercolour sketch, which does not have an entry in the *BM Catalogue*. Like Woodward's earlier image of Fox in *Reynard the Fox* (Plate 5), the sketch has a frame drawn round it and Fox is resplendent in blue and buff along with a frilly shirt. In *The Black Man of the People* (Colour Plate 1), Fox looks older and his own hair is visible. His large bushy eyebrows and five o'clock shadow both come to the fore while he stands with his left arm raised, holding his hat, mouth open as if making a speech. The word 'black' in the title appears to have been an afterthought and indicates that the print could date from *c*.1783–4.

Further evidence for this dating of the sketch is the partial portrait of a woman sporting a hat (Plate 6). It is possible that this is meant for Georgiana, Duchess of Devonshire, who was a vigorous campaigner for Charles James Fox during the 1784 Westminster election. The insertion of the word 'black' into the title of the sketch could, however, also be a reference to Fox's black appearance, linked not only to his stubble, mass of black hair and bushy eyebrows but also to his poor personal hygiene. Indeed, Stanley Ayling cites anecdotal evidence, from around 1780, referring to Fox's black appearance.[46] Fox would often receive visitors at breakfast and one of his visitors, Dr Kippis, recalled that when Fox entered, his face was unshaved, dirty and tinged with a yellowish hue, with his large bushy eyebrows adding to the darkness of his skin. His mass of black hair was uncombed and clotted with the remains of the previous day's powder and hair products. Meanwhile, his old and dirty nightgown was open at the neck, revealing a broad hairy chest.

The image of Fox as 'Man of the People' remained dominant until the French Revolution during which it was subsumed by the image of him as a Jacobin. J.R. Dinwiddy has suggested, however, that during the period of the French Revolution, there was a revival of Fox's reputation as the 'Man of the People', arguing that Fox 'appeared once more as the friend of peace and reform and stood out against the suspension of civil liberties'.[47] This suggestion is an interesting one and is evident from the satirical prints of the period. Through the 1790s the 'Man of the People' trope was again evident, interspersed with prints portraying him as a traitor and a Jacobin. The continuing use of the image of Fox as the 'Man of the People' served as an interesting juxtaposition with Pitt during the 1790s, especially after Pitt started introducing his repressive legislation.[48]

The trope of Fox as 'Man of the People' enjoyed a resurgence in 1806, when Fox's image underwent a period of rehabilitation, following his return to the Foreign Office. This revived image retained Fox's pronounced bovine jawline, bushy eyebrows and 'blue and buff uniform'; however, it moved away from the *bonnet rouge* that had become synonymous with caricatures of Fox during the French Revolution. Gone, too, was the ever-present five o'clock shadow that had been a mainstay of his visual representation since the move away from portraying him as a fox.

A good comparison of the old and new versions of the trope of Fox as 'Man of the People' is *A Man of the People in Times Past: A Man of the People in Times Present*.[49] It is a two-part print playing out the same image, with the left-hand frame portraying Fox while he was in opposition, *c*.1780s, and the right-hand frame as he was in office in 1806. In the left-hand frame, the depiction of Fox is instantly recognizable as the 'Man of the People' trope. It is complete with blue frock coat, buff waistcoat and bushy eyebrows; however, his five o'clock shadow is conspicuous by its absence, while his hair is cropped.[50] He engages John Bull, who stands at an open window. Half bowing, hat in hand, Fox is trying to persuade John Bull to support him. He says:

> Good Mr. Bull stand by me & be my Friend – depend upon it I shall ^never forget the Obligation – Instead of that Paltry Parlour you live in you shall rent the whole House!! Every thing shall be chang'd for the Better!!!

The reference to his friend could be an allusion to Lord North and the Fox–North Coalition. Meanwhile, the insertion of the word 'never' as an apparent afterthought is significant and indicates that what Fox actually said to John Bull and what he was thinking were two different things. It is, therefore, likely that the artist sought to suggest that Fox could not be trusted to keep his word. John Bull responds to Fox's overtures 'Why [– ? –] see I have experienced such chops and changes in my time – I don't dislike your looks & so I think I shall take you on trial!!!' John Bull's response indicates that Fox's overtures have been successful, showing that this scene took place during 1782–3.

While it is possible that the scene could have taken place in the early 1800s with Fox's friend being Lord Grenville, the obvious difference in age between the two images of Fox would appear to rule this out, as his hair and eyebrows have turned white during the intervening years.

In the right-hand frame, we see Fox, now in office, sporting a fancier frock coat and white waistcoat, his white hair tied back into a ponytail, with gold buckles on his shoes. He retains his bushy eyebrows; however, his five o'clock shadow is not in evidence. Time has not been so kind to John Bull who has grown poor and had to move into the cellar flat. A notice on the lintel above the now-open cellar window says, 'John Bull from Above-Stairs'. Attached to the now-closed upstairs window is a notice stating that 'This Parlour to be Lett – Enquire in the Cellar'. Again, Fox and John Bull are engaged in conversation. Fox complains, 'That man is always grumbling – Mr. Bull Mr. Bull – you are never content – I say you are very well off How should you know anything about the Matter – A Cellar is a very Comfortable Place in times like the Present!!!' In response John Bull asks him, 'Where are now all your fine promises – I wonder you are not ashamed of yourself – to drive me from my Comfortable Parlour into the Cellar!!!' From this dialogue, it is apparent that the artist is implying that once in power, Fox abandoned his previous position of standing up for the people against the government. This was in part due to the fact that the 'Ministry of All the Talents' introduced a wave of new taxes in order to pay for the ongoing war with France.[51]

Fox as a Jacobin

The French Revolution polarized political opinion and coincided with the next development in the 'stock image' of Charles James Fox. This new image, which first appeared in 1791, drew heavily upon the earlier image of him as 'Man of the People'. In these images, his distinguishing facial features of a pronounced bovine jaw, shaggy hair, bushy eyebrows and an obvious five o'clock shadow remain ever present, while he frequently retained his blue frock coat and buff waistcoat. However, it was invariably augmented by a *bonnet rouge* and/or revolutionary cockade, which completed his transformation from Fox the 'Man of the People' into 'Fox the Jacobin'. Aileen Ribeiro has argued that the red liberty cap, which is in essence the *bonnet rouge*, was the 'most universally recognized badge of liberty', whereas James Epstein has indicated that 'for loyalists, the "meaning" of the cap of liberty was unmistakable: it was the symbol of revolution, the ensign of French anarchy, the sign under which the Jacobins had orchestrated the terror of 1793 and 1794'. However, Richard Wrigley has since suggested that the liberty cap is a complex emblem, whose meaning changes over time.[52] He goes on to argue that the liberty cap was not 'understood as some kind of orthodox emblem for which there was an agreed rationale, but rather that diverse opinions were projected on to and clustered around, a generic idea'.[53] It can be argued that the caricaturists' use of the *bonnet rouge* to align an individual with the French Revolution fits within his model, especially in light of Wrigley's later argument that 'between the spring and summer of 1792, the *bonnet rouge* was transformed from a factional badge loosely connected to sans-culottes and Jacobins, to a national, republican emblem'.[54] Another characteristic of this trope is the pro-French stance of Fox and his supporters, and he is often portrayed as being closer to the interests of France than the British people, who are frequently personified in the person of John Bull. The French Revolution was a turning point in the history of the Whig Party and parliamentary politics more generally, with the party's former intellectual leader, Edmund Burke,[55] deserting the party and a new politics based upon ideological differences around the French Revolution emerging. One of Fox's biographers, Henry Offley Wakeman, puts the split down to the contrasting personalities of the two men, arguing that 'Fox could not remain Fox and not see the best side of the [French] Revolution, any more than Burke could remain Burke and not see the worst. Fox had ever been an assessor of abstract rights, just as Burke had been the apostle of practical expediency'.[56]

The attacks on Fox during the period of the French Revolution and later French Revolutionary Wars were particularly biting and voluminous by comparison to the earlier periods, save perhaps for the East India Bill crisis. Wakeman, commenting upon the caricaturists' attacks on Fox, argued that no one, no matter how level-headed or good their temperament could remain unaffected by continuous abuse from the caricaturists, even more so when so much of it was such an unscrupulous representation, seemingly excused by the perceived folly of Fox's line on events. Following the outbreak of war with France, Fox became one of the most abused men in England, being viewed by a large section of society as untrustworthy, unpatriotic and little better than a traitor. Wakeman points to the centrality of perceptions of treachery and a lack of patriotism within the new image of Fox created by the caricaturists during the period of the

French Revolutionary War, commenting that Fox was often portrayed by Gillray and others as conspiring with the French in a bid to overthrow the constitution and establish a republic according to the French model.[57]

One of the most effective examples of this 'stock image' was James Gillray's *A Democrat or Reason & Philosophy* (Colour Plate 2).[58] Here, Gillray is clearly attempting to label Fox as a sans-culotte portraying him without either culottes, trousers, breeches or pantaloons. His perceived pro-revolutionary and Jacobin tendencies are also represented by the *bonnet rouge* on his head, complete with revolutionary cockade, while a speech bubble '*Caira!*' indicates he is singing a revolutionary song, *Ça Ira*. He also has a bloodied dagger in his belt. Gillray also alleges Fox has blood on his hands, as he holds up one blood-stained hand and has the other at his waist, palm out so that the viewer can see his bloody palm. As with earlier images, Gillray has stuck with a similar extenuation of Fox's facial features. Thomas Wright has argued that this print pained the mind of Fox.[59] Indeed, he was so enraged by the print that he reputedly considered suing over it, declining when he realized that it would only increase the print's notoriety.[60]

The problem of what to do about a particularly damaging print is best exemplified by an anecdote cited by Nicholas Robinson. Hannah Humphrey had recently published a scathing attack on Edmund Burke, which was on display in her shop window. Burke and his friend Charles James Fox entered the shop and Fox announced that his friend, Mr Burke, would trounce the artist and publisher with vengeance. Burke, in a more conciliatory mood, responded that he had no such intention, for were he to prosecute it would be the making of their fortune.[61] This anecdote clearly reinforces the idea that these images were extremely difficult to repress and that such moves could prove counterproductive.

The development of the image of Fox as a Jacobin benefited from two prints that sought to deconstruct the image. The first of these was Isaac Cruikshank's *A Right Honourable alias A Sans Culotte* (Plate 7),[62] a two-part print, in which the person of Charles James Fox is divided into two with one foot on two pieces of land, between which there is a stretch of water. It is apparent that the land mass on the right is meant for England, the one on the left France, while the water between them is the English Channel. Both sides of his face retain a pronounced five o'clock shadow and bushy eyebrows. On the right, he wears a bagwig, while on the left his own shaggy black hair can be seen. His clothing is also markedly different, with the right or right honourable side resplendent in blue frock coat and cream waistcoat, black breeches, white stocking and black shoe, complete with silver buckle. On the left (or sans-culotte side) of the print Fox wears a torn red jacket over a striped shirt in the French Revolutionary colours of red, white and blue.

He wears a belt, with a pistol stuck in it, torn brown breeches and a torn brown stocking with the toes of his foot visibly poking out of a broken shoe. In his left hand, he holds a club and is saying 'Ca Ira, Ca Ira, Ca Ira'; in his right he holds a rolled-up paper, 'Association against Levellers St. Georges Hanover Square', and sings 'God Save Great George Our King'. Cruikshank is clearly trying to infer that not only Fox was in two minds politically but these two minds were somewhat incongruous. On the one hand, he was a model MP, patriotic, loyal and soberly dressed. The only thing that spoils this allusion is the heavy stubble evident on his face. On the other hand, Cruikshank attempts to convey an image of Fox as a sans-culotte, with his tatty and torn clothing, the club and pistol indicating a proclivity for violence, while the colours of his shirt provide a revolutionary link. In this half of the plate, Fox looks wild-eyed which, combined with his drooping mouth, provides a menacing effect. There is something unsettling about the size of his wide-open right eye, in comparison to his left, which is less visible as he squints through it. The positioning of the eyeball in the French half of the print gives him the appearance of glaring at the viewer from whichever angle the print is viewed, affording the sans-culotte element of the print a slightly demonic quality.

William Dent went a stage further in 1793 with his *A Right Hon*^{ble}. *Democrat Dissected*.[63] By dissecting the person of Charles James Fox, Dent is clearly attempting to analyse Fox's politics and political make-up for his readers. Through the image, he argues that Fox's political make-up is a complex mix of verbosity, hot air and republican ideals, mixed with old aristocratic and more modern democratic principles, with an intransigent dislike and distrust of the royal prerogative. The inscription of 'Commonwealth' on his heart indicates republicanism and is a throwback to Cromwell's Commonwealth. His intestines, 'French Principles', indicate his support for the French Revolution, while his kidneys are labelled 'Aristocratic' (right) and 'Democratic' (left), providing an interesting balance between Britain's more aristocratic government and post-revolutionary France's democracy. Meanwhile, his bladder is inscribed 'Reservoir for Royalty', which hints at his contempt for the royal prerogative. His lungs, represented by a pair of bellows inscribed 'Oratorical Lungs Variably Verbose', are an attack on his oratory and hints at political opportunism. The inscription on his forehead, 'Self-Interest', backs this up, insinuating that Fox was a pragmatic opportunist and lacking in political principles. This lack of principles is further reflected by the two distinct parts to his head of hair, with

Fox sporting a bagwig on the left half of his head and his own hair visible on the right. The inference appears to be that Fox was in two minds and was not operating from firm or fixed principles. Dent has, however, stopped short of portraying him as Janus, the two-faced god of Roman mythology. His other internal organs are inscribed 'Gallic', 'Aristocratic', 'Fraternity', 'Intemperance' and 'Democratic'.

Dent also intimates that central to Fox's make-up are his vices, as reflected by his ribs, which are inscribed 'Duplicity', 'Drunkenness', 'Whoredom', 'Gambling', 'Envy', 'Inconsistency' and 'Prophaness' on his right-hand side and 'Enmity', 'Cruelty', 'Madness', 'Distress', 'Treachery', 'Ingratitude' and 'Despair' on his left. The skin on his right is inscribed 'Fat of Pidgeons', indicating his love of shooting, while that on his left, 'Fat of Friends', indicates his financial reliance upon his friends. On Fox's arms, Dent contrasts British and French industry. Fox's right sleeve, embroidered 'British Industry', contains the image of a dice box and pair of dice, a link to his gambling addiction. Beneath them is embroidered 'Interest of Levellers, Jews, Gamesters, Adventurers'. Fox was often portrayed as a gamester and political adventurer, while the Jewish reference concerns the large amounts of money he owed to Jewish moneylenders.[64] On his left arm, tattooed 'French Industry', there is the image of a hangman's noose and axe; beneath this is tattooed, 'Advocate for Atheists, Jews, Papists, Dissenters &c'. Fox's right hand is clenched into a fist, underneath which is inscribed 'Argument', while in his left he holds a dagger, underneath which is engraved 'Penetration'. Through their dissection of Fox, Cruikshank and Dent attempt to highlight Fox's Francophile views. There is an internal tension within the prints between Britain and France, with British and French values balanced through their representation of him. One can surmise that with this tension, Cruikshank and Dent are questioning Fox's loyalty and calling for the reader to speculate which side Fox truly favoured. Indeed, both prints hint at treason without explicitly accusing Fox of being a traitor, instead indicating that he was teetering on the brink, which Cruikshank's image of him straddling the English Channel demonstrates to good effect. In addition, these prints accuse Fox of deceit and hypocrisy, claiming to be one thing but, in reality, being another. In *A Right Hon*[ble]. *Democrat Dissected*, Dent is evidently offering up key points of contrast between Britain and France, which he thinks Fox embodied, through his response to the French Revolution and during his Jacobin or sans-culotte phase. Unsurprisingly, Dent has also furnished Fox with a pronounced five o'clock shadow and bushy eyebrows, which had characterized prints of him since the 1780s and acted as a visual cue to the reader that they were gazing at Fox.

One of the clearest associations of Charles James Fox and the Foxite Whigs with the ideals of the French Revolution is represented in Charles Williams's *The Funeral of the Party*.[65] It invokes memories of James Gillray's *The Funeral Procession of Miss Regency* (Colour Plate 7),[66] with Fox and his colleagues forming part of a funeral procession. In this instance, the funeral is that of the Foxite Whigs, rather than the possibility of the Prince of Wales becoming Regent and installing his friends in office. The timing of the print is interesting, as one might have expected a similar print in 1784, with the Foxites mourning their fall from office and the failure of many of their colleagues to be re-elected at the 1784 general election.[67] Equally, 1798 appears a little late, with the Foxite group in Parliament having suffered a number of high-profile defections during the early 1790s.

Frank O'Gorman has argued that while Foxite unity was weakened by the Regency Crisis, it was not destroyed and that their subsequent split during the 1790s was not in any sense inevitable.[68] Edmund Burke only left the party in 1791 after a disagreement with Fox over the French Revolution, while Lord Loughborough deserted in January 1793 to become Lord Chancellor, and the Duke of Portland, Viscount Fitzwilliam, and other leading Foxites also joined Pitt the Younger's administration in 1794.[69] It would seem, therefore, that this print is a reflection on the slowly dwindling support for the Foxites in Parliament and the growing sense of futility in their opposition to the government, especially on issues affecting civil liberties, which ultimately led them to secede from Parliament in 1797 (only returning in 1801 following Pitt the Younger's resignation).

The coffin at the centre of the procession is covered in a black shroud with a red, white and blue tricolour banner at the top, middle and bottom. Between the top and middle tricolours are a number of emblems in the form of coats of arms. These coats of arms represent 'Plunder' represented by a *bonnet rouge* and crossed muskets, 'Murder' represented by a *bonnet rouge* and crossed daggers, '[P]erjury' represented by a *bonnet rouge* and crossed spears and 'Injusti[ce]', the emblem for which is obscured. On the top of the coffin sit two books: *Kentish Oaths*, a reference to the treason trials of Arthur O'Connor,[70] John Binns and a number of other suspected United Irishmen and United Englishmen, and *Toasts and Sentiments*.[71] On top of the books rest a number of old wigs and on top of this sits a skull, inscribed 'Boney-parte', with a dagger in its mouth and a *bonnet rouge* on its head. Behind the books sit a pile of worn-out *bonnets rouges*. The shroud and articles above the coffin are labelled 'Regalia of the Deceased' and indicate the nature and beliefs of the party for which Fox and his supporters mourn. The pall-bearers of the coffin are all members of the lower orders, wearing black gowns trimmed with a red, white and blue tricolour. The whole procession, with the exception of the priest, has a black scarf draped around their *bonnets rouges*. The procession is led by four citizens, each holding a meat cleaver and a bone. Next comes Charles Howard, eleventh Duke of Norfolk, as standard bearer, carrying a banner 'Majesty of the People', a reference to the toast he famously made at The Crown and Anchor Tavern on 24 January 1798, a toast which was to have him expelled from the Privy Council and Lord Lieutenancy of the West Riding and his Colonelcy of the West Riding Militia.[72] Next comes the former priest, the Rev. John Horne Tooke, dressed in cassock, surplice and preaching bands, holding a book *Rights of Man*, who reads the service. Behind the coffin stand the mournful and distressed figures of Charles James Fox and Richard Brinsley Sheridan as chief mourners, both in blue frock coats and buff waistcoats, Fox holding a handkerchief to his eyes to mop up his tears. Behind them follow a group of politicians who remained loyal to Fox during the 1790s: Edward Smith Stanley, twelfth Earl of Derby, Francis Russell, fifth Duke of Bedford, Thomas Erskine in barrister's robes and wig, James Maitland, eighth Earl of Lauderdale, and Charles Stanhope, third Earl Stanhope. This group of Fox's supporters was frequently by his side in prints during the 1790s.[73] While this image was not the last to represent Fox as a Jacobin, it is one in which the artist very clearly sought to indicate that the Foxite Whigs had adopted Jacobin principles and foretells the party's destruction because of this. The purpose of this was twofold. First, Williams is attempting to discredit the Foxites by making the terms 'Foxite' and 'Jacobin' synonymous in the public imagination. This would have had the effect of making the party appear unpatriotic and potentially treacherous. Second, Williams attempts to make the Foxites appear irrelevant, indicating that their day has passed and that their most recent chance of sweeping to power, on the back of the French Revolution, has passed. Cleverly, Williams has borrowed from Gillray's earlier *Funeral Procession of Miss Regency* and employed a funeral procession in the hope of invoking memories of the Regency Crisis of 1788–9 and the failed Foxite bid for power. By attempting to draw on perceived similarities between the two events and the Foxite's failure to come to power, one could argue that he is attempting to suggest that to fail once might be considered a misfortune, but to fail twice just looks like carelessness. Williams's print, through linking the Foxites, Jacobinism and the French Revolution together with his funeral procession, presents his audience with the clear message that all three are spent forces and that it is time to move on.

Fox as a traitor

The caricaturists were to charge Charles James Fox with treason or treacherous behaviour throughout his career; however, the methods they employed varied to suit events. During the French Revolution, many of the prints which highlighted his Jacobin tendencies hinted at treachery. This section will consider caricature as 'history painting', examining how the artists sought to highlight suspected deviant behaviour, either through substituting contemporary figures for figures from the past or by inserting their 'victims' into contemporary news items. Fintan Cullen has said of history painting that in its traditional form it was the most elevated genre within the hierarchy of academic art, providing an allegorized interpretation of events for the nation, through which heroes could be worshipped safely within the context of the past, and was, therefore, the preserve of concluded history.[74] Meanwhile, Guilhem Scherf has argued that 'the aim of a history portrait is to guarantee the immortality and exemplary status of its subject'.[75] Accordingly, its influence upon caricature, which is often viewed as the lowest form of academic art, is particularly interesting. In their efforts to ape history painting, the caricaturists turned the genre on its head. The caricaturists added their own slant to history painting, presenting their subject as the villain rather than the hero.[76] Scherf's argument that 'a historical figure is defined by the deeds that bring him glory. The portrait illustrates "a chosen moment" which fixes the deed in a decisive and expressive manner'[77] is worth considering here. In employing this device, the caricaturists use the deeds of their historical figure to bring their subject to public ridicule and disdain, mirroring high art in their efforts to ape it. It is also worth considering the ephemeral nature of caricature in contrast to the longevity of oil paintings at this point. Whereas history painters could immortalize their subject in one painting, caricaturists could make their comparisons last only through repetition.

Byron W. Gassman has argued that the act of representing an individual as Guy Fawkes was a standard trope for accusing an individual of treacherous activity and one that was used against Fox on numerous occasions during his career.[78] Indeed, caricaturists had long used visual puns when representing individuals and now returned to this, making play with the similarity of Guy Fawkes [often spelt Guy Vaux] and Fox's surname. Alarik Rynell has suggested that 'the vowel in the name *Fawkes* was evidently already then pronounced short [allowing] an interchange of *Fox* and *Fawkes* being possible. The question of the initial consonant may still have been unsettled'.[79] The use of a figure from history, in this case Guy Fawkes, in order to impart a particular message, neatly fits with the idea of caricature aping history painting.

In the wake of the collapse of the Fox–North Coalition (1783), an anonymous artist portrayed Fox destroying the House of Commons with his oratory in *Guy Vaux or F- Blowing up the Par-t House!!!.*[80] This print, while rudimentary in terms of artistic style and talent, does manage to impart its message clearly. Fox is seen in the left foreground standing on a paved area labelled 'Loyalty'. The title indicates that Fox is Guy Vaux (Guy Fawkes). He is recognizably Fox, by his bushy eyebrows and pronounced five o'clock shadow. In his left hand, Fox holds a 'Cloak of Deceit' and in his right a burning torch 'Oratory', while he is wearing the headgear of an explosives expert. There is a trail ahead of him, 'Train of False Patriotism', leading forward towards the House of Commons, which has been blown into the air by the force of 'Gunpowder or Dissention', which has been ignited by the force of Fox's oratory. Also, within the explosion are two papers, 'Pitt's India Bill' and 'Mutiny Bill' and a 'Message from the [crown]'. This message is almost certainly a reference to the backstairs intrigue that saw George III oust the Fox–North Coalition from power by letting it be known in the House of Lords of his disapprobation of the coalition's India Bill. The House of Lords acquiesced to the King's request and voted down the bill.[81] To the left of the Palace of Westminster is a group, including Lord North and Edmund Burke (dressed as a Jesuit), standing on another paved area for 'Conspirators'. This reference to their being co-conspirators with Fox refers to the coalition's failed India Bill that was widely assumed would have given them control over East India patronage, which they could have used to rival the royal patronage exercised by George III. The reference to conspirators also links Fox's colleagues with the historical event alluded to within the print. Guy Fawkes was part of a conspiracy and by placing Fox's fellow coalitionists on a 'Conspirators' pavement, they are likening them to the other members of the Gunpowder Plot. Here, the artist is seeking to use a historic event to vilify a group of individuals for recent actions and through linking these two actions together is seeking to accuse them of treachery by association.

The prominent reference to the force of Fox's oratory is significant as much of his parliamentary support and position came on the back of his personality and debating skills. While it is true that much of the Whig Party support came from seats in the gift of the Whig magnates, such as the Duke of Portland, the Cavendish family and the Earl Fitzwilliam, it was Fox's political and oratorical skills that ensured his position as head of the party. During the early part of 1784, the followers of Fox and North remained in the majority in the House of Commons, despite being in opposition to the minority administration led by William Pitt the Younger. They used this majority to disrupt the government, preventing the passage of the Mutiny Bill, which was required in order to have control over the standing army and also the budget.

The image of Fox as Guy Fawkes (again spelt Vaux) was used by James Gillray as part of his comment on Edmund Burke's desertion of the Foxite Whigs in *Guy Vaux Discovered in His Attempt to Destroy the King & the House of Lords – His Companions Attempting to Escape* (Plate 8).[82] Burke stands in the centre holding a lantern in his left hand, shedding light on Fox and his subversive activity, a night watchman's staff rests against his left shoulder, while in his right hand he holds a rattle. Behind him, Sheridan and another figure escape, leaving Fox in the guise of Guy Fawkes to answer for their actions. Fox has a red cape covering his mouth and obscuring his usual stubble; however, it remains recognizable owing to his distinctive bushy eyebrows. The cape also goes some way to covering his blue jacket and buff waistcoat. He kneels by three barrels of gunpowder, two of which are labelled 'for the King' and 'For the House of Lords'. Fox holds a burning copy of Thomas Paine's *Rights of Man*, a book he was reputed to have loathed, having only read the first part,[83] in preparation to set light to the barrels. The use of the *Rights of Man* is interesting and was an attempt by Gillray to associate Fox with Paine's ideas. Indeed, Burke broke with Fox owing to a disagreement about the French Revolution. Fox, like Paine, had greeted it enthusiastically, while Burke had condemned it.

The fact that Fox is portrayed as desiring to destroy both the King and the House of Lords is significant, not only due to the historical parallel Gillray is making between him and Guy Fawkes but also in terms of an attempt at retribution for the part they both played in the downfall of the Fox–North Coalition in December 1783. In representing Fox in this manner, Gillray is seeking to define Fox as a traitor by his deeds, providing another link to history painting, albeit a mirror image.

Burke's role in the print is equally significant, as one of the leading architects of the ill-fated Fox–North Coalition East India Bill. Although he is represented as a watchman, the audience would have acknowledged the link between him and one of Guy Fawkes' co-conspirators, Francis Tresham.[84] In choosing Burke, rather than another member of the government to discover the plot, Gillray is suggesting that he has betrayed Fox and possibly his principles in moving over to the government.

As he enters, Burke cries:

> Hold Miscreant! – I arrest thee in the British Constitution which thou art undermining – I arrest thee in the name of human Nature which thou hast most cruelly outraged – I arrest thee in the name of the Monarch whom thou dost wish to deprive of dignity & of the people whom thou hast most basely deluded? – Nay no fawning: – thy tears & thy hypocrisy make no impression on the mind and truth and loyalty: – therefore Enemy of all good! Yield to that punishment that has long waited these crimes which are 'Left as yet unwhipt of justice'.

Fox responds:

> O Lord! O Lord! that ever my aim should be discover'd when I had taken such pains to disguise myself – for Heavens sake Watchman, what have I done that I should be apprehended? – what have I done only answer me that! – dare you accuse me only for what you think I intended to do! – have I ever assassinated the King, or blown up the Lords! – as to this gunpowder here I only intended to set fire to it merely to clear the nation of Buggs: – for goodness sake do let me go: – or if I must suffer do let it without holding up my own dark lantern in my face, for my Eyes are so weak with crying to think I should be charged with such a Villainy that I cannot bear the light.

Meanwhile, the fleeing Sheridan exclaims:

> I must be off while I can as to my Friend there why if he does go to pot there's the more room for me! – I wish I could squeeze out a tear or two as well as he, it might impose on the Mob, if they should stop me: – but I've come that humbug so often before that my Eyes – Damn my Eyes! There's not one drop left in them.

In this print, the speech bubbles afford the reader an additional insight into the scene that the artist has set before them. Fox's speech is an impassioned appeal to Burke not to turn him in, while the reference to Fox's tears refers to his breaking down in the Commons chamber over his split with Edmund Burke during the Quebec Debate.[85] Burke's accusation that Fox was attempting to undermine the constitution appears to be proven through Fox's treacherous actions within the print. However, it is also a reference to their respective stances on the nature of the revolution in France and their former unity of outlook on the American colonies in the 1770s and 1780s. Sheridan's parting jibe is less simple to interpret. However, his apparent wish for the downfall of Fox, combined with his lack of remorse for the loss of Burke from the Foxites, indicated by his complaint about his own lack of tears is, in all likelihood, a comment on his personal belief that he either was or ought to be the heir apparent to the Foxites should Fox retire. During the Regency Crisis of 1788–9 there had been much jostling for position between the potential heirs apparent[86] in Fox's absence.

Another way in which the caricaturists could make individuals look unpatriotic was to apply their mirrored history painting model to current news stories, rather than to events from the distant past, continuing to represent their 'victims' as villains rather than heroes. A good example of this came after the state coach was fired upon during a possible assassination attempt while George III was en route to the state opening of Parliament in 1795. James Gillray seized upon the opportunity to portray Charles James Fox not only in a negative light but, once again, to level against him the charge of treachery in his *The Republican Attack* (Plate 9).[87] In 1797, Isaac Cruikshank sought to recall the event to the public mind.

In *The Republican Attack*, Gillray portrays several members of the opposition attacking the state coach. The Marquess of Lansdowne, a former bitter political opponent of Fox,[88] fires a blunderbuss through the state coach. Other leading members of the opposition are also present, including Fox, Sheridan, Lord Lauderdale, Lord Stanhope and the Duke of Grafton. The coach is driven over Britannia, who lies on her shield and broken spear, by the First Lord of the Treasury, William Pitt the Younger. At the back of the coach, riding as footmen are the Master of the Rolls, Pepper Arden, in his judge's wig and the Secretary of State for War, Henry Dundas, identifiable by a tartan shawl round his shoulders. In front of him is the Foreign Secretary Lord Grenville and in front of him is the Lord Chancellor Lord Loughborough. With Pitt in the driving seat there is a clear inference that he was driving the country rather than the monarch, while the combination of the opposition's actions and their sporting of *bonnets rouges* indicate that they are untrustworthy, unpatriotic and treasonous. This contrasts well with Pitt driving the state coach over Britannia, indicating that in many ways he and his government are no better than the opposition. At the same time, the insertion of leading members of the opposition as the chief protagonists again ties in with a mirroring of history painting, using events to vilify individuals. It is also worth noting the presence of a loaf of bread surrounded by a black wreath in the top left-hand corner of the print, indicating the terrible harvest of 1795 and the very high cost of bread, which led to the attack. Accordingly, it is possible to detect some sympathy for both the plight of the poor and demands for peace.

Isaac Cruikshank's *The Opening of Parliament or the Air Gun Plot or the Infamous Attack on His Majesty*[89] provides a markedly different interpretation of events from that of Gillray, as he reflected upon them two years later. In many ways the Foxites, despite not being accused of having Jacobin and Francophile tendencies, come out of his version worse. Cruikshank makes no reference to the government and, therefore, the actions of Fox and his colleagues do not have a point of comparison. Lord Stanhope and Charles Grey stand in an open window on the top right of the print, looking on as Charles James Fox stands breaking wind in the direction of the state coach, with such force that the middle window of the coach is broken. Fox is recognizable by his pronounced five o'clock shadow, bushy eyebrows and blue frock coat. George III looks on in amazement from inside the coach, indicating the newly made hole in the window to his travelling companion, whose features are obscured from the stream of wind coming from Fox's bottom. Here, Fox's behaviour is at best disrespectful to the person of George III; however, when one recalls the action that inspired this print was an assassination attempt, Fox's actions are immediately transformed from insolence and downright rudeness to the more serious charge of high treason.

While the images above do not fit the model of traditional history painting as outlined by Cullen, they do appear to turn the genre on its head, through employing similar techniques, but in reverse. The caricaturists sought to vilify their subjects, through aligning them with the villains of history, while using both current and past events to define their 'victims' through deeds that would bring them to public disdain and censure.

Pitt as minister

In contrast to Charles James Fox, William Pitt the Younger had very few 'stock images'. Pitt was elected MP for Appleby (Westmoreland) in December 1780, taking his seat in January 1781. He rose to prominence in 1782 when he entered government with Lord Shelburne as Chancellor of the Exchequer in July. He left office at the fall of Shelburne's administration in February 1783; however, he was widely viewed as the (prime) minister in waiting during the ill-fated Fox–North Coalition and became First Lord of the Treasury in December 1783. Pitt remained in office until 14 March 1801, resigning over a disagreement with the King over the need for Catholic emancipation as part of the Act of Union with Ireland. Out of office, Pitt kept a low profile, with many of his former supporters remaining in post during Henry Addington's administration. He returned to the Treasury as First Lord in 1804, following the failure of the Peace of Amiens. Pitt died in office on 23 January 1806. When he died, Pitt had spent twenty-five years and one month in Parliament, holding office for nineteen years and eight months of that time, and spending eighteen years and eleven months as prime minister. With that in mind, it is hardly surprising that the overwhelming majority of prints depicting him were published while he was in office and show him as 'Pitt the Minister'. Despite having only one predominant image, it is still important to consider it and ask the same questions of it as were asked of those of his great rival, Charles James Fox.

Pitt the Younger's first outing in caricature came on 16 February 1782 in *The Royal Hunt or a prospect of the year 1782*.[90] Pitt is depicted among a group of patriots, Charles James Fox ('F-x'), Edmund Burke ('B-k') and the Duke of Richmond ('R-d'), who are standing to the right of Lord North ('N-h') and his ministers in the foreground, offering advice. Pitt ('W-P-t') advises North to 'Shake off this Indolence'. The print, regarding the North administration and their handling of the American War, clearly places Pitt in opposition to North, standing alongside Fox. He is not alone in being identified by a redacted version of their name; however, the artist clearly feels the need to provide a W to differentiate him from his father, while at the same time aligning him with Chatham's stance. Pitt was only to appear in one further print, Thomas Colley's *War of Posts*, published on 1 May 1782,[91] prior to obtaining office. This print portrays members of the new Rockingham administration sat on small columns or 'posts'. On the right of the print a black devil, holding a trident, ushers North and three of his principal supporters, Sandwich, Amherst and Mansfield, into the fires of hell. A storm cloud hovers over the new administration, but the bolts of lightning emanating from them are directed towards the outgoing administration. Pitt the Younger is positioned immediately underneath the cloud, standing to one side of the ministers. The fact that he is standing is a reference to his refusal to accept a minor office from Rockingham; however, his presence alongside the new ministers indicates actual or implied support. This idea that Pitt would support the Rockingham ministry is reinforced by the fact that he is holding a sheaf of thunderbolts aloft. The lightning is inscribed 'Vox Populi Vox Dei' and Pitt, via a speech bubble, ascribes the lighting to his father saying, 'The Lightning [*sic*] of my father'. This could be a reference to the powerful oratory of the Earl of Chatham and suggesting that Pitt has inherited his father's skills as a parliamentary speaker. Once again, the identity of the figures is revealed through the presence of a key, providing names with letters removed. In both prints Pitt is soberly dressed in a style commensurate with the period, without being in the blue and buff of the Rockinghamite/Foxite group or the court dress of ministers.

The fact that only two prints of Pitt, prior to his obtaining office, have survived mean that there is insufficient evidence upon which to argue for a 'stock image' prior to his joining the government. This first print of Pitt as Chancellor of the Exchequer, James Gillray's *Jove in His Chair* (Plate 10),[92] shows the new First Lord of the Treasury, Lord Shelburne, seated in a triumphal car with Pitt the Younger, his Chancellor of the Exchequer riding behind in place of a footman. Shelburne had been promoted to prime minister following the death of the Marquess of Rockingham, despite the fact that the Rockinghamites were the larger group in the coalition, and following Shelburne being appointed over their candidate, many of them resigned. It is uncertain whether Shelburne had always intended to offer Pitt the Younger a senior position or whether the resignation of Fox, Cavendish and other leading Rockinghamites forced his hand. However, in *Jove in his Chair*, Gillray depicts Pitt as a callow youth in spite of being twenty-four years of age. His inexperience is further indicated by the fact that in his left hand he is holding an alphabet book. He also holds two scrolls inscribed '[Chan]cellor of Excheqr' and 'Ways & Means' indicating his now found position as chancellor. Pitt's jacket has also changed from his previous outings and resembles that of Shelburne and so could be meant for court dress or Windsor uniform.

Another early print of Pitt in office is James Gillray's *Aside He Turn'd in Envy, yet with Jealous Leer Maligne, Eyed Them Askance* (Plate 11),[93] in which Pitt is sat next to Shelburne behind a table. The visual contrast between the two foreshadows that with his rival Fox, who is also present. Although sat, Pitt is clearly the taller man and is considerably thinner than either Shelburne or Fox. Interestingly, Pitt looks considerably older in this print, published on 12 December 1782, than he did in *Jove in his Chair*, published on 11 September 1782. Both prints are by the same artist, James Gillray, and were published almost exactly three months apart, making them ripe for comparison. The first was published in the early months of Pitt's tenure as Chancellor, when there were still questions over his youth and inexperience. Undoubtedly by December, something had changed. As leader in the Commons, he would have become a better-known figure than he had been when appointed to office, while his abilities and competence as minister and administrator had been tested. By portraying Pitt as a callow youth, still learning his alphabet in *Jove in his Chair*, Gillray had insinuated that Pitt lacked experience for the office he had assumed. By portraying him closer to his true age in *Aside he Turn'd for Envy*, Gillray had begun to put those doubts behind him; however, the fact that Shelburne's hand is on Pitt's arm indicates a feeling that a steadying and guiding hand is still required. Pitt's face is, however, much more assured, and the aloof expression, which was to characterize his later representations, is beginning to take shape.

In all these early prints Pitt is portrayed as being tall and slim; however, his key facial features were still being settled. By the time the stock image of 'Pitt as Minister' had settled down, his nose had become long and pointed and he was invariable turned out in Windsor uniform, which George III had designed in 1779, in either its red with blue turnbacks and cuffs or blue with red turnbacks and cuffs version. A good example of this settled image is James Gillray's *Ministerial Eloquence* (Plate 12),[94] in which Pitt is stood as if addressing the House of Commons. He sports a wig rather than his own hair and his nose is long and pointed, thus giving him an aloof look; meanwhile, his cheeks are ruddy, alluding to his proclivity for port. Pitt is also very slender in comparison to all the other figures in the series. Despite the print being published in 1795, when Pitt would have been in his mid-thirties, he still looks youthful, another characteristic of this stock image, and a reference to his being Pitt the Younger. His buttoned-up blue frock coat with red collar and cuffs of the undress Windsor uniform is paired with a neatly tied white cravat, providing an air of his being a man of status, who is as careful and concerned about his appearance as he is with his business, namely the affairs of the state. All this is typical of images of Pitt during his tenure as prime minister. The accompanying text, concerning successes in both the East and West Indies, helps to re-enforce this image and is in stark contrast to that of Charles James Fox in the same series, which will be compared in the next chapter.

Another recurring theme within the visual representation of William Pitt the Younger is that of representing him as an animal; however, unlike his great rivals Charles James Fox, whose name conjured up animal imagery as a fox, and Charles Grey, a greyhound, for Pitt no single animal was predominant, with a variety of animals employed to suit the situation.

Conclusion

Stock images have long proved an important tool in the caricaturists' arsenal. They were not set in stone, altering over time to suit changing events and techniques. At each stage of their development, however, they retained some key features from previous stock images, thus aiding the reader's identification of the latest version. Caricaturists could take these stock images and engender them with a new meaning through the use of a number of emblematic devices. For example, if they wished to accuse their 'victim' of treachery, all they needed to do was invoke an old method, that of depicting them as Guy Fawkes. Fawkes was not, however, the only person from the past whose image was engendered with powerful images of sedition, treason and rebellion. Indeed, the image of Oliver Cromwell was also invoked from time to time along these lines. One example of this, which Fox was on record as having resented,[95] was James Sayer's *The Mirror of Patriotism*,[96] in which Fox is shown looking into a mirror from which the face of Oliver Cromwell can be seen staring back at him. The invocation of villains of the past also mirrored the high art genre of history painting, representing their 'victims' as the villains and using events to vilify them rather than as a form of hero-worship. After the French Revolution of 1789, the caricaturists were gifted a new emblem for indicating a person's revolutionary outlook. All they needed to do was include a *bonnet rouge* and instantly the figure sporting it would become suspect and their character open to question.[97] Another important aspect of the stock image in relation to accusations of treachery was the use of 'faux-history painting', in which the artists, to great effect, would cast their 'victim' as the villain of a current news story.

Stock images were not only useful for portraying individuals but also found a role in representing entire nations through emblematic embodiment. Accordingly, 'pre-Golden Age' figures such as Britannia and Hibernia remained current during the 'Golden Age', acting as a convenient (if imprecise) shorthand for Britain and Ireland. During this period, the figure of John Bull was also developed to provide a useful foil to the politicians and allowed the artists to indicate how their actions might affect the average person on the streets. Bull soon developed as a key emblem for the English masses, thanks to his standardized representation as a solid dependable farmer who, while not particularly intellectual, is brave, practical and patriotic. It is due to these characteristics that the scheming politicians are portrayed as having little difficulty in pulling the wool over his eyes and deceiving him. It is interesting to note that after the Industrial Revolution, his image moved away from that of a country yokel, becoming increasingly middle class, thus reflecting the changing nature of English society.[98]

The stock images of actual people also reflected their change in status throughout their lives and careers. The career of Charles James Fox provides a clear indication of this. His political maturity was reflected by his growing from cub to fox, while his movement from government to opposition neatly coincides with the development of the image of him as a 'Man of the People'. His return to government in 1806 is also characterized by a rehabilitation of this image, with his clothes becoming fancier, as his financial position became stronger and his ever-present five o'clock shadow became less prominent or disappeared altogether as part of his rehabilitation after the death of his great rival, William Pitt the Younger. Meanwhile, his support for the French Revolution led to his being caricatured as a revolutionary, either as a sans-culotte or else through his wearing a *bonnet rouge*.[99] The ease of this transition from the 'Man of the People' image is important and highlights the continued importance of accessories as emblems and visual shortcuts to tell the audience about an individual's views and beliefs.

A strong 'stock image' was imperative within political caricature. Once a politician had an established image in caricature they could be dropped into scenes at will and this would obviate the need for complicated and time-consuming speech bubbles and other text to explain who they were and the part they were playing. Of course, even after a 'stock image' had been created, text was still required in some prints, but this was more to develop the scene rather than identify the characters. This in turn had an important role to play in the development of a propaganda role for caricature. A strong stock image also aided the caricaturists when they sought to ape and mirror history painting, substituting their 'victim' for a villain from history, vilifying them by association, as opposed to the true history painting ideal of substituting an individual for a heroic figure from history or antiquity in order to eulogize them.

The Rivalry Begins

Introduction

The reputations of career politicians are often built upon their stance on the great issues of the day, even more so when the 'big beasts' of the age line up on opposing sides. Such periods not only captured the imagination of contemporary onlookers, including the caricaturists, but also subsequently sparked the interest of historians and political scientists. Such contests are at their most memorable when, in addition to political differences, there are obvious contrasts between the key protagonists in terms of personality, appearance or social class.[1] Not only does this make it easier to portray their battles as a struggle of class, ideology, etc., the contests become humanized and more vibrant, something that is often lacking within a period of political consensus. Samuel Rogers, a contemporary of Charles James Fox and William Pitt the Younger, commented that 'Pitt would be right nineteen times for once that Fox would be right: but that once would be worth all the rest'.[2] Inevitably, major events, such as the East India Bill crisis (1783–4), would bring these differences to the fore. Michael Wynn Jones has argued that William Pitt the Younger and Charles James Fox dominated English satirical prints during the late 1780s, highlighting their power struggle and rhetorical duels in the House of Commons as the main reasons behind this.[3]

This chapter will examine how the relationship in caricature between Charles James Fox and William Pitt the Younger developed during the formative years of their rivalry, from Pitt's first entering Parliament in 1780 to the 1784 general election. Key questions that this chapter will address are: how was the rivalry of Charles James Fox and William Pitt the Younger represented? How have their respective actions been reflected within satirical prints? Did the relationship change depending upon who was in office? Were stock images (as discussed in Chapter 1) important in the caricaturist's representation of the relationship? Why are Fox and Pitt so prevalent in caricatures of this period? Are Fox and/or

Pitt singled out as the leader of their particular political group? And finally, if so, what is the nature of the relationship of the First Lord of the Treasury and the 'Leader of the Opposition' in caricature and to what extent were political prints and/or the relationship of Fox and Pitt responsible for creating the idea of a national or modern-style party leader?

During the mid-eighteenth century, Henry Fox, later Lord Holland, and William Pitt the Elder, later Lord Chatham, emerged as two of the key figures in the House of Commons. Together they established one of the greatest political rivalries of the eighteenth century. This rivalry was to be played out by their second sons, Charles James Fox and William Pitt the Younger, during the later decades of the century.[4] The potential for this rivalry to reignite was not lost on the Fox family. Lord John Russell recalled an anecdote from a conversation in 1766, as recounted to him by Emilia, Duchess of Leinster, between her and her sister, Lady Caroline Fox. Lady Holland remarked she had, that morning, called upon Lady Hester Pitt, and that Pitt the Younger, who was not yet eight, was the cleverest child she had ever seen. His behaviour, a result of his strict and proper upbringing, convinced her that he would long be a thorn in Charles's side.[5] Within this criticism of her husband's unconventional methods of raising children, in contrast to that of his great political rival, the Earl of Chatham,[6] Lady Caroline Fox also demonstrated great foresight, in suggesting that the old family rivalry between the fathers would be played out again through their second sons. Indeed, this potentially 'throwaway' remark resonates through the political prints of the late eighteenth century, which build Fox and Pitt the Younger up into not only bitter rivals, but also political figureheads for opposition and government alike. This statement is remarkable for its accuracy as a long-term prediction, as well as the fact that the wives of the two great rivals, Chatham and Holland, appear on reasonable terms.

Early lives

Like his elder rival, Pitt the Younger enjoyed a conventional upbringing and entered Parliament at a young age; however, that is as far as the comparison goes. As a child, Pitt the Younger was sickly and educated at home before matriculating to Pembroke College, Cambridge, in April 1773, aged just 14. Upon leaving Cambridge, Pitt the Younger took rooms at Lincoln Inn and trained for the Bar, practising on the Western Circuit during the summer of 1780. Both Pitt and Fox had a keen interest in amateur dramatics,[7] which, combined with their study of the classics, played a key part in their development as orators, as did Pitt the Younger's studies at the Bar. This led to their being counted among the leading parliamentary orators of their day.[8] The poet, Samuel Rogers, noted the differences in oratorical style between Pitt the Younger and Charles James Fox, as recounted to him by Porson, who said, 'Pitt carefully considered his sentences before he uttered them; but that Fox threw himself into his and left it to God Almighty to get him out again'.[9] It is clear, therefore, that Pitt's legal training had an influence upon his oratorical style, while Fox's perceived recklessness, generally, was reflected in his style of oration. In December 1783, Horace Walpole, writing to Sir Horace Mann, sought not only to compare the oratory of Fox and Pitt, but also each to that of their fathers, suggesting that while Pitt (both Elder and Younger) had a brilliant command of language, Fox in common with his father had both solid sense and the ability to display it clearly. For Walpole, Pitt was unlikely to prove an adequate rival for Fox, owing to his luminous powers of displaying it (solid reason) clearly that mere eloquence is but a Bristol stone, when set by the diamond, reason.[10]

The oratorical ability of Charles James Fox had caught the attention of Horace Walpole very early in his career. As early as 25 January 1770, while speaking in a House of Commons committee on the 'State of the Nation', Walpole commented:

> Young Charles Fox, of age but the day before, started up and entirely confuted Wedderburn[11] even in law, producing a case decided in the courts below but the last year and exactly similar to that of Wilkes: the court, he said had no precedent, but had gone on analogy. The House roared with applause.[12]

Oratory was one of a number of areas in which Fox and Pitt the Younger provided a stark contrast, which bizarrely drew them closer together as the leading orators of their generation. Most of their parliamentary careers were spent opposite each other in the House of Commons, with Pitt as First Lord of the Treasury and Fox as 'Leader of the Opposition'. Despite their respective roles, it was Fox who headed the list of representations in caricature, featuring in 1,061 prints compared to the 699 representing Pitt between 1782 and 1806.[13] The prevalence of prints featuring both Fox and Pitt is striking and, during the early part of Pitt the Younger's career, from his first appearance in satirical prints in 1782 until 1786, Pitt was to feature in more prints with Fox than without him. Despite their constant presence and vilification in caricature, both Fox and Pitt enjoyed satirical prints, both of themselves and others, and actively collected them.[14]

Opposites attract

In addition to their political differences and divergent oratorical styles, the contrast in the personal appearances of William Pitt the Younger and Charles James Fox played straight into the hands of the caricaturists and helped make the two characters instantly recognizable within the satirical prints of the late eighteenth century. The tall and lean frame of Pitt the Younger with his prominent aquiline nose and weak chin, often depicted standing aloof, provided a distinct contrast to the shorter, rotund frame of his rival, Fox, with his pronounced bovine jawline and hirsuteness. These physical differences were augmented by their respective choice of clothing. Pitt, the King's minister, was conventionally shown sporting Windsor uniform, designed by George III to replace the old court dress. Meanwhile, Fox and his followers favoured the blue and buff colours of General George Washington, which the Opposition Whigs had adopted as their own, in solidarity with the colonists during the American War of Independence, and stuck to in the ensuing decades. These 'uniforms' proved a further gift to the caricaturists, enabling them easily to denote the political persuasion of new characters they introduced merely with the use of appropriate dress.[15] This use of dress to denote nationality or political persuasion was not, however, a new concept, with the Scots being depicted in tartan and the Dutch in clogs since the eighteenth century.[16] The use of Windsor dress and 'blue and buff' also enabled the caricaturists to use Pitt the Younger and Charles James Fox as emblems of their respective factions and build them up into the first modern political leaders. This enabled them, through one individual, to represent an entire party or faction, linking them and their followers to a set of principles and policies. This trope could then be utilized, especially at election time, to create propaganda that would have currency across the whole country, thus potentially increasing the market for the prints and help constituents, in the days before the publication of party political manifestos, anticipate how their local candidates might act on a particular issue.

Isaac Cruikshank's *John Bull Humbugg'd Alias Both Ear'd*[17] is a good example of Fox and Pitt being used as emblems for their respective 'parties'. George III stands in between Charles James Fox on the left and William Pitt the Younger on the right. Fox is dressed in his customary blue and buff with the addition of a *bonnet rouge*, indicating his support for the French Revolution. He carries a copy of the opposition newspaper, the [*Morning*] *Chronicle*, under his arm, and blows a trumpet into the King's ear, while saying 'Horrid Bloody News just arrived from France the Combin'd Armies after a Severe Engagement were all Cut into Cabbage for the National Convention too – too – too'. In contrast, Pitt the Younger, dressed in his Windsor uniform, holds a copy of the pro-ministry paper, *True Briton*, in his hand and blows his trumpet at his sovereign's other ear and says 'Great News arriv'd from France, Paris taken and more Canon, Cartridges, Balls, Bombs and Assignats than they can find room for; also 100,000 Skeletons of Sans Coulottes, Carmignols &c &c ready Dried for the Surgeons! – NB will prevent the Robbing of Church Yards & to be sold remarkably cheap too too too Rare News for Old England!!!'. In the middle, a shocked and confused George III responds to the mixed messages by exclaiming 'What _ what _ what Cabbage and Carmignols Fredderick killd ha Frederick'. The print itself relates to the campaigns against the French in May 1794, when the Duke of York suffered heavy losses while defeating the French in a cavalry action in Willems on the 10th before the English and Austrian armies were defeated at the Battle of Tourcoing. In emphasizing the defeat, Fox is clearly associated with his repeated calls for peace with France, which make him appear unpatriotic and pro-French. Meanwhile, in highlighting and exaggerating the earlier victory and making no reference to the defeat, Pitt's judgment could be called into question; however, he also appears patriotic when juxtaposed with the position and attire of Fox. The fact that they are holding newspapers is interesting. While on the one hand, in conjunction with the horns they are using, they identify Pitt and Fox as news boys, for the purposes of the print they also identify them as spokesmen for a particular side of the debate, and as such contribute to the establishment of them as party leaders within the prints.

Another good example of the visual contrast between Charles James Fox and William Pitt the Younger can be seen in James Gillray's 1798 print, '*Two Pair of Portraits: Presented to all the Unbiassed Electors of Great Britain*' by John Horne Tooke (Plate 13), originally published in the *Anti-Jacobin Review*.[18] This print shows the radical philologist, John Horne Tooke, sitting in front of an easel upon which are two portraits. On the left, Charles James Fox is characteristically corpulent and unshaved while on the right, William Pitt the Younger is visibly taller and thinner. To the right, propped up against a table, are two more portraits; on the left the first Baron Holland and on the right the first Earl Chatham. The family resemblance between the two pairs of portraits is striking, as is the fact that in both instances their poses are mirrored. Additionally, the presence of portraits of Holland and Chatham serves both to remind the reader that the rivalry has spilled over into a second generation, and that in times of war with France, it pays to have a Pitt at the helm.

While Holland and Chatham are facing one another, Fox and Pitt are standing back to back and the plinth upon which they have their hand to support themselves could almost be the same and the likenesses taken at the same time. The strong physical differences between the two men made them useful foils for each other within the caricature of the period, while the re-ignition of an old rivalry also provided some extra spice to their exchanges. This need not have been the case, however. William Pitt the Younger had been approached by the Marquess of Rockingham to join his administration of 1782, but declined when he learned that he was not to hold one of the principal offices of state.[19]

A further example can be seen in James Gillray's eloquence series, which comprised eight prints that were also published collectively as a single sheet. In this sequence, William Pitt the Younger is depicted as *Ministerial Eloquence* (Plate 12),[20] with Charles James Fox as *Opposition Eloquence* (Plate 14).[21] The others in the series are *Naval Eloquence* – William, Duke of Clarence;[22] *Military Eloquence* – Frederick, Duke of York;[23] *Fools Eloquence* – Lord Lauderdale;[24] *Billingsgate Eloquence* – Lady Cecilia Johnson;[25] *Pulpit Eloquence* – John Moore, Archbishop of Canterbury;[26] and *Bar Eloquence* – Thomas Erskine.[27] The exact purpose of this series of prints is unclear; however, it does provide contrasts between a series of 'pairs of prints'. Pitt and Fox face each other as government and opposition; the dukes of Clarence and York look at each other as brothers (both in arms and filial ties) representing the two arms of the armed forces, the Navy and the Army; Lord Lauderdale and Lady Johnson are seen facing each other too. The only 'pair' facing the same way are Archbishop Moore and Erskine, representing the Church and the Law. This is far from coincidental and demonstrates that rather than being rivals they are in fact on the same side, both being concerned with how people live and conduct themselves. The odd pair are Lord Lauderdale and Lady Johnson who alone do not represent a profession or occupation considered suitable for members of the upper classes.

The captions themselves provide an useful insight into the discussions. Fox preaches doom and gloom over Pitt's war policies, while Pitt is reeling off his triumphs: 'Success in East and West Indies', 'conquest of Corsica' etc. This almost reads like a modern-day exchange at prime minister's questions, when the leader of the opposition attacks the government's policies and the prime minister reposts by highlighting their government's successes as a way of avoiding having to tackle the opposition's accusations head on and attempt to deflect their blow by accentuating the positives. Dorothy George states that both captions relate to speeches Fox and Pitt gave in the House of Commons.[28] Pitt's phrase, 'just and necessary war', has the appearance of a pre-prepared soundbite, in an age before mass media made such things commonplace. Credence is given to this by the fact that Pitt used it in both an address to the King moved on 12 February 1793, following the French declaration of war and again in his budget speech of 23 February 1795.[29]

The Duke of Clarence's caption reads 'Damn all Bond St. Sailors I say, a parcel of smell smocks! They'd sooner creep into a Jordan than face the French! Dam me!'. The reference to a Jordan is presumably a jibe at his adulterous affair with Mrs Jordan. Dorothy George remarks that Clarence's active naval service at sea ended in December 1790 when he achieved the rank of rear-admiral with his numerous applications for employment during the war with France ignored, despite his having seen active service during the American War of Independence.[30] His brother, the Duke of York, meanwhile exclaims: 'You Lie by G – -!'. The Duke of York, in contrast with his brother, did see active service during the French Revolutionary Wars and was involved in the disastrous Flanders campaign of 1793–95, for which he is remembered in the nursery rhyme *The Grand Old Duke of York*. It is entirely possible that he is defending himself from his brother's accusations of cowardice. Certainly, his angry gesticulation indicates that he is unhappy about something.

The image of Pitt the Younger does bear a resemblance not only to a watercolour portrait of him by James Gillray, painted in 1789, but also to a portrait from the studio of John Hoppner. The image of Fox bears an even more striking resemblance to the miniature portrait of Fox by Thomas Day. Both images are kinder to Fox and Pitt than many of Gillray's other images[31] and appear to have been influenced by contemporary portraits of them. Similarly, the images in *Naval Eloquence* and *Military Eloquence* resemble portraits of the Dukes of York and Clarence. Another point of interest in relation to this set of prints is that the image of the Duke of Clarence is virtually identical to another 1795 Gillray plate, published on 28 May, *A True-British Tar*, in which the same basic image has been used, but now sits in an oval with a new title and caption.

The age difference and stature of both Pitt and Fox come out clearly and the images resemble more of a portrait than a caricature, with Pitt, for once, not appearing anorexic. Pitt is obviously better groomed, with Fox portrayed with his characteristic five o'clock shadow and messy hair. Policy differences are also picked up on in the captions below the prints. They do, however, provide a clear contrast between the two. Pitt is portrayed in a statesman like manner, seemingly holding out his hand to Fox, who is backing away, his hand held in with his fist clenched, in contrast to Pitt's open palm. Fox appears shifty and distrusting of Pitt's advance. Another reading is to see Pitt as open and trustworthy, and Fox as closed, scheming and deceitful. Fox's facial expression could also be read as embarrassed disbelief at the news of Britain's overseas success after the dreary picture he had painted for Britain's chances, in light of Pitt's speech.

Having established why Charles James Fox and William Pitt the Younger were of such interest to the caricaturists, the remainder of the chapter will consider the early stages of their joint appearance in caricature, concluding with a discussion of the East India Bill crisis.

Opening salvos

A relatively early print contrasting Fox and Pitt is James Gillray's '*Aside He Turn'd in Envy, yet with Jealous leer Mailigne, Eyed Them Askance*' (Plate 11).[32] Here, Gillray depicts a woodland scene with Lord Shelburne and William Pitt the Younger sitting behind a table and Fox standing despondently, hands in his pockets, looking over his shoulder at the table. Pitt the Younger has two money bags in front of him, not only indicating his new role as Chancellor of the Exchequer, but also denoting the fact that the new administration enjoyed the favour and patronage of George III, something that the previous administration had not enjoyed in abundance. Fox is clearly contrasted with Pitt, not just by being out of favour and out of office, but also by his obvious five o'clock shadow and their difference in stature. Pitt is portrayed as being thin while Fox and, to an extent, Shelburne, whom Pitt is sitting next to, are depicted as being more rotund. This provides a contrast which is significant due to the similarity of Shelburne's physique and that of Fox, especially in view of the fact that Pitt had declined office with Shelburne; it is probable that he would have joined forces with the Rockingham Whigs and been sitting round the cabinet table with Fox rather than Shelburne. The presence of two money bags, in front of Pitt and one in his hands, also acts as a reminder of the precarious state of Fox's finances. Indeed, he and his elder brother, Stephen, had lost some £32,000 over three nights in 1772, while on another occasion Charles lost £11,000 in a 22-hour session of Hazzard. The upshot of this sort or reckless gambling was that both brothers were regularly in debt, borrowing heavily from both Jewish moneylenders and wealthy friends, in addition to receiving bailouts from their father.[33] This could explain the mournful look on Fox's face as he gazes over towards Shelburne, Pitt and the money, which is tantalizingly close on the far side of the table. There is a sense that it is there, seeking to tempt him back. The title of the print, *Aside he Turn'd in Envy, yet with Jealous leer Mailigne, Eyed them Askance*, neatly sums up this print. Fox is jealous not only of Pitt's current position, sitting at the top table as Chancellor of the Exchequer, but also of the fact that the King chose the leader of the junior coalition partner to head the new administration upon the Marquess of Rockingham's death, rather than one of his followers. Fox's leering at the table also calls to mind the distrust that developed between him and Lord Shelburne during the Rockingham administration, over the peace negotiations to end the American War of Independence. Shelburne, as home secretary, had successfully argued against granting independence, prior to negotiating peace with the American colonies, much to the annoyance of the foreign secretary, Fox, who had argued that independence should be granted prior to opening peace negotiations. This led to two separate peace negotiations taking place simultaneously, one with the American colonies, under Shelburne, and one with France, under Fox.

Some of the early prints of Fox and Pitt focus upon Pitt the Younger's youth, which contrasted well with Fox, who had already been an MP for nearly twelve and a half years when Pitt the Younger was first elected to Parliament in 1781.[34] James Gillray's *Westminster School or – Dr. Busby Settling accounts with Master-Billy and His Playmates* (Plate 15),[35] published on 4 February 1785, provides a good example of the visualization of the age gap. Fox is portrayed as Dr Busby, a former headmaster of Westminster School and a strict disciplinarian. He is seen sitting under a statue of justice beating Pitt with a birch. In the background, North, Sheridan and Burke are in the process of carrying off John Robinson, Sir Richard Hill and Richard Atkinson, who have already been flogged by Fox. This background scene demonstrates that in addition to the comment on Pitt the Younger's youth, Gillray is also passing comment upon the unjust way in which the Fox–North Coalition was flung from office. Pitt, despite his youth, was already seen as a key player, in part due to his abilities as an orator and in part owing to his father's reputation. This was not lost on Edmund Burke. Sir Nathaniel Wraxall recorded in 1781, in his memoirs, that 'Burke exclaimed [comparing Pitt the Younger with his father], that "he was not merely a chip off the old block, but the old block itself"'.[36]

A common theme, which frequently relied upon its protagonists being easily distinguished as opposites, is that of ministers, or potential ministers, being doctors, as demonstrated in prints such as *The Rival Quacks* (Plate 16),[37] published by B. Walwn on 2 February 1784. This anonymous print can be seen as a precursor to the later propaganda battle during the 1784 Westminster election. It does, however, also tie in with the battle going on in February 1784 for supremacy in the House of Commons and control of the government. The print shows Fox and Pitt each standing on a stage, Pitt to the left and Fox to the right. Each has a parasol over them, with Pitt's being inscribed Dr Pittardo and Fox's to Dr Reynardo &c. Reynardo is clearly a reference to Reynard, King of the Foxes, and harkens back to an earlier 'stock image' of Fox as a fox. Both Fox and Pitt are clearly appealing to the crowd and although the artist does not expressly elucidate what Fox and Pitt are saying, it is evident that they are proposing rival regimens for curing the country. Fox's platform is inscribed 'The Art of Gam-g Taught and Practiced in all its Branches By', thereby highlighting his dissolute lifestyle and gambling addiction.[38] There is an implicit suggestion within this that Fox was not trustworthy, especially with regard to his financial situation, which ties in with Boyd Hilton's assertion that 'Fox was widely thought to be corrupt while Pitt enjoyed a reputation for integrity'.[39] Pitt's platform, inscribed 'Rigestir [*sic*] Office where servants may hear of good Places', contrasts with that of Fox and is a reference to royal and ministerial patronage.[40] Behind Pitt's platform is India House, an allusion to the main political issue of the day – reform of the East India Company – while between the two platforms is St Stephen's, representing Parliament. The idea of Fox and Pitt being rival doctors or quacks is reinforced by the figure of Lord North, who stands behind Fox's platform, his back to the crowd, holding a bottle 'Carthatic Drops' and a hand bill 'Motion Pills for Members'. The word 'members' and the fact he is standing facing St Stephen's are significant, referring to members of parliament, and underpin the notion of the trope of state quacks and their cures being synonymous to political leaders and their policies.

This idea of equating politicians and their policies with quack doctors and their treatments would not have been an unfamiliar one when *The Rival Quacks* was published. In 1762, Pitt the Elder was satirized as a quack in *The Cramers or Political Quacks*,[41] while Lord Bute was also depicted as a doctor in *The State Quack*[42] in September 1762, in which he was shown on a stage holding an enema syringe.

The practice of likening politicians to doctors was resurrected on 1 April 1783 when Fox and North were portrayed by James Gillray as quack doctors in *A New Administration, or – The State Quacks Administering*,[43] in which Fox and Lord North are attacked for their partnership with the suspicion that they are not to be trusted and that their alliance might be detrimental to the country. There is also a lack of dignity and decorum in the way in which they are peering up Britannia's skirt, prior to Lord North inserting an enema syringe, indicating a perceived lack of scruples and principles in the alliance between two men who had been political enemies only a short time before, with Fox being prepared to consider impeaching Lord North for his role in the American War of Independence.

East India Bill crisis

The East India Bill crisis of 1783-4 was to prove the catalyst for the re-ignition of the old Fox–Pitt rivalry. Prior to the formation of the Fox–North Coalition, Fox and Pitt held short-lived talks as to the possibility of a Fox–Pitt coalition.[44] The failure of these talks all but condemned Fox and Pitt to sitting on opposite sides of the House of Commons for much of the remainder of their parliamentary careers. The East India Bill crisis has provoked a whole raft of scholarship. For L.G. Mitchell, the crisis was an early step in the disintegration of the Whig Party;[45] meanwhile, John Cannon has argued that the manner in which George III had the Fox–North Coalition defeated over their India Bill and thus precipitated a crisis was indefensible.[46] He also commented upon the devastating nature of James Sayers's prints of Fox in connection to his India Bill before going on to cite M. Dorothy George's findings that between January and May 1784, the production of caricatures reached record levels.[47] More recently, Cindy McCreery has built on this by arguing that 'the coalition of Charles James Fox and Lord North and its relationship with the king, especially with regard to the East India Bills, almost monopolized the satiric print trade during these five months'.[48] This section will build upon this work and examine the impact of the crisis upon the representation of Fox and Pitt in caricature.

At forty-three minutes past ten on the evening of 18 December 1783, George III sat down at Queen's House to write to his home secretary, Lord North:

> Lord North Is by this required to send Me the Seals of His Department and to acquaint Mr. Fox to send those of the Foreign Department. Mr. Frazer or Mr. Nepean will be the proper Channel of delivering them to Me this Night; I choose this method as Audiences on such occasions must be unpleasant.[49]

This letter followed the defeat of the India Bill in the House of Lords. The coalition's defeat was to go down in Whig folklore as an example of backstairs intrigue and a clear example of the death of Britain's balanced constitution.[50] The message is striking for its clear display of George III's loathing of the Fox–North Coalition, which he felt had been imposed upon him and also of his personal animosity towards Charles James Fox, with whom he refused to correspond personally to advise him of his being dismissed, instead causing him the indignity of being informed second hand. Lord North dutifully responded to his sovereign, writing later that same evening, 'Lord North has in obedience to His Majesty's commands, sent Mr. Nepean with the seals of the Home department and has communicated His Majesty's pleasure to Mr. Fox'.[51]

News of the Fox–North Coalition's dismissal spread rapidly, with Horace Walpole writing to Sir Horace Mann on Friday, 19 December 1783, to inform him that 'I have only time to tell you that at *one* this morning His Majesty sent to Lord North and Mr. Fox for their seals of secretary of state'.[52] Reflecting on the fall of the Fox–North Coalition in his *Memorials and Correspondence of Charles James Fox*, Lord John Russell recalled:

> He [Lord John Townshend] said, 'He had always foreseen the Coalition Ministry could not last, for he was at court when Mr. Fox kissed hands and he observed George III, turn back his ears and eyes just like the horse at Astley's, when the tailor he had determined to throw was getting on him'.[53]

Prior to their defeat in the Lords, the coalition had enjoyed a majority of 109 in the first division on the Bill in the Commons, rising to 114 on the second division and declining slightly to 106 in the third, with over 50 per cent of the members taking part in each division.[54] Before having the coalition defeated in the Lords, George III had sounded out Pitt the Younger about forming an administration[55] to replace the coalition that he believed had been imposed upon him in contravention of the customs and practices of the time.[56] When news of the Fox–North Coalition's dismissal broke, it was widely assumed that Pitt the Younger would be installed as First Lord of the Treasury, with Horace Walpole informing Sir Horace Mann of this speculation and of the assumption that Parliament would soon be dissolved.[57] During the debate on the Bill, on 17 December 1783, Fox produced a letter from his pocket stating that:

> his majesty allowed Earl Temple to say, that whoever voted for the India Bill, were not only not his friends, but he should consider them as his enemies. And if these words were not strong enough, Earl Temple might use whatever words he might deem stronger, or more to the purpose.[58]

With Pitt the Younger waiting in the wings, it was fitting that George III chose Lord Temple, one of his favourites, and coincidentally Pitt's cousin, to be his messenger to the Lords.[59]

The problem that the Fox–North Coalition faced with regard to India, and more specifically the East India Company, was the fact that while it was generally accepted that the company could not continue the way it was, attempts to impose radical reform upon the company were always going to be problematic. Such government-imposed reforms upon a chartered company could easily be spun as a preliminary attack, ahead of a more widespread offensive on the charters of private and joint stock companies. Lord Pembroke's understanding of the coalition's plans refuted the fear that the coalition sought to take failing private companies into public ownership. He indicated that Fox's East India Bill proposed to establish two boards, one of seven nominated by the government and one of eight nominated by the East India Company.[60] It would appear, therefore, that the East India Company's directors and shareholders would have continued to have a sizeable involvement in the running of the company and of the British territories in India.

The Fox–North Coalition's uneasy relationship with George III and his disapprobation of them are evident from the lack of promotions in the peerage and lack of pensions and sinecures that were granted. These forms of patronage were seen at the change of administration as an overt demonstration of royal confidence in the new ministers.

The sheer number of anti-coalition prints did not escape the notice of Horace Walpole, who, writing to HRH the Duchess of Gloucester on 13 March 1783, commented that 'there have been cart-loads of abuse, satiric prints and some little humour on the coalition of Lord North and Mr. Fox; nor has Lord Shelburne been spared before or since his exit'.[61] Surprisingly, after his appointment to the principal political office of the land, Pitt the Younger continued to be portrayed in fewer satirical prints than Charles James Fox.

During the first two years of his administration, Pitt continued to be portrayed in more prints with Fox than without him, while it was not until 1789 that Pitt first appeared in more prints than Charles James Fox, featuring in 41 to Fox's 17. This outstripping of Fox in the caricature stakes was to be short-lived, however, with Fox continuing to dominate the visual representation stakes in 1790, 1793, 1794, 1795, 1798, 1802 and 1806.

The dominance of Charles James Fox in the satirical prints of 1783 and 1784 is easily explained through the concerted attempt to vilify the coalitionists and prevent Fox's return to Westminster in the general election of 1784. One of the key early prints to feature Charles James Fox and William Pitt the Younger in relation to the East India Bill crisis was *The Fall of Carlo Khan*.[62] It has been argued that it was a sequel to *Carlo Khan's Triumphal Entry into Leadenhall Street* (Plate 17);[63] however, they are almost certainly not by the same artist. *Carlo Khan's Triumphal Entry into Leadenhall Street*, published on 5 December 1783 by Thomas Cornell, has been widely attributed to James Sayers, whereas George credits D. Brown as the artist behind *The Fall of Carlo Khan*. *Carlo Khan's*

Triumphal Entry marked Fox's first outing as Carlo Khan, a trope that was to prove particularly damaging to him personally and the Fox–North Coalition more widely, commenting as it did upon their perceived attitudes towards the East India Company and chartered companies more broadly.[64] John Cannon has argued that it was 'one of the most influential political caricatures ever published'.[65] In making this claim, Cannon cites M. Dorothy George, who, in turn, points to Lord Eldon's recollection of Fox complaining about Sayers's prints and North and Fox's complaining to Parliament about the influence of the prints.[66] It has been widely accepted by academics that James Sayers's depictions of Charles James Fox as Carlo Khan were particularly effective. David Powell has argued that Sayer's image of Fox as Carlo Khan captured the public mood exactly, perfectly conveying the suspicion in relation to the coalition's new India board. There were concerns as to how Indian patronage might be exercised in future, with the potential for rival patronage structure to the Crown, benefiting the coalition in or out of office.[67] This does, however, fail to consider Fox's continued influence over aspects of the East India Company. Horace Walpole, writing to Sir Horace Mann on 15 April 1784 concerning the recent political developments, reported:

> The Court [of Proprietors of the East India Company] will have a great majority; but the tide, at least here, begins to turn. They did not carry a supply of six new directors of the East India Company swimmingly yesterday: Mr. Fox was within two or three voices of choosing three of those very friends who were to have been members of his bill; which proves that he has still great weight among the proprietors.[68]

The Countess of Gower, in a letter to the Princess of Brunswick on 25 December 1783, commented on the mood of the country suggesting:

> Since we came to this town it has been a constant ferment. Mr. Fox had so alarm'd the minds of the people with his East India Bill that everybody but his & Lord North's party, except those they had engaged by *ways & means*, saw destruction in the country.[69]

This observation clearly gives credence to Powell's assertion that Sayers's Carlo Khan prints had captured the public mood exactly. The arguments of Cannon and Powell tie in closely with the fact that a number of artists produced their own variants on Sayers's print. Indeed, Samuel Collings,[70] Isaac Cruikshank[71] and John Boyne[72] each published their own image of Charles James Fox as Carlo Khan, while J. Notice also published a print by an anonymous artist.[73] In 1806, Charles Williams attempted to resurrect the image, referring to Fox as Carlo the Great; however, he moved away from representing him in Eastern robes.[74]

John Boyne's *Ambitio*[75] was subsequently re-titled *Carlo Khan*, tapping into this new 'stock image'. Boyne's two plates both show Fox in Eastern garb, which was the standard representation for this image. Cruikshank, however, chose to move away from this, making Fox more Jewish than Eastern in appearance. His version of Carlo Khan bears little likeness to his other portrayals of Fox, with the reference to Westminster and the fact that Carlo Khan was becoming synonymous with Fox being the main clues as to the figure's identity.

Collings's print again portrays Fox as a 'Man of the People', astride the shoulders of Georgiana, Duchess of Devonshire, commenting on his perceived victory at Westminster, despite the furore surrounding Fox's East India Bill. It is also intended as a parody to James Sayers's print, which established the image of Fox as Carlo Khan, *Carlo Khan's Triumphal Entry into Leadenhall Street*, and thus highlighting the recycling of ideas and designs by rival artists. Both *Carlo-Khan in Limbo*, with its reference to Fox as a debtor, and Cruikshank's portrayal of Fox as Carlo Khan appear to point to Fox seeking control of East India patronage as a means of paying off his debts. This being so, the Jewish physiognomy of Cruikshank's image could be a reference to the Jewish money lenders to whom Fox owed many thousands of pounds.[76]

Fox's indebtedness was one of the reasons why his India Bill was so distrusted, as people feared he would use it not only to ensure the ascendancy of the Opposition Whigs but, through the distribution of East Indian patronage, as a method of self-aggrandizement on a level unseen since his father was Paymaster General. The argument around the damaging nature of the image of Fox as Carlo Khan is further backed up by Loren Reid's assertion that 'outside of Parliament, sentiment continued to mount against the bill and its authors'.[77]

The portrayal of Charles James Fox as Carlo Khan was an interesting construction, used by the caricaturists and writers during the East India Bill crisis to depict the attitude of Fox and his fellow coalitionists in both text and images; the character Carlo Khan appeared in songs and pamphlets in connection to Fox.[78] Unlike the caricaturists' other stock images of Fox, his depiction as Carlo Khan did not really arrive out of an earlier 'stock image', nor did it really have any currency after the particular event from which it was derived. It also differed from the other stock images, since the portrayal of Fox dressed as a Moghul leader came to symbolize an entire policy and administration rather than just the individual who was depicted.[79]

It was during this period that the true value of these prints as propaganda began to receive contemporary comment with James Sayers's prints of Charles James Fox as Carlo Khan, prompting Fox to exclaim that they 'had done him more mischief than the debates in Parliament or the works of the press'.[80] In theory, the laws on seditious libel applied equally to caricature as the printed word. However, caricature was much quicker and easier to pirate, which led to caricaturists being less likely to be pursued under this legislation as it would only serve to enhance the notoriety of the print.[81]

Such was the success of caricature as a form of pictorial propaganda that in a rare instance of the Treasury offering patronage towards artists, the administration of William Pitt the Younger granted James Sayers a pension and the sinecure of Marshall of the Court of Exchequer for his Carlo Khan prints.[82] This points to the growing realization among politicians of the impact of satirical prints as a means of disseminating views and opinions. Cindy McCreery has, however, remarked upon the lack of direct evidence of the administration of Pitt the Younger sponsoring political prints, save for the pension given to James Sayers in 1790.[83] M. Dorothy George and Michael Wynn Jones have argued, however, that Pitt the Younger did award James Gillray a pension in 1797 in return for pro-government plates.[84] John Derry has sought to downplay the influence and effect of *Carlo Khan's Triumphal Entry*, suggesting that 'compared with other attacks on Fox it was most noteworthy for its mildness', qualifying his assertion by pointing out that during his career Fox was also likened to 'Satan, Beelzebub, Belial and sinister tyrants and republicans such as Cataline and Cromwell'. Derry later cites contemporary anecdotal evidence of Fox claiming the prints were damaging,[85] which makes his earlier statement, even with its caveat, a little curious. Clearly, Derry is suggesting that during the 1790s Fox suffered far more brutally at the hands of the caricaturists than he did earlier in his career, while also indicating that Fox had been pained by some of the earlier attacks.

While unattributed in the *BM Catalogue*, *The Fall of Carlo Khan*[86] bears a certain similarity of style to Sayers's earlier effort. The main stylistic difference is in the eyes of the elephant. Sayers's elephant has wide expressionless eyes, which characterized images of Lord North, while the elephant's eyes in *The Fall of Carlo Khan* are smaller with signs of some expression. *The Fall of Carlo Khan*, although not the only print to feature William Pitt the Younger and Fox as Carlo Khan, is significant owing to its charting the fall of Fox – quite literally as he tumbles head first from his elephant, Lord North, onto a copy of his East India Bill – and the rise of Pitt. The influence of George III in the fall of the Fox–North Coalition is clearly indicated by his depiction in the front row of the crowd, where he prods the elephant with a pole and draws blood. Lord Thurlow, in his judge's wig and Chancellor's robes, is also present, as are Henry Dundas, Lord Camden and the Duke of Richmond.[87] Meanwhile, the Bill's chief architect,

Edmund Burke, reprises his role from *Carlo Khan's Triumphal Entry* of leading the elephant; however, this time he is shown fleeing the scene.

William Pitt the Younger appears in the background shoring up India House with beams of wood. This is a clear suggestion from the artist that it was widely accepted that something needed to be done about the East India Company, represented by its headquarters. It is also apparent that the artist is suggesting that Pitt, having come to power on the back of a failed attempt by his predecessors to reform the East India Company, was compelled to prop up and defend the company until he could formulate his own proposals and introduce them to Parliament. Here Dundas, with his connections to the East India Company, would prove a crucial ally.[88] It is a misnomer to argue, however, that the coalition totally ignored the East India Company with regard to its East India policy. Indeed, L.G. Mitchell points out that 'according to Robinson's List, of the 31 nabobs sitting in the Commons in November 1783, 13 only were anti-coalition'. Mitchell goes on to point out that five of its directors actually held office in the Fox–North Coalition.[89]

This was soon picked up in a print published by S.W. Fores on 24 March 1784. *Carlo Khan Dethron'd or Billy's Triumph* (Plate 18)[90] is another print that aimed to capitalize upon the earlier success of James Sayers's *Carlo Khan's Triumphal Entry into Leadenhall Street*. This print was reworked during publication, with the building on the left being reduced in length and the elephant's head moving into profile. The elephant is obviously meant to be Henry Dundas, whose head is attached to the elephant's body. This is a clear indication of his influence with both William Pitt the Younger and the company members in the House of Commons. Behind Dundas lies the sorry figure of Fox, dressed once again as an Eastern potentate, apparently having fallen from the elephant, exclaiming 'perdition Take thee for the Chance is thine'. William Pitt the Younger rides on top of the elephant, in Windsor uniform, with the Mutiny Act in his pocket, a paper – supplies – under his arm and a 'New India Bill' and 'Stamp Act' in his hands. The first two papers are clearly a reference to the coalitionists' long running attempt prior to the 1784 general election to prevent the government from renewing the Mutiny Bill and having funds to carry out their programme. Meanwhile, the 'New India Bill' is the bill introduced to the House of Commons by Pitt after the 1784 election and a clear recognition that the East India Company needed reforming, thus indicating that the coalition's fall was not entirely due to an unpopular policy.[91] This acknowledgement also casts an element of doubt upon the notion of Fox's East India Bill being the opening salvo of an attack on company charters and hints at the idea of a new 'backstairs intrigue' and Fox's unpopularity with the monarch. Indeed, writing from Paris in January 1784 to his uncle Horace Walpole, the Hon. Thomas Walpole commented, 'As for the East India Company and their charter – it is a rotten company supported by a broken charter'.[92]

Although the image of Fox as Carlo Khan was important in connection with the East India Bill crisis, it was not the only means used by the caricaturists to depict the crisis. The print, *Political Game of Shuttlecock or Fluctuation of Indian Stock* (Colour Plate 3),[93] by an unknown artist, published by B. Walwyn on 3 February 1784, was the first time, in relation to prints of Pitt and Fox, that the caricaturists had so overtly alluded to the fact that in the House of Commons they sat on the Treasury and opposition benches respectively. The first example was *The Rival Quacks*,[94] published on 2 February 1784; it was quickly followed up by *Political Game of Shuttlecock or Fluctuation of Indian Stock* on 3 February; and *Billy Lackbeard and Charley Blackbeard playing at Football*, published on 7 February 1784. Both of these later prints provide a far more confrontational example of the technique.

In *Political Game of Shuttlecock*, Fox appears in his 'Man of the People' guise and the print is noteworthy for its move away from the Carlo Khan image. The likenesses of both Fox and Pitt are crude and are evidently the work of an inferior draftsman in comparison with Gillray, Sayers and Rowlandson. In spite of this, it provides an engaging commentary upon the crisis. Pitt and Fox are shown playing badminton with India House as their shuttlecock while George III clings onto India House as it is hit back and forth between Pitt and Fox, signifying the shifting advantage within the House of Commons. Significantly, India House is just past an imaginary centre line and to the left where Pitt is standing. He is shaping up to hit India House back towards Fox, holding his racket labelled 'Royal Confidence' with a slightly apprehensive expression on his face. Fox on the other hand looks on preparing to riposte Pitt's anticipated return with his racket, which is labelled 'Majority'. The idea of a game like shuttlecock is a useful means of illustrating this sort of battle between Royal prerogative and Commons majority, with a very real expectation that eventually something will have to give and the rally will unavoidably end with either the King having to back down, or as actually happened, a shift in allegiance taking place in the House of Commons. The decline in the Fox–North Coalition's majority can be explained by the fact that many of Lord North's supporters, who were elected upon a pledge to support the King's government, could see little chance of North returning to power during the current Parliament and felt duty bound to transfer their support to the ministers who currently enjoyed the King's confidence.

Another example of the India House being moved back and forth between Pitt and Fox in order to signify the shifting advantage in the House of Commons is Thomas Rowlandson's *Billy Lackbeard and Charley Blackbeard playing at Football*,[95] published by S.W. Fores on 7 February 1784. Rowlandson portrays Pitt, once again on the left and Fox on the right, as 'Man of the People' playing football with India House, which is hovering in the centre of the print. Interestingly, there is a dice box and dice on the table behind Fox and three playing cards under his feet, indicating his return to the table of Brooks' after his dismissal from office. The sides on which Fox and Pitt are shown in these prints are significant. If one were to imagine the scene taking place inside the Commons chamber with the speaker's chair in the middle of the background, instead of the hill, then Pitt would be situated in front of the Treasury benches on the left and Fox the opposition benches on the right, making a clear allusion to their respective roles as First Lord of the Treasury and 'leader of the opposition'.

Conclusion

The fact that visually, if not politically as well, Charles James Fox and William Pitt the Younger were polar opposites was a gift to the caricaturists and enabled them to become effective foils for one another within a visual medium. In an age before television, paparazzi, photographers and 24-hour news coverage at the click of a button, many people would have struggled to pick either man out of an identity parade early in their career. Their visual contrast was particularly important given stylistic transformation of caricature during the late 1770s and early 1780s, moving away from emblems and visual puns as proxies for people to a more exaggerated portrait style. As we saw in the previous chapter, there was a need for standardized images to be quickly adopted, to enable a certain level of consistency, which would lead to ease of identification when dealing with a large cast of relatively unknown figures. This also goes some way to explaining why a void opened up for a 'party leader' to act as an emblem or proxy for a particular grouping or faction, in an age before party.

Following the East India Bill crisis and the Fox–North Coalition's removal from office, Charles James Fox invariably found himself on the wrong end of the caricaturist's etching needle. This did not bother him overly, as he remained popular in his Westminster constituency and he remained an avid collector of prints, including those which attacked him. It has been said that to be included in a Gillray print was to have arrived on the political stage, so his continued presence demonstrated that, despite being out of office, Fox was very much in the limelight. With Fox almost invariably on the receiving end, one might have expected Pitt the Younger's portrayal to have been consistently positive. Indeed, Pitt does appear to have been a darling of the caricaturists; however, this did not prevent them from poking fun at him, nor indeed attacking him and his administration's policies where needed, albeit frequently tempered by a contrast to how much worse Foxite policy, perceived or actual, would be.

1784 Election and Westminster Scrutiny

Background

The 1784 general election has provoked a vibrant historiography, with W.T. Laprade, C.E. Freyer and D.M. George engaging in a compelling debate during the early twentieth century as to the nature of Pitt's victory, how many MPs became 'martyrs' of the Fox–North Coalition's East India policy and the nature and circumstances of the Westminster Scrutiny.[1] This debate took off following the publication (in 1922) of an edition of the *Parliamentary Papers of John Robinson*.[2] At the time of the 1784 election, John Robinson was one of the secretaries at the Treasury and was tasked with compiling a study of the state of the House of Commons prior to the election and its likely state following it. Robinson was no stranger to this sort of work, having previously conducted similar studies in 1774 and 1780 for the then First Lord of the Treasury, Lord North. W.T. Laprade made the case for a Pittite landslide, with many Foxites and coalitionists being defeated at the polls, due to the fall out of the Fox–North Coalition's East India policy. D.M. George, however, argued that Laprade got the story wrong, asserting that the general election of 1784 was not really any different in essentials from any other pre-reform general election.[3] George also emphasized the fact that some defeated Foxites were returned for pocket boroughs, some withdrew from elections prior to polling, owing to a poor canvas, while also highlighting the presence in the new House of Commons of some 147 new members, in comparison with 144 new members after the 1780 election and 145 after the 1790 general election.[4]

Clearly, the 1784 general election was an election that needs to be viewed within its national context, with debates on the Fox–North Coalition and their plans to reform the East India Company being debated alongside the traditional discussions of local issues up and down the country. For the first time, the general election was also seen as a contest between two individuals,

Charles James Fox and William Pitt the Younger, for the Treasury, and as such has been viewed as the first national election. Much of the scholarship on the election has been focused upon the contest in one of the constituencies with the broadest franchise, Westminster, where Fox was himself a candidate. The issue of the Scrutiny that followed and the possible motives behind it have also occupied biographers of Fox and Pitt the Younger, and formed an important postscript to the election, the result of which would not be finally declared until 4 March 1785.

The 1784 election has become infamous for the active involvement of women. One of the most prominent was Georgiana, Duchess of Devonshire, who was a leading figure in Charles James Fox's campaign. As a leader of the Bon Ton, one might have expected her to already have been a regular within satirical prints of the day, albeit within social satires commenting upon the fashions of the day. This was not the case, however, and the Westminster election of 1784 provided Georgiana with the clear majority of her outings in caricature. Georgiana featured in 110 satirical prints during the years 1776 to 1805, with 78 of these appearing in 1784. Despite their dominance within the literature on Georgiana's involvement within the 1784 Westminster election, only 11 of these 78 prints contained butchers. It should be remembered, however, that Georgiana was not the only female to be associated with canvassing butchers, with Mrs Albinia Hobart also appearing canvassing butchers in the interest of Wray and Hood.[5]

Given the importance of this contest and the significance of the role played by women on both sides, it is unsurprising that several historians have recently revisited the Westminster contest, with a new focus on female involvement, at a time when female participation in politics was widely frowned upon. In 1993, Anne Stott was quick to acknowledge that the involvement of Georgiana, Duchess of Devonshire, within the 1784 Westminster election needed to be considered within both its contemporary context and views on politeness.[6] Her article was followed by that of Phyllis Deutsch, who was keen to emphasize the fact that the 1784 Westminster election was a fight between Charles James Fox and William Pitt the Younger, while also stressing the importance of the reckless gambling habits of Fox and his principal supporter, Georgiana, Duchess of Devonshire.[7] More recently, Renata Lana and Amelia Rauser entered the debate, assessing the importance of the role played by women within the election campaign.[8] Rauser's primary focus was the Duchess of Devonshire, whereas Lana examined the role of women on both sides. Lana's thesis was that women received a mixed reception in the popular press and that issues such as the maidservant tax and the Chelsea Hospital fell more or less within the purview of the woman's realm of hearth and home.[9]

Much of the scholarship considering the visual representation of Georgiana's involvement in Charles James Fox's campaign focuses upon prints associated with reports of her kissing butchers (and indeed other tradesmen) in return for their voting for him. The attention afforded to these prints is striking, especially since there are twelve suggesting an affair between her and Fox. In order to fully assess the impact of these prints upon the Westminster election and the Pittite attempts to keep Fox out of Parliament, or at least out of the Westminster seat, requires a more rounded and balanced assessment, looking beyond this narrow corpus of eleven prints representing her kissing butchers.

This chapter will provide a brief context to the 1784 general election, before moving on to consider three recurring themes within the visual representation of Georgiana during the Westminster election campaign: canvassing; her relationship with Fox; and the struggle between Fox and his opponents. This discussion will also consider the role of women within the Pittite campaign.

1784 Westminster election

During the eighteenth century, elections were a patchwork affair with no universal franchise and with many seats being uncontested.[10] They were generally not fought on the basis of a party manifesto, with the personality, promises and local reputation of a candidate being considered more important. A candidate's ties to a local landowner counted for far more than to which broad political grouping they belonged.[11] Accordingly, local issues were often important at election time. Even so, election years marked high points in the number of prints featuring Fox and Pitt. A good example of this was the 1784 Westminster election during which William Pitt the Younger sought to build a majority for his government, which had risen to power as a result of a backstairs intrigue. Accordingly, in some seats the election was fought along the issues of the management of India and the Fox–North Coalition.

Key issues in the Westminster contest centred upon the Chelsea Hospital, which was in the constituency, and the proposed maidservants' tax. Prior to the 1784 general election, Pitt the Younger had proposed a tax on maidservants in a bid to increase revenue and guard against a 'new pervasiveness' in London and Westminster due to sexually loose maidservants. The hope was that the tax would reduce the number of such women who were employed as maidservants. Meanwhile, the issue of Chelsea Hospital was around its funding. Sir Cecil Wray, who had sat in the last Parliament as a Foxite and now sought re-election as the Pittite candidate, thought the hospital was being mismanaged and believed that savings could be made in the cost of maintaining it.[12]

The defeat of Fox in Westminster would have been a major coup for Pitt, owing to the fact that the City of Westminster was the largest urban constituency at this time and enjoyed one of the broadest franchises within Britain, with members of the lower middle and upper working class qualifying to vote, through paying scot-and-lot.[13] In spite of this, however, it had a reputation of returning MPs drawn from the highest social level.[14] Being MP for Westminster was considered to be tremendously important for Charles James Fox and his image of being *vox populi* or the 'Man of the People'. In representing one of the more democratic constituencies, he could claim popular support, and with Parliament lying within his constituency, if things were going badly in the House, he did not need to go far to be buoyed up by his supporters.[15] Additionally, given the precarious state of his finances, being an MP was essential to avoid debtor's prison. These factors would have been influential within Pittite thinking prior to and during the Election.

Some caricaturists sought to make the coalition's East India Bill an issue in the Westminster contest, and by extension the general election more broadly. The anonymous artist of *Carlo-Khan in Limbo*[16] is one such artist. While it is true that the artist returns to the more classic image of Fox as 'Man of the People', the fact that he is referred to as Carlo-Khan in the title provides a clear reference to the East India Bill and the earlier prints of him as an Eastern despot. Fox is depicted behind bars, his jacket and waistcoat just visible, with Edmund Burke apparently coming to visit. Again, this can be interpreted as another link to the East India Bill crisis and the artist's perception that Fox and Burke were the main architects of the Fox–North Coalition's attempt to reform the governance of India and the East India Company.

Fox's incarceration is a reference to his indebtedness, a message highlighted by the inscription beneath the bars of the cell – 'Pray Remember the Poor Debters'. Fox's debts, owing many thousands of pounds to Jewish moneylenders,[17] contributed to the suspicion around his motives for the reform of the East India Company with some believing that he hoped to cash in by selling East India patronage. The failure of the India bill is reflected by the inscription upon the bag carried by Burke – 'Broken Victuals' – one possible reading of which is the fall of the coalition, but also the India bill, which had the effect of removing the source of patronage that would keep the administration together and attract new people to join it.

Burke also has a thought bubble, providing an insight into his take on events – 'Her Grace is Very good to him I think well tis an Oeconeical Situation'. 'Her Grace' is a reference to Georgiana, Duchess of Devonshire, and the 1784 Westminster election. While the suggestion that it was an 'Oeconeical Situation' could be a reflection that the Duchess of Devonshire's presence in Fox's campaign team would produce Fox a large number of votes, which if secured by the traditional 'treating'[18] of voters would have run up a large bill.[19] The title of the print, *Carlo-Khan in Limbo*, could be a reference to the close nature of the contest that was unfolding in Westminster. In the early days of the contest, Westminster looked like a lost cause for Fox. If he had lost, it would have left him needing either to retire from politics or find a new seat. The emphasis placed upon the campaign against Fox helped to reinforce the image of him as a 'modern style' leader of the opposition.

Charles James Fox was not, however, the main focus of all the attacks the caricaturists made against his campaign. The high-profile role played by aristocratic women during his campaign was the source of constant comment during the 1784 Westminster campaign, and although Fox was not represented in many of these attacks in person, he was implicated within the prints through the use of words and emblems.[20] This continued use of emblems dovetails with Nicholson's argument that their use did not die out with the stylistic changes brought in during the 'Golden Age' of the satirical print.[21] Many of the most vicious attacks were levelled at Georgiana, Duchess of Devonshire, who was often depicted wearing a ribbon bearing Fox's name, or else with fox fur incorporated within her dress, attempting to use her feminine charms to entice tradesmen to vote for Fox. The attacks on her in connection with Fox's campaign largely fall into three categories: canvassing, her relationship with Fox and the struggle with Fox's opponents.

Canvassing

Much of the scholarly attention paid to prints depicting Georgiana canvassing for Fox during the 1784 Westminster election has focused upon her supposed butcher-kissing exploits, described by Anne Stott as 'probably the most celebrated kiss of the eighteenth century ... although the Duchess denied the story'.[22] However, there are a further twelve prints connected with her canvassing individuals other than butchers, including Thomas Rowlandson's

Dark Lanthern Business, or, Mrs. Hob and Nob on a Night Canvass with a Bosom Friend (Plate 19), from the Lewis Walpole Library's collection.[23] The number of prints showing Georgiana kissing tradesmen, however, leads one to question the veracity of her denial and whether there is really no smoke without fire. In *Dark Lanthern Business*, a plump Georgiana can be seen, bare breasted and holding a lantern while taking a young man by the arm and saying to him 'Vote for whom you please but Kiss before you Poll'. The clear insinuation here is that she is seeking votes in exchange for kisses, or at least using her youth, beauty and feminine charms to proposition votes. Behind her, to the right, a couple can be seen canoodling in the doorway of 'Haddock's', while to the left, Mrs Hobart can be seen holding a lantern that shines on a negro and Chelsea pensioner and says 'D-n the Duchess, She got all the young voters'. There is a clear contrast between the two women in both dress and the manner of their canvassing, suggesting that Mrs Hobart's involvement is more respectable as she is fully clothed and not in physical contact with the voters she is canvassing. Additionally, with the remark about the Duchess winning over the *young* voters, Rowlandson can also be seen to make an aesthetic judgment on the visual beauty and perhaps virility and sexiness of the two women, hinting that it could have been her good looks and charm that helped Georgiana win the day rather than her candidate's policies and personality.

Aside from kissing tradesmen, two other recurring themes of prints depicting the Duchess canvassing are the handing over of money by her to tradesmen in exchange for goods or services as a way of effectively bribing voters[24] and immodest or unladylike behaviour.[25] A good example of this is *The Tipling Dutchess Returning from Canvassing*,[26] in which an intoxicated Georgiana, with her breasts exposed, is assisted home by two male figures, one of whom is Fox. Sam House leads the way, holding a blazing torch, indicating the lateness of the hour. This print is highly critical of the perceived moral looseness and abandon of women such as the Duchess of Devonshire, who became involved in electioneering. The lack of probity of her behaviour is implied through the exposure of her breasts in a very public scene, an act which also questions her fidelity. This print also reveals something of the electoral practices of the time, particularly the practice of treating, whereby candidates and their campaign team would hold mass entertainments for voters and non-voters alike. At these events, usually held in public houses, the candidate and their well-to-do supporters would wait at table, serving the people of the constituency with food and drink.

The supposed lack of decorum exhibited by women actively engaged in electioneering can also be seen in *The Covent Garden Deluge*,[27] originally published in *Rambler's Magazine*. The Duchess appears alongside Fox on a balcony in Covent Garden, attempting to enlist support from passers-by, encouraging Fox and informing him 'You shall come in Charley' while urinating upon a figure below. That figure is intended for Sir Cecil Wray, a onetime Foxite who was standing against Fox in the Pittite interest. Wray protests against his treatment indicating that Georgiana's target ought to have been Admiral Hood who was following close behind. Georgiana's urination on Wray is symbolic of the way his support began to suffer upon Georgiana's entry into the fray, as she actively canvassed for Fox, who in the print is clearly encouraged by the early progress the Duchess's support was showing, exclaiming 'Drown the Rascal'. This print can, however, also be viewed as a warning of the pitfalls of female political involvement and the adverse impact upon the morals and behaviour of women who crossed the line between active and passive involvement within politics. The masculine nature of Georgiana's behaviour, actively canvassing tradesmen on behalf of a non-relative, and the imagined consequences of this are expressly indicated in *The Political Shaver* (Plate Colour 4),[28] in which Fox, with the assistance of Sam House, can be seen shaving the Duchess of Devonshire. This has the effect of making the reader question her femininity and indicates that there are certain side-effects for women embarking upon masculine pursuits, such as electioneering. Interestingly, Fox's five o'clock shadow is not as prominent as usual, while stubble is visible upon the Duchess's cheeks and neck. Linda Colley has pointed out, however, that through her role in the Westminster election, the Duchess of Devonshire 'crossed the divide separating private female influence on male politicians (which was acceptable) from autonomous and political action (which was not)'.[29] She went on to argue that it was not unusual for women to canvas on behalf of male relations.[30]

Elaine Chalus has indicated that politically involved women had to tread carefully along a fine line of acceptable levels of political engagement. She argues that it was socially acceptable for women to support relations, as this fell within the traditional female role of familial duty. On the other hand, Chalus asserted that those women who effectively became politicians in their own right crossed this line and were seen to pose a threat to the polity and the place of women in relation to men.[31] Georgiana was not the first woman to involve herself in an election campaign. During the 1774 general election, Georgiana's mother, Lady Spencer, visited Northampton, where her husband's nominee, Mr Tollemarche, was facing a challenge from Sir James Langham, a newcomer to Northampton politics. She wrote to Georgiana, informing her that 'I have dined each day during the Poll at the George with all the gentlemen and am extremely popular among them'.[32] Amelia Rauser has argued that the Duchess of Devonshire's role in Fox's campaign was unprecedented and that her 'avid canvassing of votes provoked much outrage and amusement among her contemporaries'.[33] Accordingly, it would seem that appearances alongside male relations during elections were acceptable, so long as they remained inconspicuous, whereas, working independently for the benefit of candidates to whom they had no filial ties was not.[34]

From these prints, it is clear that the caricaturists were critical of female involvement in election campaigns and the threat that such behaviour posed to the social norms. There are clear gender politics in play, with politics being viewed as a man's world. Indeed, on occasions, women who crossed the line into active political engagement can be seen to take on masculine qualities and characteristics within the prints, such as in *The Political Shaver* where the Duchess of Devonshire requires a shave to remove her beard. Additionally, the caricaturists asserted that women who were out on the election trail were little better than whores, prostituting themselves to secure votes for their candidate, who in turn effectively become their pimp, amassing votes rather than wealth in this instance.

Relationship with Fox

In his biography of William Pitt the Younger, William Hague asserted that Charles James Fox had an affair with Georgiana, Duchess of Devonshire.[35] Although he does not produce any evidence for this, he is not alone in presenting a case for an affair, with S.A. Hunn indicating, in his 1997 thesis on 'Negative perceptions of Whiggery', that there was a common belief that Fox was having an affair with Georgiana.[36] On the other hand, Amanda Forman has argued that 'there is no evidence to prove or disprove the notion that Georgiana and Fox had become lovers'. She does, however, insert an important caveat, pointing out that Georgiana's correspondence with Fox for the early to mid-1780s has not survived.[37] It is, therefore, impossible to judge with any degree of certainty whether there is any truth within the assertions of numerous satires produced during the 1784 Westminster election hinting at the Duchess's infidelity.

One such print, *The Devonshire Amusement* (Plate 20),[38] published by John Wallis on 24 June 1784, provides a very strong hint. While the main thrust of this two-part print criticizes the Duchess for stepping away from the female sphere of hearth and home by engaging in the male preserve of politics, thus effectively defeminizing her, there are several layers that need to be explored. The left-hand pane shows her out on the campaign trail in a state of abandon, her hat having fallen, skirts raised revealing her ankles, the name 'Fox' emblazoned on a belt around her minute waist, holding a pole with a depiction of Fox's head on top with a crosspiece inscribed 'Liberty' and a fox's brush hanging from either end of this.

The birds in the cloud above the Duchess also refer to the maidservant tax, one of the main issues of the Westminster contest. They exclaim, 'No Tax on Maidenheads no Wray', a reference to Sir Cecil Wray and his stance in favour of the maidservant tax and plans for reforming Chelsea Hospital.[39] The use of the word 'maidenhead' is a double entendre, on the one hand referring to maidservants and on the other indicating a woman's virginity and purity; it is a thinly veiled insinuation that the Duchess was cheating on her husband. The insertion of a pair of cuckold's horns to the duke's portrait, which hangs behind him in the right pane, provides further evidence for this. This raises a further question of who the artist believed the guilty party to be? While it is unclear, from the print, exactly who the artist suspects of engaging in criminal conversation with the duchess, two contenders quickly emerge. The fact that in the left-hand portion of the print she is out campaigning for Fox implicates him in the affair, and she can be seen holding a portrait of the Prince of Wales, a prominent supporter of Fox to whom she was a confidante, could also imply that she was the prince's mistress.[40]

While the cuckold's horns could be used to suggest an affair between Georgiana and Charles James Fox, as Hunn and several prints have hinted at, they could be a comment upon the belief that she was securing votes through offering sexual favours to tradesmen, something indicated in the prints.[41] They could, however, also be present to indicate that the duke had been duped by his wife into staying at home and caring for their child, while she was electioneering. This role reversal, while making comment upon the Duchess's 'masculinity', also suggests that the duke is subservient and slightly effeminate. It should be remembered that while politics was the preserve of men, members of the House of Lords were not supposed to campaign during elections.

Fox is strongly implicated within this role reversal and, by highlighting the inverted roles, the artist is attempting to discredit Fox through attacking his campaign team and tactics. This image goes against Renata Lana's suggestion that some artists sought to undermine the political credibility of the Duchess of Devonshire by suggesting that her independence was a mere illusion.[42] This assertion is not, however, borne out within the prints of her in connection with Charles James Fox in the 1784 Westminster election. Lana does point out that Pittite propaganda did on occasions target individual Foxite women, thus acknowledging their importance within Fox's campaign.[43] Lana's argument about Pittite propaganda attacking the prominent role played by women in Fox's campaign is a compelling one and one which the number of anti-Fox prints from the election containing women would seem to confirm.[44]

Other prints indicating an affair between Fox and Georgiana achieve this in a number of other ways. J. Barrow's *Parliament Security or a Borough in Reserve*, shows Fox as a fox, whose head appears from within the Duchess's skirts.[45] This print was re-issued the following month under a new title, *A Borough Secur'd or Reynard's Resource*.[46] Meanwhile, in *Reynard put to his Shifts*, Thomas Rowlandson has Georgiana sheltering Fox beneath her skirts.[47] This print followed on from his *Political Affection*, in which Georgiana neglects her daughter, instead holding a fox to her bosom to breastfeed.[48] Another example of her becoming intimate with Fox can be seen in William Dent's *Nil Desperandum or the Hands of Comfort*, in which both Georgiana and her sister, Henrietta, have an hand in Fox's breeches seeking to arouse him and distract him from his poor showing in the early stages of the polls.[49]

Henrietta was also implicated in *The Devonshire Method to Restore A Lost Member* (Plate Colour 5),[50] in which she stands behind Fox, who is led into an apothecary's shop by her sister. Both have fox brushes in their hats, which hang limp and are intended to not only indicate their support for Fox's election campaign, but also to be phallic symbols. The limpness of these brushes is not only a reference to Fox's poor progress in the election, but also suggesting that he has lost his virility. As she hands a purse to the apothecary, Georgiana says 'His tail restore, you shall have more', while Henrietta says 'Oh Poor Fox will loose his tail'. Here, the tail is also being used to indicate Fox's seat in Parliament, representing Westminster. The payment to the apothecary could be of an inflated price in an attempt to bribe him into voting for Fox, thus helping him to recover and retain his seat, something that also featured in other prints, such as *The Duchess Canvassing for her Favorite Member*.[51] While accepting payment, he replies to the women, 'My famous pills cure many ills', possibly indicating his agreement to vote for Fox. Meanwhile, the paper under Fox's foot, 'Dr Leakes Antivanerial Drops', also gives credence to the reading suggesting his inability to perform sexually owing to venereal disease, and so along with the limp phallic brushes suggesting a possible affair with either or both sisters. These suggestions of effectively bribing the electorate aimed to damage Fox's campaign through discrediting the votes that were cast for him by insinuating that they had not been fairly won and or had come from illegal means. The overt bribery of voters was illegal, even in eighteenth-century elections, while one of the accusations levelled against the Foxite campaign, by Sir Cecil Wray, when he called for a scrutiny of the result, was that Fox had illegally polled Catholics.

Struggle between Fox and his opponents

In addition to prints depicting Georgiana canvassing, consorting with tradesmen, kissing butchers and implying an affair with Fox, there are several prints that bring her into the struggle with Fox's opponents. These prints took in a range of locations and conceived the contest in a variety of ways. One of the more interesting tropes within these images represents the election as a boxing match. This occurs in three of the thirteen prints on the broad theme of the struggle in which rival candidates or their female supporters feature.

In *The Westminster Election*, published in the *Rambler's Magazine*, Georgiana and the Duchess of Rutland are restrained by two male figures, preventing them from engaging in the masculine pursuit of boxing.[52] *The Rival Canvassers* (Plate 21) also depicts Georgiana engaging in a sport of pugilism, this time fighting Albinia Hobart, with the candidates as seconds for their female supporters.[53] The use of the masculine pursuit of boxing provides a metaphor for the election that is heavily laden with symbolism. It conceives the election as a contest between two figures, which is particularly apt for the 1784 Westminster election, which despite having three candidates notionally vying for two seats was, in fact, viewed as a contest between the incumbents, Fox and Wray, for the second seat, with Admiral Hood considered a shoe-in for the first. Additionally, boxing, like elections, was very much a male preserve, thus the caricaturist's use of the visual metaphor of Georgiana, Duchess of Devonshire, fighting or attempting to fight female supporters of Pitt's candidate, Sir Cecil Wray, illustrates how they had crossed or were seeking to cross from passive to active involvement in the election campaign and, therefore, forfeiting their feminine sensibilities, and instead taking on more aggressive male characteristics. Through directly fighting one another, they were clearly seen as having moved from a more passive attempt to influence and sway, and instead become politicians in their own right, standing as effective proxies for their principles, namely the candidates themselves.

A satire on the Westminster Scrutiny, *A New Way to Decide the Scrutiny*,[54] continues the boxing theme; however, this time Georgiana is not fighting. The bout instead is between Fox and Sir Cecil Wray. Georgiana is instead Fox's second while Admiral Hood acts as Wray's second. Again, through acting as second, she is assuming an active role rather than the more a passive role of an observer. Fox himself appears in tartan, a reference to his representing Tain Burghs in the House of Commons during the scrutiny. Fox's transfer to another seat for the duration of the Westminster Scrutiny also had both personal and political ramifications. His continued membership of the House of Commons was essential for him, from a personal point of view, as it enabled him to hide behind parliamentary privilege to avoid prosecution for his debts. While his transfer to the remote constituency of Tain Burghs did prevent Pitt the Younger from excluding him from Parliament, which had been one of the motives behind the scrutiny, Fox's continued presence within the House of Commons also provided him with an important advantage over his rivals for the Westminster seat, that is the ability both to speak and vote in the ensuing debates about the Westminster election and scrutiny.[55]

Fox's exclusion from the Westminster seat did, however, provide Pitt with a temporary coup, as Fox was no longer able to appeal directly to his constituents when things were not going well in the House of Commons, as he had been able to do when representing Westminster. He was also denied his previous claim, a popular mandate for his actions, which came from representing the largest electorate in Britain, namely Westminster. Indeed, it can be viewed as humiliating for the erstwhile 'Man of the People' to be required to seek an alternative seat to Westminster, which had one of the widest franchises of any seat in Britain with some 12,000 voters, by comparison to Tain Burghs, a remote seat in the far north of Scotland controlled by half a dozen families, which it is unlikely he ever visited.[56]

Another trope that was used by the caricaturists was to portray the election contest as a race, with three prints being produced portraying the 1784 election as a race.[57] While one might have expected the caricaturists to use this as a vehicle for criticizing the gambling habits of Fox and his chief supporter, Georgiana, the reality is that none of these prints make a direct link between the election as a horse race and Fox's love of the turf. In Isaac Cruikshank's *Westminster Races* (Plate 22),[58] all three candidates can be seen mounted, riding along as if in a race. The position of the poll at the time is effectively provided, with Hood out in front with Fox on his tail and Wray juddering to a halt. The caption below reinforces this idea of a race being run, reading: 'A Political Heat, run in Covent Garden, between Old Veteran a famous Horse the Property of his M ....y, Dutchess [sic] a Filly, the Property of the Duke of D .....e, and Judas an Obstinate Ass, who was clearly distanced.' This caption clearly locates the race to the Westminster constituency with a reference to Covent Garden, the traditional site of the hustings for elections in the Westminster constituency. The caption also identifies the candidates through their horses: Old Veteran being the horse of the naval veteran, Admiral Hood; Dutchess [*sic*], a reference to the Duchess of Devonshire, Charles James Fox's mount; and Judas that of Sir Cecil Wray, who had deserted the Foxites in favour of Pitt the Younger prior to the election. Isaac Cruikshank was clearly having fun with the close association the Duchess of Devonshire had with Fox's campaign, while the suggestion of Fox being mounted upon the Duchess raises many questions about the nature of their relationship. It is striking that in common with Fox's mount, Hood's is the property of another. In the case of Hood, a naval officer by profession, his steed belongs to his lord and master, the King, in whose service he is in his professional life. On the other hand, Fox's mount is intimately connected to the Duke of Devonshire. The question here is whether Fox is in the duke's pay, or whether an affair is hinted at. Sadly, the remainder of the print does not provide a clear answer and it is left to the reader to draw their own conclusions.

Another print up this theme is *Ride for Secret Influence Rewarded*, published by Edward Shirlock on 25 May 1784.[59] At first this print is a little curious, as it features both Fox and Georgiana twice. In the foreground, Fox gives Georgiana a piggyback, which has the effect of hoisting her skirts up to reveal not only her ankles, but her garters and thighs as well. In the background, it is she who is mounted upon a fox, which is clearly intended for Fox, leading a procession with Lady Salisbury following on an animal with the head of Admiral Hood, with Mrs Hobart trailing behind on another animal with the face of Sir Cecil Wray. Again, the artist is critical of the involvement of women within the election campaign. The print clearly points to the perceived unladylike behaviour of active participation in elections by both Mrs Hobart and Georgiana shown riding astride their mounts, and only Lady Salisbury adopting the customary ladies' riding pose of side saddle. This comment echoes one referenced by the curator that 'according to a newspaper paragraph Lady Salisbury "is the only woman of rank who has interfered on the Ministerial side ... But her proceedings have been marked with such delicacy and dignity, as to shame the mobbing conduct of her rivals"'.[60] From this difference in portrayal it is apparent that while the anonymous artist is no fan of women involving themselves in politics, one could surmise that they were a supporter of Hood, given that both he and his female supporter are cast in a better light than his rivals and their female supporters. On the other hand, this could also have been owing to Hood's position as a naval officer, as he might have been viewed, at that point, as being above party politics.

Westminster Scrutiny

The decision to hold a scrutiny of the vote in the Westminster constituency at the 1784 election delayed the return of MPs for that constituency and so had the effect of leaving both the people of Westminster unrepresented at Westminster and Charles James Fox out of Parliament and divested of the protection that membership entailed. The privileges afforded to MPs at the time, which included immunity from prosecution for indebtedness, made a seat in Parliament imperative for Fox, given the nature of his debts and the fact that for Fox 'gambling became a disorder he could not shake, an obsession that weakened him financially and politically'.[61] It is little surprise, therefore, that a number of the prints published on the topic of the Westminster Scrutiny comment on his indebtedness.

A good example is *The Mumping of Fox or Reynard Turn'd Beggar*,[62] an anonymous print published by E. Rich on 22 June 1784. In the centre of this print, Fox is shown in a dishevelled state. His jacket is torn, breeches and stockings are holed and part of his left shoe is missing; meanwhile, his five o'clock shadow is so pronounced that it more closely resembles designer stubble. This, combined with the begging box he is holding, inscribed 'Fox's Begging Box For the Good of my Self. Let my Country be D-D', helps to reinforce his impecuniousness. There is a clear suggestion that Fox's contesting of the scrutiny was entirely self-seeking. His support within Westminster is evident from the presence in the background of three butchers, brandishing cleavers and marrow bones, with one exclaiming 'Fox for ever', while one of Fox's chief supporters, the publican Sam House, can be seen next to them holding a flag 'Standard of Sedition'. From the tone of the print it is apparent that the anonymous artist was no fan of Charles James Fox, as they sought to associate him and his supporters not only with sedition, but also through his speech bubble ['My worthy Geese &, Ganders, although I have every reason Imaginable To believe, that I have not one real vote in a Hundred yet if you will put your Mite into my Box I will endeavour all I can to Bother my opponents and you into the Bargain. Pray remember the poor Fox'] with electoral fraud. This print also draws on earlier prints on the Westminster election in which the electors of Westminster are likened to geese.[63] Another nod to earlier prints comes in the text underneath the print, in which Fox is also compared to Reynard, king of the foxes. Here, reference is made to the poverty of Fox's position, in terms of both his financial position and political capital. The verse is clear that Fox would face severe financial hardship, from which he might not recover, should the scrutiny go against him. Ultimately,

Fox's friends and supporters managed to shore up his position, courtesy of some quick thinking. Prior to the 1784 election there had been an agreement between the two leading families in the constituency; however, by 1784 there had been realignment within the political landscape of the constituency, with the Pitt-supporting Sinclairs failing to come to an agreement with the Fox-supporting Ross's. Both sides were preparing for a contest in which the incumbent MP, Charles Ross, was expected to seek re-election, standing against Sir John Sinclair. Shortly before the election, Fox's position in Westminster was beginning to look doubtful and he was swiftly declared a candidate and sworn in as a burgess of Kirkwall. He was elected by three votes to two on 26 April.[64] Fox's presence in the new Parliament, representing a remote Scottish constituency, did not go unnoticed by the caricaturists.

Fox's temporary transfer to Tain Burghs during the Westminster Scrutiny[65] was essential for him to avoid prosecution for his debts and this switch was commented upon by George Murgatroyd Woodward in his *A View of the Orkney Isles with one of Mr. Fo-x's New Constituents* (Plate 23).[66] It is unclear whether Woodward ever published the print, which does not appear in the *BM Catalogue*. There is, however, a preliminary ink and watercolour sketch in the Woodward Collection at the Derbyshire Record Office, which Woodward would almost certainly have sought a publisher for, given the attention surrounding the Westminster election of 1784 and the ensuing scrutiny. While Fox is not represented in person, the reference to him in the title is significant, as it is one of the few known images that referred to his return for the remote Scottish constituency of Tain Burghs. Fox's return is significant, as not only did it in part prevent Pitt the Younger from excluding him from Parliament,[67] it also enabled him to speak and vote in the ensuing debates about the Westminster election and scrutiny, a luxury not afforded to the other candidates in the disputed election.[68] At the same time, it can be seen as humiliating to the erstwhile 'Man of the People' to be required to seek an alternative seat to Westminster.[69]

The remoteness of Tain Burghs is reflected in this print not only by the isolated island in the background and desolate rocky foreground, but also by the emaciated state of the Scotsman and his dog. The disdainful expression on the face of Fox's new constituent clearly reflects the way in which the constituency is being used; having an Englishman imposed on them could also reflect the fact that the new member for Tain Burghs was rapidly sworn in as a burgess of Kirkwall after the announcement of a scrutiny at Westminster.[70] It is also apparent that, in the new Parliament, Fox would be more concerned in contesting the Westminster Scrutiny than looking out for the needs of his new constituents.

Another print that refers to Fox's transfer to Tain Burghs is *Paul before Felix or the high Bailif disconcerted*,[71] another anonymous print, published by S.W. Fores. Here, Fox is portrayed in Highland dress, tartan jacket, waistcoat, kilt and stockings, in place of his standard blue and buff. He stands addressing a meeting, chaired by Thomas Corbett, high bailiff of Westminster, who was responsible for not returning any of the candidates when declaring the scrutiny. The other figures around the table are sat holding their noses, with one of the figures complaining that 'this business smells horridly', while another states that 'I can smell how matters goe [*sic*]'. Clearly, there is a feeling that, while not breaking any rules, seeking election in multiple constituencies, in the same election, was not an entirely honourable thing to do, especially as the upshot was that he had a place and a voice in Parliament in the debates over the conduct of the Westminster election, a luxury his fellow candidate did not have. In front of him is an open book with 'Eloquence or the Art of making wrong appear right' visible on the page. Clearly, the suggestion is that, such was Fox's power of speech, he could successfully argue that black was white. Fox's presence and involvement in the debates around the Westminster Scrutiny, owing to a technicality, did not sit right with people, hence the suggestions within the print that the whole thing stank. The stench could also have been due to the bailiff, who incidentally is not holding his nose and who refused to return any of the candidates. Some see this as part of a deliberate ploy to keep Fox out of Parliament and that he should be imprisoned as a debtor and therefore out of politics for some considerable time. This view is backed up by the high bailiff's stuttering attempt to counter Fox's accusations that his failure to return members for Westminster, because of the scrutiny, was mischief-making and a deliberate ploy to keep him out. This is further borne out by the paper in front of Corbett, 'A political plan of the Present M-y'. Accusations of underhanded dealings in this matter could be applied equally to both sides of the debate and therefore the scrutiny takes on the appearance of an underhand attempt to subvert the will of the people to achieve a political goal, namely the exclusion of Fox from Westminster.

The theme of pungency as a metaphor for electoral fraud and malpractice was picked up on in an earlier print, *The Scrutiny, or, Examination of the Filth* (Plate 24),[72] published 24 April 1784. In this print, five figures are huddled around two stacks of chamber pots holding their noses. All six pots are inscribed 'Poll Book 1784' and stand on a plinth 'The Scrutiny, or, examination of the Filth', which clearly ties it in with the 1784 Westminster election. At first glance, it is difficult to tell whether the print is in favour or against the scrutiny, which was demanded by Sir Cecil Wray, as soon as it looked likely that Charles James

Fox was likely to be returned. While this call succeeded in keeping Fox out of Westminster, albeit only temporarily as it turned out, it did afford him and his supporters time to secure his election elsewhere until matters had been settled in Westminster. The figure on the left vomits into the chamber pot on the top of the left-hand stack, while holding a spoon. As he does so he says:

I already am sick
Of this poisonous trick
The busines so thick
T'would weary old Nick
With spoon or stick
Right from wrong to pick

The figure immediately opposite him stands stirring the chamber pot on the top of the right-hand stack while stating:

The cause I may gain,
Though with labour and pain
I can hardly refrain,
From Puking amain
Thro such filth for a tag
Is wares [*sic*] than euphorbium bag

Meanwhile the man in the centre of group says 'A hogo here is. Worse than Cats pis Than Devils Spew. Or Asafoetida'. Clearly, the stench of the chamber pots is obnoxious, and there is perhaps a certain reluctance on the part of the enquirers to look into them. There is some question as to whether the stench emanates from illegal and dubious practices in Westminster, or from the obvious political nature of the call for a scrutiny. A clue to the thoughts of the anonymous artist is undoubtedly the presence of two devils, one on either side, who are in the process of placing a net around the figures examining the issue. The left-hand devil says 'Ay Brother and by my tail, The Sheriffs shall admit no bail' with the other replying 'Spread the net and you shall see Many a false oath will come to me'. From the right-hand devil's response, it is clear that they suspect that there were a number of dubious votes cast during the election. This could be viewed as evidence that the artist was in favour of the scrutiny, especially given the large number of prints that alleged Fox was in league with the devil. The fact that they are trying to capture the scrutineers, owing to a fear of what they might find, is clear evidence that the artist is warning over attempts to stop or prevent the scrutiny. The use of spoons, however, by two of the scrutineers is indicative of a view that by calling for a scrutiny Wray was stirring things. The reference to vomiting on the part of the two stirrers, as well as the fact that all five scrutineers are holding their noses, suggests that they are not entirely willing participants in the drama. The reference by the figure on the left that the scrutiny is a poisonous trick clearly infers that the whole episode was a low piece of politicking and an underhand attempt to keep Charles James Fox out of Parliament. The thickness of the business also refers to its murky nature and a suggestion that the scrutiny was based on a false prospectus. This sentiment is echoed by his opposite number, who claims that they can hardly hold back from puking because through their efforts examining the poll books, they might bring in Wray and put out Fox. It is unclear, however, which of these was the most unpalatable into them. *The Scrutiny* is a good example of the multi-layered nature of satirical prints produced during this period, as well as the continuity of tropes and borrowing of ideas from other artists and earlier prints.

When one considers the vehemence of the opposition to Fox and his fellow coalitionists and the fact that his notoriety was increasing, as were the frequent attacks upon him in the satirical prints, it is surprising that he managed to retain his Westminster seat. However, as discussed earlier, the active assistance of Georgiana, Duchess of Devonshire, and her sister, Lady Duncannon, played an important role in Fox's return. One should also consider the argument of Penelope Corfield, Edmund Green and Charles Harvey that 'Westminster opinion was not deterred by Fox's notoriety'.[73]

Conclusion

The 1784 Westminster election was an hard fought contest that effectively pitted Fox against Pitt the Younger. In many ways, it can be viewed as the first national election, with the common issue across the country being the record of the Fox–North Coalition, as well as being viewed as a contest for the Treasury between Fox and Pitt. The contest prompted a large number of satirical prints, many of which featured Fox's chief ally in the campaign, Georgiana, Duchess of Devonshire. Most of this output was in opposition to Fox, and more specifically the central role of the Duchess of Devonshire and several other women within the campaign. This sustained attack on the Duchess and her active canvassing in Fox's interest led her to feature in more prints in 1784 than in every other year combined. It is clear, therefore, that the election represented a significant event within her life in the public eye.

Through levelling accusations of infidelity at the Duchess, in both these prints and those hinting at an affair with Fox, it is likely that the caricaturists sought to blunt the Fox campaign's most potent weapon, that is, the Duchess. This could have been achieved in a number of ways: (1) through her leaving the fray voluntarily; (2) being forced home by a jealous husband; or (3) The Duke of Devonshire withdrawing his support, and more importantly cash, from Fox and his campaign, owing to a belief that Fox had engaged in criminal conversation with his wife.

It is important to note that Georgiana was not the only woman to be involved with the 1784 Westminster election. Nor was she the only female attacked in satirical prints; however, she does provide a central figure for these attacks and as such she is able to act as a barometer of public opinion on female participation. Undoubtedly her position as a leader of fashion and the wife of one of the wealthiest men in England might explain why she came to dominate the prints, as she was already in the public eye. Georgiana had a reputation as a political hostess and so had form for dabbling in politics, something that would have influenced the caricaturists' response to her electioneering. This track record of political engagement, combined with her involvement with the campaign of a non-relative, explains why she could be viewed as a threat to the natural order of things.

In response to this challenge, the caricaturists sought to pour out their disapprobation upon women who sought to become politicians in their own right through entering into the male preserve of politics and electioneering. In part, these attacks were aimed at undermining the campaigns these women supported, and in part act as a warning to other women as to the dangers and potential side-effects of direct political engagement. It is apparent from the prints of Georgiana that one of the principal methods of doing this was to play down their femininity and to embody them with masculine characteristics. Accordingly, Georgiana was often portrayed with masculine traits or engaged in masculine activities in prints on the election. There is also a tendency to depict her as being more 'manly' than men around her while she is engaged with election-related activities. The nature of these attacks include having a more pronounced five o'clock shadow than Fox,[74] boxing,[75] abandoning her daughter to her husband's care while canvassing[76] and defending Fox from his pursuers.[77] Alongside prints depicting Georgiana as being more 'manly' than the men she is with, there are other prints in which her political actions have caused her to lose or abandon her feminine graces, for example, public drunkenness[78] and urinating in public.[79] Both these sets of prints should be examined alongside one another to create a more complete picture of the criticism and imagined consequences of active female participation in elections. The warning from the caricaturists about active involvement within the political process is that females who overstepped the line between acceptable and unacceptable behaviour would suffer the following: losing their femininity, gaining masculine features such as a beard and behaving in a lewd and unladylike way, not riding side-saddle, getting drunk in public and exposing themselves to all and sundry. This in turn would cause the men they associated with to become more feminine and hints towards a brewing crisis of masculinity. This latent crisis was fuelled by active female political engagement and women encroaching into other hitherto male preserves, thus forcing men into more passive or subservient roles.

Many of the attacks on the Duchess of Devonshire did not directly feature Fox and yet they were still biting and aimed at disrupting his campaign. The fact that prints did not need to attack the candidates themselves in order to pass negative comment upon them is interesting. It provides comment not only on the nature of elections in the late eighteenth century, but also upon the personalities involved in the election campaigns and how well their political sympathies were known. It can also be used to demonstrate that the use of emblem remained an important tool in the caricaturist's armoury, with fox's brushes frequently standing proxy for Fox. The continued use of emblem during the 1784 Westminster contest is significant and clearly demonstrates not only the fact that the genre was still in a transitional phase, but also the allegorical nature of late eighteenth-century election campaigns. The invocation of sexually charged double entendres and innuendoes was not uncommon within eighteenth-century satirical prints.[80]

Prints of Georgiana consorting with tradesmen had the effect of questioning the morals and scruples of Fox and his associates concerning the means with which they secured votes, as well as the validity of those votes that were secured. Arguably this contributed to the decision of Wray to demand a scrutiny. This decision of the defeated candidate to call a scrutiny prompted a second wave of prints on the election, with the whole business, including Fox's temporary return for Tain Burghs, being viewed as a dark and murky business, with nobody emerging from the whole affair with much credit. That said, what the 1784 Westminster election does point to is the biting nature of caricature and its ability not only to report but to shape and direct the nature of debates.

Despite the vilification of Georgiana and the implied attacks on his masculinity, Fox was still able to retain his seat, albeit in second place to Admiral Hood and after a politically motivated scrutiny failed. Accordingly, one could surmise that these prints had little or no impact upon the election, in spite of the fact that

Westminster and indeed seats in Middlesex as a whole were well placed to be affected by prints, with London being the centre of the print trade. The potential for prints to have an impact on elections more widely, however, is unlikely. What these prints do highlight is the conservative nature of society in the late eighteenth century and the fact that gender politics played an important role in late eighteenth-century life. The masculinization of women by the caricaturists, in their portrayal of their political activities, suggests that the masculine world felt threatened by this incursion of women into the male sphere and this would help fuel a crisis of masculinity.

Pitt the Younger's First Administration

Charles James Fox and William Pitt the Younger: 1784–8

The period following the East India Bill crisis and general election of 1784 proved a spell of relative calm in British political prints. In the autumn of 1788, this was shattered by the news that George III had fallen ill and the subsequent jockeying for position, which took place when it became apparent that his indisposition was likely to be prolonged. The fact that there were only five recorded divisions in the House of Commons between the vote on Pitt's India Bill on 16 July 1784 and the vote on 16 December 1788 on 'Parliamentary Competence to Regulate Regency'[1] goes some way to explaining the low number of prints featuring Fox and Pitt during this period, as might the fact that much of the opposition's attention was focused on their bid to impeach Warren Hastings, a former governor-general of India, which began around February 1786. The low number of divisions, given Pitt the Younger's landslide victory in the 1784 general election, is relatively unsurprising, as his overwhelming majority would undoubtedly have had an impact not only on the frequency of divisions, but also upon the ability of the opposition to catch the public eye. Notably, 1785 marked an exceptionally high output during this period and this spike in prints output can be partly explained by the repercussions of the Westminster Scrutiny, which was not finally settled until 1786.

Impeachment of Warren Hastings

The fall of the Fox–North Coalition did not mark the end of Indian affairs dominating parliamentary business. Soon after assuming office, William Pitt the Younger put forward his own India Bill, which was unopposed at first reading on 16 January 1784; however, his hopes of a speedy resolution of the

East India Question were dashed on 23 January when his bill was defeated in the Commons. Pitt would return with a new India Bill later in 1784 and continue to tinker with things through the remainder of the 1780s.[2] The impeachments of Warren Hastings and Sir Elijah Impey were time-consuming ventures and followed the 1784 election. Moves to impeach Warren Hastings, who had been governor-general of India from 1773 to 1784, began in earnest in February 1786, with Edmund Burke making much of the early running in the campaign.[3] The impeachment of Sir Elijah Impey, the Chief Justice of Bengal, followed in 1789. L.G. Mitchell has convincingly argued that the East India Bill was a catalyst for these two impeachments, as the Fox–North Coalition attempted to salvage their reputation by demonstrating that India had indeed been oppressed and misruled during the Hastings governor-generalship. Instrumental to the charge was the conduct of the trial, in 1775, of Maharaja Nandakumar, who was accused of attempting to deprive a widow of more than half her inheritance through the forging of a bond. Given that the coalition India Bill was ostensibly presented as a measure of reform of both the East India Company and the general governance of India, any proven misconduct by the company or its officials in the years preceding the coalition's bill would justify their actions.

The attempted impeachment of Warren Hastings, therefore, became an important aspect of Foxite policy in the immediate aftermath of the Fox–North Coalition's demise. The pursuit of Hastings was felt to be the perfect opportunity to exonerate themselves over their East India policy and remove questions over their judgement and motivations. The fact that Pitt the Younger had introduced his own India Bill early in his premiership demonstrated that there was a consensus that the whole governance of India was in urgent need of reform, but this did not help to restore the Fox–North Coalition's reputation. Should the impeachments succeed in proving that India had been misruled under Hastings and the East India Company Rule, then the coalition hoped their actions would have been vindicated and their arguments that their India Bill was merely an attempt to 'clean up' the administration of India, and not an all-out attack on chartered companies, might just appear to stand up.[4] Between the Westminster Scrutiny and the impeachment of Warren Hastings, Pitt the Younger and his administration managed to keep many Foxite MPs occupied within extra-parliamentary proceedings for much of the session. Even so, the changes to the make-up of the House of Commons occasioned by the 1784 general election were dramatic and when Pitt the Younger moved his second East India Bill on 16 July 1784 his administration recorded a 211 vote majority.[5]

Despite Charles James Fox and William Pitt the Younger being on opposite sides about the necessity of impeaching Warren Hastings, they only featured in eight surviving prints together on the subject and one on the impeachment of Elijah Impey, all of which were published between 1787 and 1788. Therefore, this episode can only provide a small sideshow within the overall representation of their rivalry within caricature. Even so, as a significant event within the politics of the period, it is important to give it consideration.

The first print on the broad topic of the impeachment of Governor Hastings was published as early as 7 January 1785, by G. Wallis, and entitled *The Fall of Achilles*.[6] Charles James Fox, Edmund Burke and Lord North can be seen fleeing across the scene, as Pitt the Younger (front left) fires an arrow at the group, striking Fox in his right Achilles tendon. As he looses his arrow, Pitt exclaims 'Thus do I strive with heart and hand To drive Sedition from the Land'. Meanwhile, Burke shouts at Pitt 'Before thy Arrows Pitt, I fly O D—n that word prolixity'. Dorothy George cites this outburst by Edmund Burke with his speech in the House of Commons on 30 July 1784, in which he had brought forth a motion, calling for papers on the conduct of Governor Hastings to be placed before the House. Pitt was critical from the opposition benches, claiming that 'if the Hon. Gentleman went on in that manner, making motions for which there were no parliamentary grounds, there would be no end to it'.[7] Criticism of Burke's actions was not limited to Pitt the Younger, with William Wyndham Grenville shouting him down and exclaiming that his pressing 'himself so frequently on the House [was] contrary to all rule, and if tolerated, there was an end to all debate.'[8] These reproaches were, arguably, not entirely around the issue of East Indian Affairs, but also more generally about the fact that whenever Burke took to the floor of the House, he generally held forth at some considerable length.

William Dent sought to characterize the debate in historical terms in his *The Battle of Hastings*,[9] in which two opposing armies – the 'Bengal Battalion' on the Treasury benches and the 'British Battalion' on the opposition benches – do battle in the House of Commons. Each army is urged on by their 'expert on Indian Affairs' in the guise of musicians with Dundas playing the bagpipes and Burke the drum. Meanwhile, their 'Champions', Major Scott and Richard Brinsley Sheridan, do battle in the foreground, immediately in front of an oversized Hastings, who stands on the table of the House of Commons. Behind Hastings, the Speaker can be seen between his legs paraphrases Hamlet's soliloquy asking, 'To be, or not to be, Impeachment is the Question'. The rank and file of both sides produce a lot of hot air in responding with 'Aye' or 'No' which links with the forcefulness of their declarations, also keys in with the lengthy speeches delivered on both sides.

The print is interesting for a number of reasons. First, that the artist has provided a key to individuals at the bottom of the plate, owing to the crowded and complex nature of the print. Secondly, in this instance Fox and Pitt are not depicted as the principal protagonists. Indeed, they are not even the first of the supporting cast. It would, therefore, be very easy to overlook this print, dismissing it for lending nothing to any discussion of the relationship between Charles James Fox and William Pitt the Younger in caricature. To do so, however, would miss the point that William Dent is making. By depicting Pitt the Younger and Fox in their places, on the Treasury and opposition benches, respectively, while their lieutenants are engaged in the main cut and thrust of the fight, creates the impression that the impeachment of Hastings is nothing more than a sideshow and a distraction. With Fox and Pitt in their places this can be viewed as a skirmish. Money is clearly viewed as a motivating factor behind the defence of Hastings, with Pitt, Thurlow and other ministerialists being paid off in rupees from Hastings' mouth, right hand and side, which has been pierced by Pitt's spear 'refined candour'. Meanwhile, Scott's shield is a full money bag and Dundas's bagpipes are full of coin. In contrast with Pitt, Fox's presence is more passive sitting on the front row of the opposition benches, alongside North, shouting no and watching on as Sheridan and Scott fight to his left and supporters to his right attempt to club Hastings. There is clear criticism of the opposition from the Treasury benches to the coalition's attempt to impeach Hastings, with allegations of corruption made through the Bengal Battalion being awash with coin from India. This accusation is particularly striking, given that the coalition was effectively accused of trying to line their pockets via their India Bill.

The suggestion that the Pitt and his fellow ministers had been paid off in exchange for opposing the Foxite's impeachment attempt is picked up upon by James Gillray in his *The Bow to the Throne, – alias – the Begging Bow* (Colour Plate 6).[10] Here, Hastings in oriental dress sits upon a close stool surrounded by gold coin. Behind him George III has his hand inside Hasting's throne and is in the process of scooping gold coin out of it exclaiming 'I am at the bottom of it'. Meanwhile, Hastings hands over full money bags labelled 'Pagodas' and 'Rupees', to Thurlow and Pitt respectively, while beneath them Queen Charlotte grovels before Hastings, kissing his toe, as she surreptitiously attempts to remove a large money bag of '£200000'. Behind these figures are several hats being held out upside down, including a bishop's mitre, in the hope of their being filled with coin.

Clearly, money and the balance of power were viewed as key motivators in the debates on the impeachment of Warren Hastings and Elijah Impey. It is also apparent that control of the East India interests was a way of accruing wealth, something that led the caricaturists to raise the question of corruption. Air and wind feature heavily within prints on the subject, perhaps intended to represent the overly long speeches on the topic, which was seen as a sideshow to the main issues affecting the nation. The caricatures on the impeachments brought both Richard Brinsley Sheridan and Henry Dundas to the fore, with Pitt and Fox looming in the background, something that helps to cement, rather than undermine their image as party leaders. Indeed, the caricaturists reverted to them when placing the sideshow within the context of the broader debate of who should govern the nation, as characterized by James Gillray's *State-Jugglers* (Plate 25).[11] The scene takes place outside of St James's Palace. George III and Queen Charlotte can be seen on either end of a plank, dressed as Punch and Judy balancing upon a beam from which a sign bearing the image of a crown hangs, giving the illusion that the royal palace has become the Crown Inn. Queen Charlotte, despite her slenderer figure, is heavier and she is in the process of taking a pinch of snuff from a golden snuff box, while her husband, the king, is higher and appears alarmed or dismayed by what he sees, either across from him or below. Underneath the sign, Warren Hastings kneels on a platform and is flanked by the standing figures of William Pitt the Younger and Lord Thurlow. Around the front of the platform are several figures seeking patronage. Pitt pulls two ribbons from his mouth and three figures before him, two of which are Admiral Hood and John Wilkes, reach up to take hold of them. Meanwhile, Hastings exhales a flow of gold coin which the remaining supplicants, including a bishop, Dundas, Lansdowne and Sydney, endeavour to catch in upturned hats, while Thurlow exhales fire, adding to the carnivalesque atmosphere. In the background, Fox, riding on top of Burke and supported by a figure, possibly the Duke of Norfolk, places his hat beneath the legs of Thurlow. It is debatable whether Fox is also trying to climb onto the stage, but the gesture of placing his hat upon it could be read as his throwing his hat into the ring and demonstrating a willingness to return to office. In the foreground are two curious figures, a fishwife and a ragged chimney sweep, who are looking on in wonder at the scene before them. Their presence can be seen to pass comment on the ridiculous behaviour of the politicians at this time, who are supposed to be their social superiors, but are acting in the manner of street performers, an entertainment form for the lower orders.

Regency crisis 1788–9

The regency crisis of 1788–9 was one of the more troubling episodes of the late eighteenth century and saw the Opposition Whigs caught unawares and largely leaderless, with Fox away on the Continent. Fox's absence led to a crisis of leadership with several leading figures vying for influence with the Prince of Wales, who as heir apparent was a leading candidate for the Regency, and given his closeness to leading Foxites, their preferred candidate. It was widely felt that should the Prince of Wales be installed as Regent, with no restrictions upon the exercise of the royal prerogative, he would dismiss his father's ministers, replacing them with his 'friends'. Undoubtedly, this fear of losing office to Fox prompted Pitt the Younger's cautious attitude to the issue of a regency, as well as his casting around for an alternate candidate in whom he could be sure of his own position due to his enjoying their confidence. This scramble to seize the initiative, in the rapidly unfolding and relatively unprecedented crisis, badly exposed the weakness and divisions within the Opposition Whigs. Without Fox to unite and lead the 'party' the weakness and political naivety of their nominal leader and probable candidate for the post of First Lord of the Treasury, the third Duke of Portland, quickly became apparent as he failed to show effective leadership and prevent infighting between rival factions within the party. Within this leadership vacuum, members of the old guard such as Edmund Burke, who had provided much of the intellectual leadership in the old Rockingham Connection and the 'young guns' such as Charles Grey and Richard Brinsley Sheridan, jockeyed for influence and position in the hope of securing a plum job in the new Foxite administration, whose commission was viewed as being a question of when and not if. Both sides informally held talks and the new guns sounded out Lord Chancellor Thurlow, a veteran of numerous administrations, about staying on, much to the irritation and frustration of the leading Foxite lawyer, Lord Loughborough, who had long held ambitions for the woolsack and indeed Fox, who mistrusted Thurlow.

Meanwhile, Fox's ability to quickly come up to speed with events after his return to England was hampered by the fact that his journey had left him exhausted and suffering from dysentery.[12] Accordingly, it took some time for the Foxites to arrive at a unified position on the emerging crisis. S.A. Hunn has argued that 'Foxite policy, for what it was worth, was based upon the fact that it became clear in November 1788 that the King was unwell'. George III's distress of mind became increasingly apparent and was unmistakable when he 'called Mr. Pitt a rascal and Mr. Fox his friend'. As is became clearer that the King's illness was not going to be brief, the Foxites began to formulate plans based upon the assumption that the King was as mad as a March hare, with no hope of his recovering.[13]

Having been out of office since 1783, their baser political ambitions came to the fore, and rather than expressing concern for the health and well-being of their sovereign, acting in a statesmanlike fashion and playing the long game, they quickly began making plans for office. Arguably, this contributed to Pitt the Younger pursuing a policy of making slow steps, while seeking another candidate for the regency, namely Queen Charlotte, to whom he was quite close. When it became apparent that the only viable option for regent was to be Prince George, Pitt sought to write restrictions to the regent's powers into his Regency Bill to prevent his immediate removal from office. The behaviour of the Foxites also left them wide open to criticism within satirical prints on the crisis and cemented the view, left over from the Fox–North Coalition, that they were self-serving rather than working for the greater good of the nation, and working for themselves and their own self-interest. Unsurprisingly, therefore, the regency crisis marked a temporary spike in Fox's appearance in satirical prints.

The Prince of Wales was a known drinking and gambling companion of Fox and a keen supporter of the Foxite Whigs. Indeed, he had hosted a party following the close of voting in the 1784 Westminster election and Fox's supposed return.[14] It was widely believed that upon becoming regent, he would immediately remove Pitt and invite Fox to form an administration. This belief is given credence by a letter from the Prince of Wales to Fox from as early as 1782–3, informing him that he would 'rejoice not a little if I again see you in Administration'.[15] This is backed up by a letter from Sheridan to Lord Palmerston in 1788, in which he informed him that the Prince of Wales had in his mind rejected the notion of continuing with his father's ministers and advisers and in a very open manner instructed the Duke of Portland and Charles James Fox to draw up their own plans for government in the event of him being appointed regent.[16]

The regency crisis of 1788–9 provoked the caricaturists into action producing a series of prints, both for and against the positions adopted by Charles James Fox and William Pitt the Younger. Indeed, Hunn draws attention to Burke's view of the regency crisis as ignorant as opposed to barbarous times, owing to people in general drawing their information from newspapers and magazines. Also highlighted is the warning from Burke, and possibly others, that since the press was the only source of information on the views and actions of politicians and parties available to all but those at the heart of affairs, Fox ought to treat them with more respect.[17] After his treatment at the hands of the caricaturists over the

East India Bill crisis, Fox's carefree attitude towards the press, considering reports of him in the popular press to be beneath his notice, appears a little incongruous; however, it was entirely consistent with his response to George Selwyn in 1781, when informed of an attack on his character in the *Public Advertizer*. Fox replied that he did not care what was said about him, nor how he was represented in prints. If he was portrayed erroneously as ugly, those who knew him would do him justice and as for the rest, he did not care what they thought of him.[18]

One of the enduring quotations of the regency crisis of 1788–9 was a remark by William Pitt the Younger, directed at Charles James Fox, that he would 'un-Whig the gentleman for the rest of his life'.[19] This remark was prompted by Fox's avocation of the Prince of Wales's constitutional right to be regent.[20] This played into Pitt's hands, as it was well known that he was seen as the tool of the King, a point well illustrated in 1795 by the Irish artist William O'Keefe in his *Farmer George's Wonderful Monkey* (Plate 26),[21] through the placing of a chain around his neck attached to a crown. The print hints at Pitt being the creature of his master, George III, as well as hinting at Pitt's perceived aspirations to play at being king with his holding of the orb, a symbol of royal power, in his right hand. While the print does not seek to contrast Pitt the Younger's naked ambition with that of his arch-rival Charles James Fox, it was a scathing attack on Pitt and his supposed intent. The sense of naked ambition is characterized through the fact that except for his bearskin hat and red jacket, Pitt is naked. His facial features have been grotesquely exaggerated; however, in contrast with his monkey body, they have not been simonized. O'Keefe clearly understands the visual conventions of the time and has made a conscious decision to do this, so as to not suggest any stupidity on the part of Pitt. The fact that Pitt is running through Windsor Great Park with the crown jewels about his person could ascribe an alternate or additional meaning to the crown around his neck. The print interpreted as an attack upon Pitt for stealing the crown jewels, crown, orb and sceptre, either to crown his own preferred candidate or to hold them in trust and make himself regent. The way in which the crown is around his neck, the orb in hand and the sceptre at his waist, shows Pitt holding and exercising royal power in trust. The text at the bottom of the print is of itself intriguing: 'the Naturalist's of this Country is at a Loss how to give an Account of this Extraordinary Animal, therefore we may Suppose it to be an Offspring of the Devils, & that he = Shit it Flying'. Clearly, there is a sense that Pitt has departed from his previous principles and conduct and transformed into a different 'animal'. There is an allegation that Pitt, like Fox, has become self-seeking and willing to do a deal with the Devil to shore up his own position once the position of his patron, George III, came into question owing to his illness and prevent the Prince of Wales from becoming regent.

Pitt was not the only politician accused of betraying their former principles in exchange for power during the regency crisis. Indeed, Pitt's observation of Fox having betrayed his principles with his advocacy of the natural right of the Prince of Wales to the regency was picked up in an anonymous print in January 1789, entitled *The Veil being Removed: in his TRUE Colours, appears The PRETENDED MAN of the PEOPLE: Alias the WORD-EATING MONSTER from BOLOGNA!*,[22] published by 'a lover of his King and Country'. It is possible, however, to suggest that far from betraying his Whig principles outright, Fox merely saw the long-term incapacity of a monarch as being tantamount to their death and proposed that the most appropriate course of action would be to proceed as if the monarch were physically dead.[23]

The Veil being Removed is a very powerful print with its clear biblical allusions. The fact that Pitt is pulling the curtain aside and thus making Fox visible to the viewer is significant. It creates the impression that he is exposing Fox and his deviation away from the traditional Whig principles and sentiments, which he continually espoused in his rhetoric. While unveiling Fox, Pitt exclaims 'Ecce MONSTRUM!' which literally translated means 'behold the monster'. This phrase has an interesting parallel to the passion gospel when Pontius Pilate exclaims 'Ecce Homo!',[24] something that would not have been lost on its eighteenth-century readers. It is possible, therefore, that the anonymous artist is trying to equate Pitt with Pilate and Fox with Christ. This ties in with contemporary comment about Fox and his nephew, Henry Fox, Third Baron Holland, who was described by Fox as 'a *Second* Messiah come to plague you all'.[25] Horace Walpole exercised his wit along similar lines when, in a letter to Lady Ossory on 28 November 1773, he informed her that 'I told Lord Ossory I call it [Henry Fox] a Messiah come to foretell the ruin and dispersion of the *Jews*'.[26]

In the print, both figures are espousing views that one might commonly think belong to the other. Pitt holds a paper outlining his view that the Prince of Wales had no greater right to be regent than any other citizen. Fox, on the other hand, is busy eating a paper outlining his view that the Prince of Wales had the constitutional right to be regent without needing the consent of Parliament or the people. Fox also suggests that Bolognia sausage was more palatable than having to eat his words. This clearly is a reference to his being in Italy when the crisis broke. He was also forced to backtrack on this assertion, which was viewed as incongruous with his Whig principles and his frequent challenges to the royal prerogative throughout the early part of his career.[27]

The Veil being Removed drew on a number of themes from an earlier print by James Gillray, *Bolognia-sausages, or opposition flux'd*, published on 12 December 1788.[28] In common with the later anonymous print, there is a clear suggestion that Pitt was making Fox eat his words and a link between Fox's 'misguided' assertion of the Prince of Wales's natural right to the regency and his being absent on the Continent at the outbreak of the crisis. James Gillray portrays Fox fleeing the chamber of the House of Commons, slightly fearful, excreting small sausages all the way, with Pitt's profile just visible in the doorway, as he asserts that:

> The Prince of Wales has no more right to a 'succession to the Regency, than any other Subject*, and whoever asserts the 'contrary, speaks little less than Treason! – I repeat, than Treason!'
> *without the consent of Parliament (BM 7476).

Pitt's speech bubble is interesting for a number of reasons. From a purely design aspect, it is clear that, such was the haste at which the print was put together, he missed a crucial phrase 'without the consent of Parliament' when he etched the plate and had to add it afterwards. From a political slant, we have Pitt, seemingly defending the sovereignty of both Parliament, and by extension, the people's elected representatives, while Fox appears to be defending the prerogative powers of the monarchy, backtracking as he exits, saying 'I never said he had a right to the Regency I didn't indeed! indeed I didn't!'. Not only is Fox undertaking a U-turn in terms of what he said or was supposed to have said, but by supporting the royal prerogative over the will of Parliament, he was effectively performing a U-turn on one of the cornerstones of Whiggism. The shock of what has come to pass with Fox and Pitt having almost exchanged metaphorical positions, with Pitt upholding Parliament's rights, having been put in power over the 'elected' Fox–North Coalition in 1784, and Fox's long-held view that Parliament should choose who governed, is illustrated by Speaker Cornwall, who arms raised in astonishment, exclaims, 'Lord! Lord! What will this House come to?'

One of the defining prints of the regency crisis of 1788–9 was James Gillray's *The Funeral Procession of Miss Regency* (Colour Plate 7), published on 29 April 1789.[29] Here, Gillray astutely assessed the political situation, as both Fox and Sheridan look as though their last real chance for office has just disappeared with the King's recovery, while there is also a hint of animosity between them. The print depicts a funeral procession, marking the end of the regency crisis and with it any real chance the Foxite Whigs had of getting into power, as George III, who had an intense personal dislike and distrust of Fox, continued to be capable of ruling Britain. This print also pokes fun at the Irish Parliament, represented by six bulls acting as pallbearers. Early in the crisis, the Irish Parliament, seeking to assert their independence from Westminster, speedily pushed through their own Regency Bill before dispatching a messenger to the Prince of Wales, offering him the regency of Ireland. This move, combined with the representation of Ireland and their Parliament, in *The Funeral Procession of Miss Regency*, reinforces the fact that Ireland was still very much a part of British politics.[30] Indeed, there were close links between Fox and Henry Grattan, a leading Irish politician.[31] While the Irish Regency Bill can be seen as somewhat premature, as the full extent of the King's condition had not yet been established and nor was the likely timescale of any recovery known, their messenger only arrived in London as news of the King's recovery broke. This can clearly be seen as an attempt to establish both the sovereignty of the Irish Parliament and a bid to clarify the constitutional position of Ireland in relation to the rest of Britain, portraying the relationship as that of a sister kingdom, rather than a parent–child relationship.[32]

The Funeral Procession of Miss Regency can also be seen to make light of the Opposition Whigs, who forfeited their early advantage through indecision and poor judgement, which was personified by Fox's natural right blunder.[33] In this drama, the procession is being led by Edmund Burke who is dressed as a Jesuit, while the part of the chief mourner is played by the Prince of Wales's illegal wife, Maria Fitzherbert. Fox's position directly behind Mrs Fitzherbert along with Richard Brinsley Sheridan, who was closely tied to the Prince of Wales, clearly reflects the sense of a missed opportunity on the part of the Opposition Whigs to return to power. Fox and Sheridan are described by Gillray as 'Second Mourners' and 'The Rival Jacobites'. The second of these two descriptions is an allusion to the fact that they were the two leading negotiators within the Foxite camp, the term Jacobite indicating their desire to depose George III and potentially begin a Catholic succession with the Prince of Wales and Mrs Fitzherbert. With a Roman Catholic as chief mourner and the priest in Jesuitical garb, the procession takes on a flavour of a Catholic funeral and so the notion of the recovery of George III delivering the nation from the tyranny of Roman Catholicism is strong. Deliverance from poor judgement and political and personal gambling is also apparent from the presence of a pair of dice, a dice box and empty purses on the top of the coffin.

The notion of Fox and Sheridan as rivals in *The Funeral Procession of Miss Regency* is an interesting one. At this time, Fox was the clear leader of the Opposition Whigs. Early in the crisis, during Fox's absence, it was Sheridan and Grey who were jockeying for position. Both Fox and Sheridan were close associates of the Prince of Wales, but by this period, arguably it was Sheridan who was closer. It is not impossible to see, however, where this notion of a Fox–Sheridan rivalry sprung from. They were seemingly working independently, receiving separate instructions from the Prince of Wales. Additionally, they provided the House of Commons with differing versions of the Prince's marital status during the debates over it in 1786.[34] The ambiguity of the exact nature of the Prince of Wales's relationship with Mrs Fitzherbert and the need to clarify the position once a statement had been made to the House of Commons were a significant cause for embarrassment, both to Charles James Fox and the Prince of Wales personally and to the Foxite Whigs more generally. It has been generally accepted by historians that Fox knew nothing of the Prince's secret marriage at the time of his first statement; however, this did not prevent the caricaturists from making the most of the situation or from suggesting that Fox was closely embroiled in the whole affair and that his denial of the marriage was both deliberately misleading and a considerable misjudgement. It certainly seems to have been questionable whether Fox had been willfully blind to the closeness of the Prince of Wales's relationship with Mrs Fitzherbert, and was working on a don't ask, don't tell policy. What we do know is that Fox cautioned the Prince of Wales against marrying Mrs Fitzherbert, knowing that it would remove him from the line of succession, thus at a stroke dashing his best hope of a return to office. Fox's council against the union might well be the reason behind his being unaware of the secret marriage, with the Prince being unwilling to risk his friendship with Fox.

Clearly, the embarrassment caused by this episode, to both sides, was avoidable had the Prince of Wales heeded the advice contained in Fox's letter of 10 December 1785 not to marry Mrs Fitzherbert.[35] Fox pointed out that 'a marriage with a Catholic throws the Prince contracting such a marriage out of the succession of the crown.'[36] In this letter, Fox also informed the Prince that it had come to his attention that he was contemplating marrying Mrs Fitzherbert and enquired him whether 'is this really in your mind.'[37] Had the Prince of Wales been entirely truthful in his reply, dated 11 December 1785, four days before his secret marriage on 15 December 1785,[38] then Fox would have been able to avoid the embarrassment that he was caused by denying in Parliament that the Prince of Wales and Mrs Fitzherbert were married when in fact this was not the case.

This question of the Prince of Wales' marital status prompted a number of prints, including James Gillray's *WIFE & No WIFE _ or _ A Trip to the Continent* (Plate 27), published on 27 March 1786,[39] in which he imagines a wedding scene involving many of the Prince of Wales' closest associates and allies, with the notable exception of Richard Brinsley Sheridan. The fact that Fox was unaware that the Prince had secretly married Mrs Fitzherbert on 15 December 1785 must have made Gillray's print particularly galling. The print imagines a Roman Catholic marriage ceremony between the Prince of Wales and Maria Fitzherbert, being conducted by Edmund Burke with the aid of a choir of monks. As an Irishman, Edmund Burke was always open to suspicion of latent Roman Catholicism and was often portrayed as a Jesuit, as he was on this occasion. Fox himself is afforded a central role in the scene, giving the bride away. On the one hand, Gillray is clearly seeking to infer that Fox was in full knowledge of the marriage and therefore complicit in the Prince's flouting of the Royal Marriages Act by marrying without the King's permission.[40] On the other hand, there is also a sense that he had been betrayed by his friend, as the image hanging immediately over his head is that of Judas's betrayal of Christ in the garden of at Gethsemane. It is equally possible, however, that the image is implying that just as Christ knew that he would be betrayed and by whom, Fox was in possession of the facts, but continued on his path nonetheless. It is somewhat surprising that Fox, who was not exactly a virtuous figure, should have been equated with Christ in two prints at this time, when only a few years earlier he had been accused of being in league with the Devil. The exact reason for this resurrection of his character is unclear.

While Richard Brinsley Sheridan is conspicuous by his absence, the presence of Lord North, dressed as a coachman, is somewhat incongruous. His sleeping suggests that he is unaware of the events that are taking place around him, but he was always seen as a friend of the King prior to his ill-fated coalition with Fox and although George III had felt betrayed by that junction, it did not push North into the arms of the Prince. In all likelihood, Gillray has included North in the scene in order to warn of a possible return of the Fox–North Coalition should the Prince of Wales ascend to the throne and his being asleep defends him, to a certain extent, from knowledge of the events taking place.

Meanwhile, during the regency crisis there was some confusion over who the Foxite Whigs should have approached to fill the post of Lord Chancellor. Sheridan sought to persuade Lord Thurlow,[41] the existing Lord Chancellor, to carry on, while Fox had previously promised the Great Seal to Lord Loughborough, the Foxites' leading lawyer and long-time candidate. Fox's reluctance to accept Thurlow was in part owing to not wishing to offend Loughborough by reneging on his earlier promise to him, and in part a continuation of his personal distrust and suspicion of Thurlow, which dated back to the second Rockingham administration. Thurlow was himself a veteran of a number of administrations across the spectrum of English Whiggism. He was very much the King's man and owed his longevity to George III's belief that just as the choice of Chief Minister was his, so was that of Lord Chancellor, who had the care of the Great Seal of State. Indeed, it was a combination of the George III's belief that the appointment was his and Fox's disregard for Thurlow that led to the Great Seal being held in commission during the ill-fated Fox–North Coalition. Arguably, the refusal to have Thurlow contributed to the King's animosity towards the coalition. Lord Thurlow's willingness to change horses mid-stream, breaking with Pitt when he appeared to be on the way out, switching allegiance, temporarily, to the Foxite Whigs, and then moving back again when it became apparent that the King would recover in order to remain in office, was picked up by the caricaturists. This episode clearly damaged the trust between Pitt and his Lord Chancellor and ultimately contributed to Thurlow's removal by Pitt in 1792, despite having no ready replacement. The lack of unity within the Opposition Whigs played into Pitt the Younger's hands and he was able to exploit this division and confused opposition line to drag out events in the hope of an improvement in the sovereign's health.[42]

In *Dead, Positively Dead* (Plate Colour 8),[43] Lord Thurlow is depicted in the centre of the print turning his coat round back to front and exclaiming that 'this side will do as well as the other'. The Prince stands next to him weeping into a handkerchief, while Sheridan scurries through the open door laden with a trunk inscribed 'Dispatches for C. F'x'. By portraying Lord Thurlow in the process of turning his coat, the artist passes comment upon his duplicity during the regency crisis, negotiating with both sides until the end in the hope of remaining in power, an action which later contributed to him losing his position as Lord Chancellor. Another significant feature of the print is Queen Charlotte being crowned behind Thurlow. While this act could be in response to Pitt the Younger's plan to place the care of the person of George III into the hands of the Queen during his illness, it could be speculation on the part of Gillray that Queen Charlotte was poised to be made regent. This idea is given credence by the Prince of Wales's order to Sheridan to 'make haste' as he rushes out with dispatches for Fox. Presumably this is to brief Fox, so that he can mount a rebuttal of the plan to make the Queen regent and to enable him to better make the case for the Prince of Wales' claim. If this is so, then the print is also passing comment on Charles James Fox's abilities as an orator. Indeed, the fact that the Prince of Wales is depicted crying suggests a fear on his part that his supporters are losing the argument. The fact that Prince George is standing on a paper 'prayer for the Restorat[io]n of his Maj[esty's] health' suggests a certain frustration on his part on both the length of delay in making him regent and also the length of time he has already had to wait even to get close to ascending to the throne. His second speech 'We must keep up appearances' could demonstrate a perceptiveness that it was in his interest to not appear too grasping of the throne. If this is indeed the case, then the holding of the handkerchief to his eyes could be the Prince going through the motions of public grief for his father's present illness or indeed crocodile tears, rather than genuine grief. The title of the print, *Dead, Positively Dead*, is a clear reference to the Foxite position, that in the event of the King's long-term incapacity, then events should proceed as if the King were in fact deceased, and in the event of the heir apparent being of age (which he was in this instance), then the search for a regent should stop with them. It is also possible, however, to read the print instead as suggesting that the Queen would prove a better choice for the position of regent than her dissolute son, George, Prince of Wales, who was too closely tied to the Foxite Whigs for some people's liking. The fact that Queen Charlotte is being crowned by two women emphasizes the sense of urgency that was developing for finding a solution. This action could be read as an attempt to chivvy Pitt the Younger along while he retained the initiative, or as a warning to the Foxites as to what would happen if they did not act quickly. Given the situation of where the crown was likely to rest, it is unclear exactly which way Thurlow is turning his coat and the fact that he is mid-turn could indicate that he is at that moment in two minds as to which side to lend his support to. The likely role of the Queen in any regency settlement was a topic of much contemporary speculation. Lady Stafford, writing to Granville Leveson Gower on 18 August 1788, suggested that 'after violent altercations a modified Regency was settled in favour of the Prince of Wales; the Queen to have the care of the King and the right of appointing his household'.[44]

While *Dead, Positively Dead* does not directly feature Charles James Fox or William Pitt the Younger, it is nonetheless a useful print for garnering the caricaturist's assessment of the situation. It also provides comment upon the motives behind some of the political manoeuvring that was taking place, namely the Lord Chancellor's desire to remain in post at all costs and Pitt's determination to keep Fox and his friends as far away from office as possible by using any means at his disposal. This comment regarding Pitt's determination to keep Fox out is also picked up on by Thomas Rowlandson in *Suitable Restrictions* (Plate Colour 9),[45] portraying William Pitt the Younger as a manipulating puppeteer.

In this print, the Prince of Wales is dressed as a child with a soft cap with three ostrich feathers pluming from the top and petticoats. He attempts, unsuccessfully, to reach for the crown on the floor, which is surrounded by marbles. The prize which the Prince of Wales had craved for so long, the chance to rule, had been made tantalizingly close by his father's illness and continued to be so, owing to the restrictions to the regent's powers proposed by Pitt the Younger when it became apparent that he would be unable to block the Prince of Wales from becoming regent. The leading strings being used by Pitt the Younger to restrain the Prince of Wales are clearly a visual metaphor for those restrictions. As he pulls the Prince back, Pitt exclaims, 'hold, not so fast Georgy', indicating that his path to full use of the prerogative powers would not be a straightforward as the Prince might have anticipated or desired. The use of a diminutive form of the Prince of Wales's Christian name further emphasizes his portrayal as a child, while the leading strings, which prevent him from both reaching the crown and reaching out to the Foxites, are indicative of some of the restrictions Pitt was planning to bring in as part of the Regency Bill, which it was anticipated would soon be before Parliament. Through this representation of the Prince of Wales and associated attribution to him of child-like qualities and characteristics, by implication, question his readiness for the regency. Clearly, his judgement, maturity, both political and personal, and experience are called into question. This is personified through his friendship with Charles James Fox and his associates, something that clearly he and the country are in need of protection from. Under Pitt's plans, the regent would be prevented from making appointments for life and restricting the appointment of people to positions that were not vacant, or to become so by the death or resignation of the incumbent.[46] Another reading of this print would place Pitt as a scheming and self-interested puppeteer, attempting to build enough restrictions into his Regency Bill to enable him to continue to pull the strings. The contrast between the normally youthful Pitt and the Prince of Wales is particularly striking, with Pitt looking calm, assured and older than his years. This has been achieved through the positioning of his wig, suggesting that he had gone bald through age-related hair loss, while in contrast the Prince has long, flowing youthful locks. This has the overall effect of making the age gap appear considerably larger than the three years it actually was.

While all this is going on, Fox, Burke and Sheridan are depicted playing marbles, seemingly oblivious to what is going on around them. The smug expressions on the faces of the Foxites, who clearly believe that it is only going to be a matter of time before they take office, provide a stark contrast with the worried look on Pitt the Younger's face and create the impression that was widely felt at the end of January 1789, that a regency under the Prince of Wales was inevitable, as was the return to power of the Opposition Whigs. The Foxites do not come out of *Suitable Restrictions* particularly well, as their playing marbles can be seen to depict them in an arrogant manner, demonstrating a trivialization of the issue and a complete ambivalence to the health of their sovereign. Additionally, through turning the whole question into a game, they can be seen as political gamblers, thus Rowlandson succeeds in questioning their political maturity and suitableness for office.

This sense that a regency under the Prince of Wales and with it the return of the Opposition Whigs to power was an inevitability is reflected in *The Tories and the Whigs Pulling for a Crown*,[47] published on 2 January 1789 by J. Aitken. In the centre of the print, the Prince of Wales sits on a throne under the Prince of Wales's feathers watching on as Lord Thurlow and William Pitt the Younger are having a tug of war with Edmund Burke and Charles James Fox for the crown. Lord Thurlow is depicted wearing his Lord Chancellor's robes and has his arms locked round the thin waist of Pitt, who is leaning back and tugging vigorously for all he is worth. In stark contrast are Burke, dressed as a Jesuit, a common theme throughout the prints of this period,[48] and Charles James Fox, whose fat belly can be seen bulging through his waistcoat and how is only holding onto the rope with one hand. In spite of this, the crown remains ever so slightly on their side of the Prince of Wales's throne. While on the face of it Fox looks ambivalent, the speech bubbles above the heads of the figures portray a different story. Thurlow encourages Pitt to keep pulling, for fear of losing his position as Lord Chancellor,[49] while Pitt attempts to reassure him that he will not give in. The Prince of Wales comes across as non-partisan and aloof, sitting back and claiming that he must wait for a winner to emerge from the contest. This is in stark contrast to events, as the 'heady excitement of Cabinet-making almost drove other pleasures from his mind', as he discussed potential cabinets with senior members of the Foxite Whigs.[50] Burke, meanwhile, encourages Fox to keep pulling as he was not strong enough to withstand the collective might of Pitt and Thurlow, in spite of the fact that he appears to be doing just that. Fox's caption is intriguing as he appears to have given up, claiming that he never dreamed of treason. It is clear, therefore, that in this instance the text provides for another reading of the image, in which case the reader can surmise that the artist is attempting to impart the shifting of the initiative away from the Foxites, back towards the government. The dejected look upon Fox's unshaved face could be read in such a way as to back this up, rather than his being ambivalent. The fact that two diametrically opposite readings of this are possible, by including or excluding the text in the analysis, emphasizes the importance of text and the ability to read in fully understanding eighteenth-century satirical prints.

When *The Tories and Whigs Pulling for a Crown* is viewed alongside other prints on the regency crisis, such as *The Funeral Procession of Miss Regency, Dead, Positively Dead* and *Suitable Restrictions*, it is clear that no politician could claim to have emerged from this episode with much credit. That said, Pitt the Younger did prove himself an astute political tactician, using every means open to him to delay the passage of a Regency Bill, in order to give time for the doctors to attempt a recovery.[51] This policy, however, did leave him open to the accusation of being a very controlling and manipulative figure, anxious to cling to power by utilizing every means at his disposal. On the other hand, Charles James Fox's political judgement was again called into question and his behaviour could be perceived to have bordered upon treasonable in the distasteful speed at which he attempted to capitalize upon the King's illness, while his close personal ties with the Prince of Wales led some to question his motives. Whether or not Fox and Pitt would have acted similarly had they found their roles reversed is impossible to tell. The intrigue that the regency crisis occasioned would have long-lasting repercussions including a heightening of George III's distrust and personal dislike of Fox and his being forced to dispense with the services of Lord Thurlow. The diarist, Joseph Farington, recorded in May 1797 that 'The King has a steady objection to Fox; and is said to believe that were He to yield in this respect He might experience the fate of the French King'.[52]

Conclusion

The attempted impeachment of Warren Hastings and Sir Elijah Impey can be viewed as an attempt by the Fox–North Coalition to justify their East India policy following their removal from office in December 1783. The fact that Pitt the Younger, eventually and with some reluctance, was finally forced to consent to this action demonstrates that the move was not entirely baseless and self-serving. It is therefore arguable that these proceedings would have occurred irrespective of the coalition's downfall. Both the impeachments and the ongoing Westminster Scrutiny occupied the energies of the leading Foxites for much of the new Parliament and Pitt's landslide victory in the 1784 election helped to keep down the number of divisions. Whether or not the coalitionists were ultimately successful in recovering their reputation is unclear, however, for as the impeachment process dragged on the caricaturists interest waned.

The Regency Crisis of 1788–9 helped to reignite the rivalry between Charles James Fox and William Pitt the Younger, as it occasioned the possibility of a change in administration. Pitt's shrewd tactics ultimately led to the Foxites proving themselves as divided and unready for office, and opened them up to appearing unsympathetic to their sovereign's health and lacking in judgement. The opposition's disarray was not aided by Fox's absence at the start of the crisis and the unwillingness of the young guns, Grey and Sheridan, to wait for his return before acting, did little to aid the Foxite cause. The closeness of Sheridan to the Prince of Wales and their misleading of Fox over the exact nature of the Prince's relationship with Maria Fitzherbert also harmed the Foxite cause. The prints on this are also interesting for two reasons. First, in the *Funeral Procession*, for the comment on Ireland's renewed attempt to assert her sovereignty and secondly, for Lord North's presence in *Wife and No Wife*. Fox's badly expressed assertion of the Prince of Wales's 'natural right' played into Pitt the Younger's hands and enabled him to suggest that Fox was a political chameleon, willing to abandon his colour and principles if it meant an opportunity for office and power.

The role of Lord Thurlow in the regency crisis comes to the fore in many of the prints and his duplicitous behaviour can be seen as the start of his demise. His power and influence arose through his being very much the 'King's Man' and the Fox–North Coalition knew to their cost what his forced exclusion could mean in terms of royal favour. Certainly, it required much political capital to forcibly remove him against the King's wishes, which certainly strengthened his hand during the regency negotiations. It is interesting, however, that while it is apparent that he could be painted as being as self-serving as Fox, if not more so, he is not vilified to the same extent in the prints.

What the prints on the regency crisis highlight the most is that at times of political uncertainty and contest, the Fox–Pitt rivalry comes to the fore, with Fox and Pitt the Younger serving as emblems for the rival factions or 'parties' jockeying for position and power.

5

Divisions Emerge

Introduction

The relationship in caricature between William Pitt the Younger and Charles James Fox altered following the East India Bill crisis and the 1784 election, with Fox constantly being criticized for the manner of his opposition to Pitt the Younger. This heralded a move towards a more formalized opposition towards the King's government. Fintan Cullen has argued that it is impossible to fully understand the political rivalry between Charles James Fox and William Pitt the Younger, and the cult status they enjoyed into the nineteenth century, without acknowledging and understanding their visual representations, which were numerous and ranged across mediums and genres. Within the more ephemeral world or caricature, Cullen argues both supporters and rivals vied for the numerous images which pitted the two men against each other, whereas only supporters would purchase a bust of their hero.[1]

The French Revolution not only brought about fresh divisions between Charles James Fox and William Pitt the Younger, but also within the Foxite Whigs, and these divisions were to fundamentally change the nature of British politics. The revolution in France polarized opinion and provided space for a new conservative ideology to emerge. These divisions were long-lasting with many of Pitt's acolytes coming together as a nascent Tory Party in the early nineteenth century.

This chapter will examine what the divisions which opened within British politics in the wake of the French Revolution were, what their causes were and examine how this was all represented within contemporary satirical prints. Consideration will also be made of the importance of the role played by caricature in the move towards the creation of the 'Modern Party Leader' and the importance of the personal relationship of William Pitt the Younger and Charles James Fox within that process.

French Revolution

The French Revolution of 1789 was a massive turning point in the history of the long eighteenth century and completely redefined the term revolution. The event polarized political opinion and was the catalyst for the disintegration of the old Whig connection in Parliament.[2] Henry Offley Wakeman, one of Fox's biographers, has argued that:

> Fox could not remain Fox and not see the best side of the [French] Revolution, any more than Burke could remain Burke and not see the worst. Fox had ever been an assessor of abstract rights, just as Burke had been the apostle of practical expediency.[3]

Indeed, Herbert Butterfield has argued that 'repeatedly Fox betrays the fact that, far from realizing that the French Revolution had altered the character of the English political scene, he interpreted the political history of contemporary France in terms of English constitutional history'.[4] That is to say, Fox firmly believed the French Revolution was akin to the Glorious Revolution of 1688 in England and that the French were merely attempting modest reform in removing a despotic and morally bankrupt monarch.[5] Meanwhile, E.A. Smith has argued that 'Fox's error was to see French politics in terms of English political ideas and to see in the revolution the transference to France of English Whiggism'.[6] Fox greeted the French Revolution enthusiastically, rhetorically asking 'How much the greatest event it is that ever happened in the World! And how much the best!'[7] This was a view that L.G. Mitchell has argued Fox still espoused as late as 1792, reiterating his view that the French Revolution was a French version of 1688 and, as such, had not substantially challenged the Whig party's principles. Mitchell argues that Burke was just as adamant that the opposite was the case.[8] So out of step was Fox with the majority of opinion within the political classes, he was vilified and much abused by the caricaturists for his views on the revolution which led to the creation of a new stock image of him: Fox the Jacobin.

One of the most effective examples of this 'stock image' (Plate Colour 2) was James Gillray's *A Democrat or Reason & Philosophy*.[9] Here, Gillray aligns Fox with the revolutionary sans-culottes, portraying him without culottes, trousers, breeches or pantaloons. His perceived pro-revolutionary and Jacobin tendencies are also represented by the *bonnet rouge* on his head, complete with revolutionary cockade, while a speech bubble has him singing a revolutionary song, *Ça Ira*. Gillray also suggests that Fox has the blood of the revolution on his hands through the presence of a blooded dagger in his belt and bloodstained hands.

Thomas Wright has argued that this print pained the mind of Fox.[10] Reputedly, Fox was so enraged by the print that he repeatedly considered suing over it, only declining when he realized it would only increase the print's notoriety.[11]

The image of Fox as a Jacobin was aided by two prints that sought to deconstruct this image. The first of these was Isaac Cruikshank's *A Right Honourable alias A Sans Culotte* (Plate 7),[12] a two-part print in which Fox is divided into two with the land at his feet bisected by a stretch of water (the English Channel), rendering that on the right England and the one on the left France. Both sides of his face retain a pronounced five o'clock shadow and bushy eyebrows, while he has a wig on the right and his own hair cut in the cropped revolutionary style on the left. His clothing is also markedly different, with Fox in his 'Foxite uniform' in the right or right honourable half and as a ragged revolutionary in a torn red jacket over a striped shirt in the French Revolutionary colours of red, white and blue on the left. On the left he has a pistol and carries a club, rendering him aggressive and barbaric while singing 'Ca Ira, Ca Ira, Ca Ira'. On the right he holds a paper, 'Association against Levellers St. Georges Hanover Square' and is singing 'God Save Great George Our King', making him appear more of a patriot than a reactionary. Here, Cruikshank infers that Fox was at a watershed having to decide between respectability and opposing the revolution and being seen as a barbaric thug by supporting it. In the revolutionary half of the plate, Fox looks wild-eyed which, combined with his drooping mouth, provides a menacing effect. There is something unsettling about the size of his wide open right eye in comparison to his left, which is less visible as he squints through it. The positioning of the eyeball in the French half of the print gives him the appearance of glaring at the viewer from whichever angle the print is viewed, affording the sans-culotte element of the print a slightly demonic quality.

William Dent went a stage further in 1793 with his *A Right Honble Democrat Dissected.*[13] By dissecting Fox, Dent attempts to distil Fox's politics and political make-up for his readers, offering up key points of contrast between Britain and France, which he thinks Fox embodied. For Dent, Fox's political make-up is a complex mix of verbosity, hot air, republican ideals mixed with old aristocratic and more modern democratic principles, with an intransigent dislike and distrust of the royal prerogative. The inscription of 'Commonwealth' on his heart indicates republicanism and is a throwback to Cromwell's Commonwealth. His intestines, 'French Principles', indicate his support for the French Revolution, while his kidneys are labelled 'Aristocratic' (right) and 'Democratic' (left), providing an interesting balance between Britain's more aristocratic government and post-revolutionary France's democracy. Meanwhile, his bladder is inscribed

'Reservoir for Royalty', which hints at his contempt for the royal prerogative. His lungs, represented by a pair of bellows, inscribed 'Oratorical Lungs Variably Verbose', are an attack on his oratory and hints at political opportunism. The inscription on his forehead, 'Self-Interest', backs this up, insinuating that Fox was a pragmatic opportunist and lacking in political principles. This is further reflected by the two distinct parts to his head of hair with Fox sporting a bag wig on the left half of his head and his own hair visible on the right. The inference appears to be that Fox was in two minds and was not operating from firm or fixed principles. Dent has, however, stopped short of portraying him as Janus, the two-faced god of Roman mythology. His other internal organs are inscribed 'Gallic', 'Aristocratic', 'Fraternity', 'Intemperance' and 'Democratic'.

Dent also intimates that Fox's vices were central to his make-up, as reflected by his ribs inscribed: 'Duplicity', 'Drunkenness', 'Whoredom', 'Gambling', 'Envy', 'Inconsistency', 'Prophaness' [sic] etched on his right-hand ribs and 'Enmity', 'Cruelty', 'Madness', 'Distress', 'Treachery', 'Ingratitude', 'Despair' on his left. The skin on his right is inscribed 'Fat of Pidgeons' [sic], indicating his love of shooting, while that on his left, 'Fat of Friends', indicates his financial reliance upon his friends. On Fox's arms, Dent contrasts British and French industry. Fox's right sleeve, embroidered 'British Industry', contains the image of a dice box and pair of die, a link to his gambling addiction. Beneath them is embroidered 'Interest of Levellers, Jews, Gamesters, Adventurers'. Fox was often portrayed as a gamester and political adventurer, while the Jewish reference concerns the large amounts of money he owed to Jewish moneylenders.[14] On his left arm, tattooed, 'French Industry', there is the image of a hangman's noose and axe, and beneath this is tattooed, 'Advocate for Atheists, Jews, Papists, Dissenters &c.' Fox's right hand is clenched into a fist, underneath which is inscribed 'Argument', while in his left he holds a dagger, under which is engraved 'Penetration'.

Through their dissection of Fox, Cruikshank and Dent highlight Fox's Francophile views. There is an internal tension within these prints between Britain and France, with British and French values balanced through their representation of him. One can surmise that through this tension, they are questioning Fox's loyalty and asking the reader to decide which side Fox truly favoured. Both prints hint at treason, without explicitly accusing Fox of being a traitor, instead suggesting that he was teetering on the brink. In addition, Fox is accused of deceit and hypocrisy, claiming to be one thing, but in reality being another.

It is unsurprising that an event that polarized opinion to the extent that the French Revolution did was met by a barrage of satirical prints. The importance of the growing print trade during this period should not be underplayed. However, care should be taken not to overemphasize how seriously much of it was taken by the public. In this battle in print during the course of the French Revolution and the French Revolutionary Wars, no political figure was immune from attack. Indeed, Michael J. Turner and Fintan Cullen have argued that during the 1790s, the impact of printed material on the public was increasing.[15] Turner also points to evidence that even a popular patriot leader could still fall victim and that Pitt was quick off the mark in understanding the importance and potential of satirical prints.[16] As early as the East India Bill crisis, Pitt had seen fit to reward the caricaturist James Sayers after his highly successful and damaging attacks on Charles James Fox, whom he had portrayed as Carlo Khan. Pitt the Younger sought to reward James Gillray, the foremost caricaturist of his generation, on a number of occasions. Gillray, however, was not averse to biting the hand that fed him if he believed that comment deserved to be made. Henry Offley Wakeman argued that following the outbreak of war with France, Fox became 'one of the best abused men in England', with large sections of society swayed by images depicting him as untrustworthy, unpatriotic and little better than a traitor. For Wakeman, the caricatures of James Gillray were at the vanguard of this, with Fox consistently portrayed at the head of a party conspiring with the French to overthrow the English Constitution in order to establish a republic based on the French model.[17] Wakeman's suggestion that during the 1790s Fox was 'one of the best abused men in England'[18] is born out within the satirical prints, while his assertion that Fox was depicted by the caricaturists as a traitor links in to one of the 'stock images' of him. Fox's image during the 1790s was not aided by his views on the French Revolution, which were diametrically opposed to those of Pitt the Younger. Fox greeted the revolution enthusiastically, rhetorically asking 'How much the greatest event it is that ever happened in the World! And how much the best!',[19] while during a debate on war with Russia on 15 April 1791, Fox informed the Commons that he 'admired the new constitution of France, considered altogether, as *the most stupendous and glorious edifice of liberty which* had been erected on the foundation of human integrity in any time or country'.[20] Fox was also a lover of peace and frequently called for an end to hostilities during the French Revolutionary Wars. John Derry has pointed out the 'poignant irony in the fact that Charles James Fox, who eventually became the greatest critic of the influence of the crown and avowed friend of the French Revolution, was himself descended from the Stuarts and the Bourbons'.[21] Derry has also argued that Fox's sympathetic attitudes towards the French Revolution were part of a broader worldview on reform and that Fox was devoted to civil and religious liberty.[22] Indeed, it has been argued that Fox was anti-Bourbon rather than anti-French, with L.G. Mitchell arguing that in his speeches 'the word "France" becomes interchangeable with the phrase "House of Bourbon"'.[23]

Charles James Fox's anti-Bourbon views were translated by James Gillray in *The Hopes of the Party, Prior to July 14th _ 'From Such Wicked Crown and Anchor-Dreams, Good Lord Deliver Us'* (Colour Plate 10),[24] to anti-monarchist or republican views, reminding viewers of his earlier representation as the regicide and former Lord Protector, Oliver Cromwell, during the East India Bill crisis.[25] For Diana Donald, Fox's championing of the dissenters' campaign to repeal the Test and Corporation Acts helped to fortify the revival of this old image of Fox as a Cromwellian republican.[26] The link to Cromwell is enhanced by the speech bubble emanating from the mouth of Fox, who is cast as Royal Executioner, complete with mask:

> Zounds! What the devil is it that puts me into such a hell of a Funk? – damn it, it is but giving one good blow, & all is settled! – but what if I should miss my aim! – ah! It's the fear of that which makes me stink so! – & yet what should I be afraid of? If I should not succeed, why nobody can find me out in this Mask, any more than the Man who chop'd the Calf's-head off, a Hundred and Forty Years ago – and so here goes!

The irony here is that the mask Fox is wearing has fox's ears, thus making him instantly recognizable. Indeed, Fox's appearance is characteristically rotund, with his usually pronounced five o'clock shadow in evidence along with his unkempt hair, while sporting his trademark blue and buff 'uniform'. Meanwhile, through the large eyeholes of the mask, Fox's bushy eyebrows are visible. The clear implication is that Fox's disguise is not as effective as he believes, owing to the fact that Gillray has seen right through it and in consequence been able to render both Fox's aim and belief into pictorial form.

The title of the print is particularly intriguing with the first part very definitely drawing Fox and his followers together into a distinct grouping or party, in an age before formal political parties. Meanwhile, the second half takes the form of a versicle and response. The response 'good Lord, deliver us' invokes the litany in the *Book of Common Prayer*, a reference that would not have been lost upon a contemporary audience, in an age where regular attendance at church was still the norm and all Church of England services came from the *Book of Common Prayer*. Indeed, the litany was appointed to be said or sung at morning prayer on Sundays, Wednesdays and Fridays, and at other times commanded by the

Ordinary.[27] The 1662 litany had several versicles with the response 'good Lord, deliver us':

From all evil and mischief; from sin, from the crafts and assaults of the devil; from thy wrath and from everlasting damnation,
Good Lord, deliver us.
From all blindness of heart; from pride, vain-glory, and hypocrisy; from envy, hatred, and malice, and all uncharitableness,
Good Lord, deliver us.
From fornication, and all other deadly sin; and from the deceits of the world, the flesh, and the devil,
Good Lord, deliver us.
From lightning and tempest; from plague, pestilence, and famine; from battle and murder, and from sudden death,
Good Lord, deliver us.
From all sedition, privy conspiracy, and rebellion; from all false doctrine, heresy, and schism; from hardness of heart, and contempt of thy Word and Commandment,
Good Lord, deliver us.
By the mystery of thy holy Incarnation; by thy holy Nativity and Circumcision; by thy Baptism, Fasting, and Temptation,
Good Lord, deliver us.
By thine Agony and bloody Sweat; by thy Cross and Passion; by thy precious Death and Burial; by thy glorious Resurrection and Ascension; and by the coming of the Holy Ghost,
Good Lord, deliver us.
In all time of our tribulation; in all time of our wealth; in the hour of death, and in the day of judgment,
Good Lord, deliver us.[28]

The last of the versicles with the response 'good Lord, deliver us' would appear particularly apt for this print, beseeching the Lord God to deliver us from both times of tribulation (revolutionaries and sans-culottes have taken control of London) and 'at the hour of our death' (George III is about to be executed). The final bidding within this versicle, to be delivered 'in the day of judgment', could, if the litany is being invoked, be a veiled criticism of George III, who, it can be assumed, at the day of judgement would have to account for his actions and those of his ministers acting in his name, including the loss of the American Colonies. Additionally, there are a number of diverse factors within the litany from which the petitioners seek deliverance, which could be said to have been embodied by the French Revolution and its supporters on both sides of the

Channel, namely, all evil and mischief; all deceits of the world; and all sedition, privy conspiracy and rebellion. Additionally, the crafts and assaults of the Devil could provide a tie-in with Fox, owing to accusations of his being in league with the Devil at the time of the Fox–North Coalition, and may, therefore, have caused viewers to substitute the Devil for Fox. The incantation of the Devil in Fox's speech bubble is interesting and suggests that if such a scene were to come to pass, then it would have had the Devil's fingerprints all over it, thus providing a link back to both the title of the print and to the litany. Indeed, a litany against the revolution in France could read: against the assaults and deceits of Fox, *good Lord, deliver us.* For Diana Donald, this print has strong elements of the theatrical, arguing for an element of play-acting within Gillray's prints during the 1790s, while also arguing that Fox and Sheridan were opportunists, taking advantage of circumstance, rather than being genuine opponents of the system abused.[29]

Richard Brinsley Sheridan, one of Fox's key acolytes, has a central role, holding George III's head steady on the block in readiness for his execution. He is clearly playing second fiddle to his leader, cast as executioner, in spite of being the more radical and keener supporter of the French Revolution. As he steadies the King's head, Sheridan seeks to reassure Fox saying, 'Hell & Damnation, don't be afraid give him a stroke, & then throw off the Mask – Zounds, I wish I had hold of the Hatchet'. From this speech and that of Fox, it is apparent that Fox is wracked with doubt over this course of action and that he is being carried along by the young cubs of his party, Sheridan and the absent Charles Grey, who were waiting in the wings and vying to be seen as heir apparent. Fox's being led by the younger members of his party echoes his own childhood and his father's pandering to his sons, and belief that the young were invariably right.[30]

The religious undertones of the print are further developed by the presence of John Horne Tooke, a radical and former clergyman (pictured holding the King's legs), while the non-conformist Dr Joseph Priestly, in the guise of a clergyman, seeks to comfort the King, saying:

> Don't be alarmed at your situation, my dear Brother; we must all dye once; and, therefore what does it signify whether we dye today or tomorrow – in fact, a Man ought to be glad of the opportunity of dying, if by that means he can serve his Country, in bringing about a glorious Revolution; – & as to your Soul, or any thing after death don't trouble yourself about that; depend on it, the Idea of a future state, is all an imposition: & as every thing here is vanity & vexation of spirit, you should therefore rejoice at the moment which will render you easy and quiet.

Priestley's invocation of the Glorious Revolution of 1688–9 is striking, given that the Hanoverian reign was a by-product of it. Clearly, he is suggesting that like the Stuarts before him, George III had turned into a despotic monarch, which the people ought to mobilize against and replace. Horne Tooke's words of comfort to the King also contain a degree of heresy (again, something which the litany calls for the Lord to defend us from), in that it appears to deny the existence of heaven and hell, suggesting, therefore, that the King can rest easy with no need to worry about his soul, as with no future state, it all being imposition, he will not be called to make account for his life.

The presence of Sir Cecil Wray on the scaffold alongside Charles James Fox is curious, given the fact that he had transferred his allegiance to Pitt at the 1784 election. It is entirely possible that he is being attacked as an opportunist who would readily switch sides when the wind changed; however, it should be remembered that he retired from active politics following his defeat in the Westminster Scrutiny. Wray has clearly abandoned Pitt, who can be seen over his shoulder hanging from a lamp bracket attached to the wall of the Crown & Anchor Tavern,[31] in a death agony, head back and sharp nose pointed directly towards the sky, his fingers clasped together. There is an irony that Pitt should be depicted hanging outside the Crown & Anchor, given that it was a centre for loyalism. Queen Charlotte, cruelly caricatured with a haggard face, hangs from a lamp bracket directly opposite Pitt. Their close proximity, with Pitt's breeches touching the Queen's skirts in a suggestive manner, indicates not only their closeness politically, harkening back to the regency crisis, but is also suggestive of an inappropriate degree of intimacy. Images of the regency crisis are further drawn upon, through George III exclaiming, 'What! What! What! – what's the matter now', totally oblivious to what is going on and his impending death.

Wray stands with his right hand on Sheridan's shoulder saying 'Here do give me a little room Joseph that I may be in readiness to catch the droppings of the Small Beer when it is tapp'd; I never can bear to see the Small Beer wasted Joseph!'. Here, Wray is invoking one of Sheridan's characters, Joseph Surface, from his 1777 play *School for Scandal*. The reason for this is unclear, especially in light of the fact that it is Joseph Surface's brother, Charles, who stars in the famous drinking scene in the play and is the more dissolute of the brothers.[32]

Another print that drew upon the Crown & Anchor Tavern, while passing comment on Charles James Fox, William Pitt the Younger and the French Revolution, was James Gillray's *The Crown & Anchor Libel Burnt by the Public Hangman* (Plate 28),[33] which also provides a good example of the return of the image of Fox as 'Man of the People' during the French Revolution. In the print, Pitt the Younger appears as the public hangman, hatchet in one hand and noose acting as his belt. In his pocket he has a book, *Ministerial Sincerity and Attachments: A Novel*, and is in the process of dropping another open book onto a fire. The left-hand page of the falling book reads 'No Lords No Commons No Parliament', while on the right-hand page is an illustration entitled 'Royal Stump'. As he does this Pitt offers a warning to would-be traitors:

> Know, villains, when such paltry slaves presume
> To mix in Treason, if the plot succeeds,
> You're thrown neglected by: – but if it fails,
> You're sure to die like dogs!

This print provides comment upon Pitt's desertion of John Reeves (1751–1829)[34] after the publication of his *Thoughts on the English Constitution*, which emphasized the power of the King and relegated the role of Parliament to that of branches of the tree of the constitution. The book being dropped onto the fire is intended for Reeves's book and the flames are being fanned by the breath of Fox, Sheridan and Erskine, who are seeking to increase the size and intensity of the fire. The opposition were incensed by Reeves's book and its attack on Parliament and called for it to be burnt publicly. Reeves can be seen fleeing into the Crown & Anchor Tavern protesting 'O Jenky! Have I gone through thick and Thin for this?' Protruding from his pockets are a list of spies, informers and reports of Crown & Anchor agents, indicating his support for the government and their repressive legislation passed during the period known as 'Pitt's Terror'.[35] In spite of the minor success in getting Pitt to drop a key ally in the conservative reaction to the French Revolution, there is also a sense of this being only a partial victory, as Reeves was acquitted at his subsequent libel trial.

Another common theme of the satirical prints featuring William Pitt the Younger and Charles James Fox is the contrast between Pitt taking advantage of John Bull, while Fox is seen as pro-French and often paying more attention to France than the perceived abuses of Pitt's administration. A good example of this is James Gillray's *Opening of the Budget – or John Bull Giving His Breeches to Save His Bacon* (Plate Colour 11),[36] in which Pitt the Younger can be seen fleecing John Bull down to the clothes he is standing up in. He is aided and abetted by his supporters, who are themselves declaring a divvy on the proceeds. Pitt explains to John Bull, who here is standing proxy for the nation:

> More money, John! – more Money! To defend you from the Bloody, the Cannibal French – They're a coming! – why they'll Strip you to the very Skin – more Money. John! – They're a coming – They're a coming.

Dundas echoes Pitt's warning to John Bull exclaiming 'Ay! Ay! They're a coming! They're a Coming!' while filling his Scots cap full of gold coin. Lord Grenville also chimes in, lending his voice and support to Pitt's message, 'Yes! Yes, They're a coming', as does Edmund Burke, who reassures John Bull of the urgency of the situation exclaiming, 'Ay They're a coming'. In common with Dundas, both Grenville and Burke are also seen helping themselves to gold coin, which falls through a slit in the side of Pitt's money bag. In response to the government's demands John Bull asks Pitt and his supporters somewhat incredulously while handing his trousers over to Pitt:

> A coming? – are they? – nay then, take all I've got, at once, Measter Billy! – vor its much better for I to ge all I have in the World to save my Bacon, – than to stay & be Strip'd stark naked by Charley, & the plundering French Invasioners. As you say.

The irony of this is that in making John Bull give up his breeches, Gillray is suggesting that Pitt the Younger is in danger of literally turning him into a sans-culotte, while doing to him that which he is warning Fox and the French would do if he failed to comply. In the background, Fox can be seen with his back turned, ignoring the plight of John Bull and instead looking towards France, with whom Britain was at war, for salvation. In desperation, Fox shouts towards the French fortress at Brest:

> What! More Money? – O the Aristocrat Plunderer! – Vite Citoyens! – vite! – vite! Depechez vous! – or we shall be too late to come inn for any Snacks of the l'argent! – vite Citoyens! Vite! Vite!

Once more the stark contrast between the physique of Fox and Pitt is emphasized, as is Pitt's nose which is very pointed and makes him appear aloof. Burke, Dundas and Grenville can be seen with their hands in the side of the money bag siphoning off money from the 'Requisition Budget', to which John Bull has just sacrificed his breeches and effectively filling their pockets. There is a clear suggestion that while the ministers are feathering their own nests and making a profit from public service, Fox is to be trusted even less, owing to his being in league with the enemy.

Recurrence of the trope of politician as doctor

Caricaturists of the late eighteenth century were not afraid of recycling old ideas or tropes and applying them to new individuals, situations or contexts. A good example of this is the representation of politicians as doctors, suggesting this regimen of treatment or that to cure their patient, who was often an embodiment of the nation. These 'cures' might make reference to the policies being proposed or the competence or character of the politician concerned. The resonance of this metaphor grew as the concept of the 'Modern Party Leader' became increasingly apparent and was used to good effect in James Gillray's *Doctor Sangrado Curing John Bull of Repletion – with the Kind Offices of Young Clysterpipe & Little Boney – with a Hint from Gil Blas* (Plate 29),[37] published in 1803 and in Charles Williams's 1808 print *Political Quacks, or the Erfurth Copartnership Commencing Business*,[38] in which Napoleon Bonaparte was portrayed as a quack doctor.

In *Doctor Sangrado*, Prime Minister Henry Addington, himself the son of a doctor,[39] is depicted bleeding John Bull while a diminutive Napoleon is poised ready to catch his blood. The ineffectiveness of the opposition is made clear through Charles James Fox and Richard Brinsley Sheridan watching on without either intervening or offering up an alternative cure. The print is a comment on the Peace of Amiens (1802–3) and the fact that Britain had been heavily taxed to pay for a war that achieved nothing before a peace settlement, which gave Napoleon's administration time to establish themselves, regroup and build up their forces. The negative nature of this print is apparent from the weakness of John Bull during this process, giving the impression that he is being bled dry, while the words 'West Indies', 'Cape of Good Hope', 'Malta' and 'Ceylon', etched into the stream of blood pouring into Napoleon's upturned hat, indicate the favourable nature of the peace to France.[40] This process also has the effect of casting those present in a negative light, especially the opposition, represented by Fox and Sheridan, who offer bowls of hot water that would have made him bleed more. The clear inference here is that the Foxite opposition were not competent to deal with the situation and that while Addington's policy might be painful, Fox's policy would have been far worse.

In James Gillray's *Britannia between Death and the Doctor's* (Plate Colour 12),[41] published on 20 May 1804, there is a sense of contrast between Pitt the Younger, Charles James Fox and Henry Addington. Britannia sits on the foot of a bed in the centre of the print, resting her arm on her shield. The emaciated skeletal figure of Napoleon Bonaparte peering around the bed's curtain and holding a spear in an aggressive manner was clearly the reason behind Britannia's melancholy state. Seemingly oblivious to Napoleon's presence, but determined that he has the answer to Britannia's woes, Pitt the Younger tramples over Fox in his effort to remove Henry Addington from the room. The ushering out of Addington represents his replacement as First Lord of the Treasury by William Pitt the Younger.[42] Gillray's clever use of a visual simile in likening Addington,

Pitt and Fox to rival doctors, each proposing a different course of treatment, is particularly effective in relaying his views on the debates over the governance of the country at that time.

Pitt holds a medicine bottle labelled 'Constitutional Restorative' high in the air, a reference to the idea that Pitt was best placed to lead the country in a war with France[43] and that with the renewed outbreak of war a return to his policies was the best cure for the nation. Fox, on the other hand, holds up a bottle labelled 'Republican Balsam' in one hand, his *bonnet rouge* in the other, while a dice box, inscribed 'Whig Pills', and two dice have fallen out of his pocket. The balsam and hat are clear references to Fox's stance in favour of the French Revolution and provide a good visual metaphor for his desire for peace with France. Meanwhile, the dice allude to his addiction to gambling and their presence is designed to infer that just as he was reckless in his gambling at the tables of Brookes', by extension his judgement could not be trusted in the affairs of state. Addington, on the other hand, drops the bottle of 'Composing Drops' he was holding as he is kicked through the door by Pitt, indicating that he was a safe pair of hands during the Peace of Amiens and following Pitt's resignation, but lacked the ability to lead the country in times of war. Clearly, therefore, Addington, Fox and Pitt's suggested treatments can be linked to their views on the war with Napoleonic France.[44] Addington presided over the Treaty of Amiens and peace with France, Pitt the Younger was First Lord of the Treasury when France declared war on Britain in 1793 and returned as First Lord of the Treasury after the resumption of hostilities between Britain and France, while Fox was in favour of peace with France. Evidently the different treatments Addington, Pitt the Younger and Fox were proposing to Britannia can be seen to reflect the different policies they advocated in the House of Commons. During the Peace of Amiens, Pitt had been concerned about the ambition of Napoleon, whereas Addington was concerned about the possibility of a renewal of hostilities and was anxious to avoid it. Pitt became convinced that the government did not possess the necessary talents to prosecute war successfully, should war be renewed, and so reconciled himself to return to office, in spite of his poor health, should there be a resumption of hostilities and the King require his services.[45]

1797 Invasion crisis

Gwyn A. Williams, in his *When Was Wales?*, gives over a handful of lines to the 'farcical French Landing near Fishguard in 1797, when the Directory under cover of its Irish campaign, dumped a gaggle of criminals led by a paranoid American'.[46] Williams argues that the run on the Bank of England, which the invasion precipitated, was imminent in any case and that it strengthened British patriotism while provoking a witch-hunt against local radicals.[47]

The idea of a crisis at the Bank of England being imminent prior to the French invasion was developed by R.G. Hawtrey in his 1918 *Economic Journal Article*, 'The 1797 banking crisis', in which he argues: 'In England the currency difficulties began just when those of France ended. The restriction of cash payments by the Bank of England occurred on February 27th, 1797, and continued throughout the war'.[48] In outlining this argument, Hawtrey made no reference to the French invasion at Fishguard but instead focused on how the war with France was paid for.[49] This argument was also picked up on by Ian Christie, who contended that until 1797 Pitt had no difficulty in financing the war as money always seemed to be available, although it was expensive. The difficulty arose as Pitt preferred loans to increasing taxation at a time when there was already tremendous pressure on the financial markets, while at the same time as obstinately adherence to his sinking fund. By the beginning of 1797, Christie argued that 'the delicate mechanism of a gold-backed currency fell out of balance, and news of the landing of a small French raiding expedition at Fishguard in February provoked a run on the banks'.[50] By the end of February, the government was forced to rush through an emergency bill authorizing the Bank of England to suspend cash payment and issue small denomination notes (£1 and £2) as legal tender.

In his *History of Modern Wales*, Philip Jenkins, in a passing reference to the invasion, argued that the invasion 'caused real panic among the authorities about the danger of fifth column activity among Welsh nonconformists', as part of a broader point on the radical nature of Welsh non-conformity during the period.[51] Meanwhile, Gwyn A. Williams, in his *Artisans and Sans-Culottes*, also used the invasion as a source of comment upon the radical nature and treatment of non-conformists in Wales: 'The persecution of South Wales Baptists after the French landing at Fishguard at [*sic*] 1797, while unjust, was not pure hysteria'.[52]

Within the British Museum's collection of eighteenth-century caricature there are seven prints relating to the French invasion of Fishguard and subsequent suspension of gold payment by the Bank of England. These prints were published between 1 and 22 March 1797, and are dominated by the work of James Gillray. Many of these prints sought to compare and contrast the position of the First Lord of the Treasury, William Pitt the Younger, with that of the 'Leader of the Opposition', Charles James Fox. While a number of Pitt's policies were unpopular and portrayed as such within the prints, it was invariably Fox, owing to his support of the revolution in France, who comes off second best. A common theme of the satirical prints featuring William Pitt the Younger and Charles James Fox is the contrast between Pitt taking advantage of John Bull, while Fox is seen as pro-French and often paying more attention to France than the perceived abuses of Pitt's administration.

The first print on the 1797 invasion crisis, published on 1 March, was James Gillray's *Bank-Notes – Paper Money – French-Alarmists – O the Devil! – Ah! Poor John Bull,*[53] which provides a specific comment on the decision to suspend gold payment from the Bank of England and instead issue paper notes in an attempt to prevent a run on the bank's supply of gold in the wake of the French landing in Pembrokeshire, Wales. This print also contrasts both the behaviour and policies of Fox and Pitt the Younger.

A confused John Bull is portrayed as a simple yokel farmer, flanked by Richard Brinsley Sheridan, sporting a *bonnet rouge* and Charles James Fox in a bicorn hat with a revolutionary cockade in it, indicating their pro-revolutionary views. They both urge him to refuse the notes being offered to him by the bank clerk, William Pitt the Younger. Fox, wearing a hat in the style of a military officer, clearly a reference to the recent French landing, says to John Bull, 'Don't take his damn'd Paper, John! Insist upon having Gold, to make your peace with the French when they come'. Sheridan, bending towards John Bull, also attempts to dissuade him from accepting the paper notes he is being offered saying, 'Dont take his Notes! nobody takes Notes now! They'll not even take Mine!'.

Underneath the bank's counter, Pitt has six padlocked bags containing coin, while in the background the Lord Chancellor, Loughborough, Lord Chief Justice, Lord Kenyon and Foreign Secretary Lord Grenville are carrying in more bank notes of different denominations. The clear inference of the print is that Fox, Sheridan and their associates are unpatriotic in attempting to dissuade John Bull from accepting paper money, while John Bull indicates that he feels it his patriotic duty to accept the paper money in lieu of his gold, as the gold was needed to pay for continuing prosecution of the war. In contrast to the image of Fox as unpatriotic for advocating peace with France, Britain's natural enemy and urging John Bull to demand his gold over the new banknotes, Pitt the Younger is portrayed as the great patriot, as indeed his father the Earl of Chatham had been viewed.

It is particularly interesting that the main thrust of the print is an attack on the opposition, rather than a criticism of the government for not adequately protecting Britain from invasion. There is, however, an implied criticism of

Pitt the Younger and his government, through the hoarding of coin under the counter, picking up on a pre-crisis theme in *Opening of the Budget* (Plate Colour 11) that the government were feathering their own nests. The silence of the government ministers is also telling, while the red face of Pitt, possibly a reference to his heavy drinking, also could be a sign of embarrassment. There is also an interesting sideswipe at the level of Sheridan's debts,[54] when he explains to John Bull that 'nobody takes Notes now! They'll not even take Mine!'.

This suggestion of government ministers lining their own pockets (at John Bull's expense) is provided in Richard Newton's *The New Paper Mill or Mr Bull Ground into 20 Shilling Notes*,[55] in which John Bull finds himself in a mill, being ground down into paper money (20 shilling notes), which is bagged up for the use of government ministers. The bag in front of Pitt is labelled 'Specie For Our Own Use' while the bag Dundas carries away is labelled 'Specie for Wimbledon'. The print not only comments through the inscription on the mill 'By Royal Authority' on the act of 3 March 1797 authorizing the issue of paper money, but also criticizes the exploitation of the people, represented by John Bull, by Pitt and his government.

Another print from 1797 on the same theme is Isaac Cruikshank's *Billy a Cock-Horse or the Modern Colossus Amusing Himself* (Colour Plate 13),[56] which imitates James Gillray's *The Giant-Factotum Amusing Himself* (Colour Plate 14)[57] produced prior to the invasion. In both prints, Pitt sits astride the Speaker's chair, dangling a globe from his right hand while his ministerial colleagues hero-worship their leader. In *The Giant-Factotum*, the opposition are crushed under Pitt's left boot while in *Billy a Cock-Horse*, Fox's side is pierced by Pitt's spur as he and his colleagues attempt to flee the House of Commons, possibly heralding the Foxite secession of 1797–1801 in the wake of their consistent defeats over Pitt's repressive legislation and failure in censuring his government. There is also an indication of a strengthening of the opposition or waning of Pitt's power, as the opposition go from being downtrodden to their leader alone being wounded. Both *The Giant-Factotum* and *Billy a Cock-Horse* comment on the ongoing war with France, while *Billy a Cock-Horse* also comments on the suspension of gold payments by an Order in Council of 26 February 1797.[58] In both prints, Pitt is depicted with papers bulging from his left coat pocket and gold coin bulging from his right. While the accompanying text in *The Giant-Factotum Amusing Himself* points to resources for prosecuting the war, in *Billy a Cock-Horse* the accompanying text indicates the requirement for additional part-time forces and the nation's dwindling levels of gold and silver. Significantly, Pitt's gaze in the two prints is directed in different ways. Pitt's focus shifts between the two prints, looking to his own benches while things were going well and shifting his gaze to the opposition after the French have landed in Fishguard. This switch in Pitt's focus from his own supporters and Britain's dominance of the globe to the opposition is telling. While on the one hand it could be viewed to signify concern over renewed opposition confidence in the wake of the French landing, it could also be an accusation that it had occurred through Pitt taking his eye off the ball.

The fact that Pitt the Younger is represented towering over his colleagues indicates his dominance over Parliament, something that is emphasized by his holding a sceptre and dangling a globe from his right hand. MPs from his own benches are also kneeling at his foot and looking up expectantly as if seeking favour of patronage, a clear comment from Cruikshank on the traditional methods of maintaining support for an administration. This concept of Pitt as a domineering figure was not a new one and can be dated back to his actions during the regency crisis.[59]

James Gillray's *Midas Transmuting All into Paper*[60] is another take on the theme and is clearly inspired by the legend of King Midas from Roman mythology, as the title alludes to and maintains some of the imagery from *The Giant-Factotum*, which depicted Pitt in a similar pose over the Speaker's chair. Indeed, Gillray helpfully supplies a reference to Ovid's *Metamorphosis*.[61] According to Greek and Roman mythology, King Midas was rewarded by Bacchus, the Roman god of wine and inebriation, for reuniting him with his foster father, Silénus. His reward for this service to the god was that he could 'choose any boon he desired'. Midas responded, asking, 'Grant that whatever I touch with my body may turn to gold'.[62] This gift was in fact a mixed blessing as it prevented Midas from being able to enjoy food and drink since it turned to gold in his mouth. Midas soon came to despair of his situation and requested that Bacchus take away this ability. Later on, while walking in the mountains, Midas disparaged Apollo's[63] playing ability. Apollo was suitably enraged by this and turned his ears into those of an ass; later, when the wind passed through the reeds, they would say 'King Midas has ass's ears!'.[64]

Pitt is portrayed sitting on the Bank of England, wearing a crown that does not cover his asses' ears. He has a padlock inscribed 'power of securing public credit', locking a chain round his neck and the key of public property at his waist. His belly is swollen and full of gold coin. Indeed, his belly is vastly out of proportion with the rest of him, his arms and legs retaining their usual pencil thin size and resembles more what is usually ascribed to Fox. Pitt is depicted excreting and exhaling coin, which miraculously transforms into bank notes in mid-air. This is a clear reference to the Bank of England's issuing of paper notes in order to stave off a run on the nation's gold reserves. The heads of Fox, Sheridan, Erskine, M.A. Taylor and Grey can be seen in the reeds, all sporting *bonnets rouges* exclaiming, 'Midas has Ears'.[65]

The overbearing size of Pitt can be viewed as a comment upon the government's increasing control of all areas of life. In the background one can see the French port of Brest, from which a fleet has set sail, presumably to invade Britain, while an explosion has forced hundreds of *bonnet rouge* sporting *sans-culottes* into the air. Pitt is clearly oblivious to this and the inference is that not enough is being done about the nation's defences. By furnishing Fox and his colleagues with *bonnets rouges*, Gillray is attempting to suggest that they are in league with the French, a common theme within his prints during the 1790s.[66] The fact that none of them is looking out across the sea, like Pitt, could be read as a criticism of their failure to hold the government properly to account over the French landing at Fishguard. The likening of Pitt the Younger to King Midas could also contain a veiled comment by Gillray on Pitt's proclivity for claret and port, owing to the close links between King Midas and Bacchus. All three prints can be seen to comment on the overbearing nature of Pitt the Younger personally and his administration more generally, and this is reflected by the image of Pitt the Younger towering over two of Britain's principal institutions, the House of Commons and the Bank of England. The lack of a robust opposition is another theme of these three prints and the opposition's pro-French stance is clearly illustrated by the insertion of a *bonnet rouge* in both of Gillray's prints and the Foxites fleeing in that of Cruikshank.[67]

Split-Plate Designs

During the period of the French Revolution, split-plate designs became a popular method employed by caricaturists to portray contrast.[68] James Gillray's *Hanging: Drowning (The Fatal Effects of the French Defeat)*, (Plate 30)[69] was an early example of artists applying this method of representation to the Fox–Pitt relationship. Fox is depicted hanging himself from the rafters, while Pitt the Younger and his good friend, drinking companion and colleague, Henry Dundas, are portrayed enjoying a drunken evening with the table overturning, wine spilling everywhere and them being reduced to sitting on the floor on account of their drunken state. The catalyst for their actions would appear to be contrasting newspaper reports of the same event from their respective sides. On the left, Fox drops a newspaper 'Account of the Republican Overthrow', while on the right, Pitt clasps a newspaper 'News of the Victory over the Carmagnols'. The fact that the catalyst is a newspaper is significant as it highlights the growing importance of the press. Pitt and Dundas's drunken Bacchanalian orgy can, however, also be read as a criticism of them, suggesting the pair are drunkards and questioning their ability to govern the country. Both Pitt the Younger and Dundas were well-known as heavy drinkers. Indeed, S.A. Hunn has indicated that it was Dundas who first introduced Pitt to heavy drinking and was the only man who could out-drink Pitt, who was himself a six-bottle [of port] man.[70] Hunn also points out that criticism of heavy drinking during this period needs to be discussed within the context of the time when 'Three-bottle men were accounted little better than milksops'.[71]

Press reporting is again an important factor in *The Table's Turn'd* (Plate 31).[72] On the left of the plate, Fox, as a winged devil in a blue top and *bonnet rouge*, symbolizing his shared Opposition Whig and Jacobin credentials, clasps a rake-thin Pitt round the waist in one hand. The subtitle of this panel is 'Billy in the Devil's claws', while the subtitle of the plate on the right is 'Billy sending the Devil packing'. These subtitles, combined with the print, demonstrate a pro-Pittite line. On the left Fox exclaims 'Ha! Traitor! – there's the French Landed in Wales! what d'ye think of that, Traitor?' This speech is a clear reference to the French landing of 1797. On the right of the print, Pitt has freed himself from Fox's grasp and holds a copy of the *Gazette*, reporting Admiral Sir John Jervis's victory over the Spanish fleet, aloft. This news has quite literally taken Fox aback, his *bonnet rouge* falling from his head as he leaps into the air in shock. Pitt continues to goad him saying 'Ha! Mr. Devil! – we've Beat the Spanish Fleet what d'ye think of that Mr. Devil?' It should be remembered that the first duty of any government is the defence of their people. The French invasion at Fishguard had highlighted the weakness of Britain's defences.[73] However, the swift rounding up of the French troops, combined with news of victory over the Spanish, prevented the opposition from fully capitalizing on the event and enabled the government to breathe a sigh of relief.

The portrayal of Fox as a devil is also significant, as not only does it contrast him with Pitt, it also suggests that Fox is in league with the Devil, a visual accusation that the caricaturists levelled at Fox on numerous occasions throughout his career. An early example is found in a print published in the *London Magazine* in March 1777 to accompany the 'Diaboliad'[74] accusing Fox of being in league with the Devil, by depicting him waiting at the back of a queue to pay homage at the Devil's throne. Gillray associates Fox with the Devil on a number of occasions, including in *Gloria Mundi or the Devil Addressing the Sun*,[75] 'Crumbs of Comfort', or – Old-Orthodox, Restoring Consolation to his Fallen Children,[76] *The Coalition*,[77] which was also published as *Junction of Parties*[78] and perhaps most significantly in *Phaeton Alarm'd*,[79] in which he continues to associate Fox with the Devil, even after his death. Fox is shown in the bottom right of the print as a ghostly devilish figure clutching a trident and surrounded by flames, while at the same time contrasting him with the angelic figure of Pitt the Younger in the opposite corner of the print clutching his harp.

Anti-Jacobin Review

In addition to one-off and occasional negative prints attacking individuals on certain topics and in response to certain policies, there were also publications whose aims were to push a particular agenda. One such publication was the *Anti-Jacobin Review*, which sought to promote loyalism and attack Jacobinism through articles, poetry and prints.[80]

The *Anti-Jacobin Review* was set up in 1797 in order to provide a conservative voice amid the radical agitations of the 1790s, following the unsuccessful treason trials of 1794. Jennifer Mori has argued that it was established with the aid of the government.[81] How much direct involvement the Pitt administration had with the *Anti-Jacobin Review* is hard to quantify, but certainly George Canning, an adviser and disciple of Pitt, was heavily involved with the magazine from the outset. Pitt did pen some financial articles for the *Review* between November 1797 and July 1798; however, this should not be used to suggest that the *Anti-Jacobin Review* was a government mouthpiece.[82] It had an interesting subscription list with several notable figures of all political persuasions listed as subscribers, including Thomas Paine Esq., William Cobbett, Georgiana, Duchess of Devonshire,[83] George Canning, Viscount Castlereagh and Lord Camden.[84] The artist James Gillray, who contributed a number of illustrations to the magazine, was also a subscriber.[85] George Canning was at the head of the team whose brainchild the *Anti-Jacobin* was. Other influential figures were George Ellis and John Hookham Frere.[86] The periodical was the successor of a newspaper, the *Anti-Jacobin; or, Weekly Examiner* and according to de Montluzin the successor paid less attention to the Foxite Whigs and the 'Lake School' poets.[87]

Fox and his followers were 'victims' of some of Gillray's plates within the journal. One of them was *Two Pair of Portraits* (Plate 13).[88] Some plates, such as *New Morality; – or – The Promis'd Installment of the High-Priest of the*

Theophilanthropes, with the Homage of Leviathan and His Suite,[89] *Evidence to Character; – Being a Portrait of a Traitor, by His Friends & by Himself* (Colour Plate 15)[90] and *Doublûres of Characters; – or – Striking Resemblances in Phisiognomy* (Plate 32),[91] were also issued as standalone prints. These prints, when produced in the *Anti-Jacobin Review*, should have been bound alongside a poem or some explanatory text; however, the plates were not always bound in the right place.[92]

Evidence to Character attacks Fox and his colleagues for their role in Arthur O'Connor's trial for treason in May 1798. Fox, Moira and Sheridan all acted as character witnesses for O'Connor, who later confessed to having been a member of the United Irishmen. Frank MacDermot has suggested, however, that they might have perjured themselves on account of the fact that a copy of a letter from O'Connor to Fox, informing him that the 'United Irishmen's test or oath was quite harmless and that he himself had taken it',[93] was found when his house was searched in 1797. Fox stands at the bar of the court with a book in his pocket, 'Letters to Lord Ed[ward] F[itzgerald] Mr. O'Conner etc. etc.' Fox informs the court, 'I SWEAR that he is perfectly well affected to his country! – a Man totally without dissimulation – I know his principles are the principles of the Constitution'. Sheridan has a paper in his pocket entitled 'List of Irish Directory' and is holding a book entitled *Four Evange Lists*. He informs the court that 'I know him intimately: – I treated him & he treated me with Confidence! – & I SWEAR that I never met with any man so determined against encouraging French assistance'. Erskine, in legal robes and wig and apparently defending O'Connor, claims 'His friends are all MY friends! – and I therefore feel MYSELF intitled upon MY Oath to say that he is incapable in MY judgment of acting with treachery & upon MY Oath I never had any reason to think that his principles differed from MY own so help ME God'. The speeches from three of the Foxites' strongest and most talented speakers all appear to have laboured in vain, on account of O'Connor's confession:

I confess that I became an United Irishman in 1796 & a Member of the National Executive from 1796 to 1798. I knew the offer of French assistance was accepted at a meeting of the executive in the Summer 1796: I accompanied the Agent of the Executive (the Late Lord Edward Fitzgerald) through Hamburgh to Switzerland, had an interview with General Hoche (who afterwards had the command of the expedition against Ireland) on which occasion everything was settled between the parties with a view to the descent. I knew that in 1797 a Fleet lay in y⁰ Texel with 15000 Troops destined for Ireland I knew of the loan negociating with France for Half a Million for the Irish Government.[94]

While delivering his confession, O'Connor half bows, hands clasped together and above him two hands appear out of a cloud, one holding the scales of justice and another a noose around his neck. The hands appearing out of the cloud are suggestive of divine judgement. The irony of Gillray's image is that in the actual trial of O'Connor, a verdict of not guilty was returned, whereas in the print O'Connor appears to be condemned by his own mouth.[95] The upshot of the print is that Fox and his colleagues appear foolish for their attempt to convince the court of O'Connor's virtues. The print also leads the viewer to question the trustworthiness of Fox and his colleagues, especially considering their ties to several leading Irish politicians, something that Erskine's speech particularly highlights. The references to constitutional principles, made by Fox and Norfolk, were intended to remind the viewer of the earlier treason trials, especially that of John Horne Tooke who had called the First Lord of the Treasury, William Pitt the Younger, as a witness in his defence in an attempt to prove that the reform he advocated in his speeches and writings was no different in substance from the Reform Bills that Pitt had put before Parliament during the 1780s.[96] *Evidence to Character* is a very verbose print that relies upon the reader having a good level of literacy in order to understand and interpret it.

Doublûres of Characters is another important anti-Foxite print produced by James Gillray for the *Anti-Jacobin Review*. The print is based on a quotation attributed to Lavater, 'If you would know mens hearts, look in their faces'. Rather cleverly, Gillray introduces his viewers to physiognomy, providing two images each of the figures depicted. The first is designed to represent how they might appear should the viewer run into them in the street. The second image, behind the first, is designed to provide an insight into the character of the individual concerned and is based on the ideas of physiognomy, as laid out by Lavater. Helpfully, Gillray includes an explanatory note at the bottom of the print.

The first figure to be represented is Charles James Fox, dressed in his traditional blue jacket and buff waistcoat as the 'Patron of Liberty'. Behind him is his *doublûre*, the 'French Arch-Fiend'. Here there are flames behind him and he has what looks to be a snake draped round his naked torso. Second is Richard Brinsley Sheridan, as a 'Friend to his Country'. His *doublûre* is 'Judus Selling His Master' for which he is shown holding a money bag, presumably holding his thirty pieces of silver, and it is likely that this also contains a subtle dig at his frequent impoverishment. Sheridan's *doublûre* has a scheming covetous expression almost as if it is a side of Sheridan that he needs to keep in check. Third is the Duke of Norfolk as 'Character of High Birth'. His *doublûre* is 'Silenus Debauching'. Here Norfolk is depicted looking considerably older, drinking a glass of wine with a bunch of grapes, complete with leaves on his head. Fourth is George Tierney as a 'Finished Patriot' whose *doublûre* is 'The Lowest Spirit of Hell'. Here Tierney is depicted looking even more hawk-like than usual, eyes set close together and a long hooked nose. Fifth, Sir Francis Burdett, resplendent in green frock coat, red waistcoat and neatly tied cravat, stands in profile as 'Arbiter Elegantiarum'. His *doublûre* is 'Sixteen-String-Jack'. Here Burdett looks rather less well groomed, his coiffure has come forward and is overhanging his forehead, coming down past the level of his nose. Also gone is the exquisitely tied white cravat, to be replaced with a simple country patterned neck cloth. Sixth is the Earl of Derby, again in profile as 'Strong Sense'. His *doublûre* is 'A Baboon' in which he has a naked torso and sports a *bonnet rouge*. His features have been slightly simianized, giving his *doublûre* an ape-like quality. Last is the Duke of Bedford in top hat, brown jacket and red waistcoat, who is 'A Pillar of the State'. His *doublûre*, 'A Newmarket Jockey', is dressed as a jockey with a striped jacket and jockey's cap. His *doublûre* is visibly shorter, unshaved and has a determined expression.

David Bindman has argued that *Doublûres of Characters* was a brilliant response to the English translation of Lavater's *Pyhsiognomische Fragmente*, using his phrase 'If you would know Mens Hearts, look in their faces', as both an epitaph and inspiration, imagining the hearts of the Foxite leaders from their caricatured faces. For Bindman, the juxtaposition of their 'real' countenance and supposed moral being was perfectly summed up with the *doublûre* of Fox, 'The Arch-Fiend'.[97] The stark contrast between the caricatures of the individuals and that of their souls is striking and makes the print very effective.

The whole image serves to undermine the public's trust in the opposition and make them appear shady individuals who were not up to running the country. This is an interesting statement to make in the aftermath of Pitt's 'Terror' and in some ways could be viewed as a means of attempting to justify it, as Gillray did in *Evidence to Character*. It is also interesting to note that Lavater considered a receding forehead to be a sign of intelligence, something that does not come out in Gillray's *Doublûres of Characters*, with neither Fox, Norfolk or Derby looking particularly intellectual.[98] H.T. Dickinson has argued that conservative propaganda was more substantial during the 1790s than that disseminated by the radicals, before going on to highlight the *Anti-Jacobin Review* as one of the great conservative triumphs in this area.[99] The fact that the *Anti-Jacobin Review* continued into the 1820s indicates its longevity and therefore suggests that it was successful and well received. It is questionable how much the success of conservative propaganda affected the Opposition Whigs during the 1790s. While the decision to secede in 1797 was predominantly due to Fox's following being much reduced in the House of Commons and the perceived futility of opposing the measures of the administration of William Pitt the Younger, the effect of negative propaganda might have also fed into this decision. The question of the effect of conservative propaganda is difficult to quantify, owing to a lack of evidence as to the number of prints produced, while publications such as the *Anti-Jacobin Review* would have naturally appealed to a more conservative readership who did not need convincing of the dangers of revolutionary principles.

Conclusion

The French Revolution has rightly been viewed by historians as one of the key turning points of European history. It was an event that polarized opinion and arguably led to the emergence of the modern Conservative Party. It was an event that tore the Foxite Whigs apart, with Pitt the Younger able to tempt the more conservatively minded and aristocratic members away from Fox, although many personal friendships endured this political break. The revolution took place at a time when the potential of satirical prints to have an impact on and help shape debates was becoming known, and prints such as James Gillray's *A Democrat or Reason & Philosophy* (Colour Plate 2) caused Fox much distress, to the point where he contemplated legal action, then declining as to do so would only serve to increase the notoriety of the print. The inclusion of specially commissioned prints, albeit in loose-leaf form, in the loyalist periodical *The Anti-Jacobin Review*, is clear evidence of the important role it was felt such images could play alongside articles and portray the loyalist response to events in France.

The development of Charles James Fox and William Pitt the Younger as emblems for the two sides of political debate continued apace and is particularly apparent with the return of the trope of the politician as doctor, seeking to cure the nation of its ailments. Meanwhile, the French Revolution, with its iconography, made comparing and contrasting the views of Pitt, Fox and their respective followers particularly easy, as the insertion of a *bonnet rouge*, loaded with meaning, could not only demonstrate whether a figure was pro- or anti-revolutionary, but could also be utilized to create an impression of unpatriotic and treasonous activity. Indeed, no matter what Pitt did to the long-suffering John Bull during the period of the French Revolution, all the caricaturists had to do was place a *bonnet rouge* on Fox and immediately his actions became more suspicious and invariably he became the enemy of the piece.[100] The fact that their fathers before them had been engaged in a rivalry was also helpful to the satirical artists, as it gave them a history and meant that little explanation was needed for the tension between the two men.

While it would be easy to suggest that the relationship in caricature between Fox and Pitt's successor, Henry Addington, does not at first appear to build upon the Fox–Pitt relationship within the creation of the 'Modern Party Leader', but a few caveats need to be considered. Henry Addington was elevated to First Lord of the Treasury from the obscurity of the Speakership of the House of Commons, which does not make this a fair test, while the Fox–Pitt rivalry had entered its second generation. In many ways, unlike Addington, who as Speaker had no personal following,[101] Fox and Pitt were used by the caricaturists as emblems of their respective sides of the political divide, a device commonly employed by political commentators and cartoonists today with reference to the leaders of modern political parties.[102] Equally, Fox's relationship with Lord North, after his initial break with him in 1774 and his becoming the principal Commons spokesman of the Rockingham Connection by 1777, does point to a significant development in the creation of the image of the 'Modern Party Leader' during the rivalry between Pitt the Younger and Charles James Fox.

The creation of the image of the 'Modern Party Leader' was a significant step forward within caricaturing the individual and built upon the use of 'stock images'. The use of 'party uniforms' and leaders as emblems for their parties and policies had an impact upon the methods through which individuals were represented in caricature. This new concept relied on the special relationship between Fox and Pitt in caricature, which itself was heavily reliant upon their strong physical differences and the history of rivalry between their two families. The French Revolution also had an important part to play and fundamentally changed the political landscape of Britain, with politics becoming ideologically polarized for the first time since the end of the Jacobite cause. The Fox–North Coalition also played a significant part in the changing nature of how individuals were represented in caricature.

Reform, Abolition and Legacy: The Final Salvo

Charles James Fox and the Opposition Whigs seceded from Parliament in 1797 owing to a number of factors. These included their unsuccessful opposition to Pitt's repressive legislation of the mid-1790s, their failure to push parliamentary reform through the House of Commons and their opposition to assessed taxes. Following Pitt the Younger's victory in the 1784 general election, Foxite support slowly leeched away and following the 1790 election they had been reduced to a rump group of around sixty-seven MPs with another thirty providing occasional support in the period from 1794 to 1796.[1] They returned to Parliament sporadically until 1801 and Pitt the Younger's resignation from office. Fox's representation in caricature continued to flourish during the early years of his secession, rising significantly in 1798 owing to the French Revolutionary War, before tailing off during the first two years of the nineteenth century. Pitt the Younger's resignation appears to have resulted in a greater contraction in his representation in caricature with Fox, with the two only featuring together in three prints in 1802 and 1803. Unsurprisingly, Pitt's representation increased significantly in 1805 upon his return to office.

The relative peak in the visual representation of Fox and Pitt during the mid- to late-1790s is not unexpected owing to these years being turbulent. There was unrest and rebellion in Ireland in 1798, and there was also a loyalist backlash against Jacobin ideas. The 1790s also saw the launch of a number of journals that included satirical prints, thus potentially widening readership and consumption of these images. Many of these loose-leaf journal illustrations were included within the *BM Catalogue* and as such artificially inflate the figures, but these prints have been included owing to the fact that the version in these periodicals was not always published at the same time and also they had the potential to reach readers outside of London. The *Anti-Jacobin Review* was first published in 1797 and carried numerous plates by James Gillray, while the German journal *London und Paris* began publication in 1798 and carried reproductions of a number of British prints, along with an explanatory text.[2]

While Pitt's individual figures dropped off from the 1790s they are broadly comparable to those for 1800, the last full year of his first administration. The fact that these figures are so low suggests that Pitt and Fox's joint interest stems from their being viewed as leaders of their respective sides of the House as well as debates. They do, however, make interesting reading when juxtaposed with those for Fox and Addington during the same period. Fox seldom featured in more prints with Addington than he did with Pitt the Younger during Addington's administration. Meanwhile, Pitt the Younger featured in more prints than Addington in every year from 1801 until 1806 when Addington featured in three more prints than Pitt (see Table 2). During the same period, Fox only featured in more prints than Pitt in 1802 and 1806, while being represented in more prints than Addington in every year with the exception of 1803. The fact that Fox and Addington appeared in so few prints when leader of the opposition and prime minister, respectively, is surprising. It would appear, therefore, that Fox and Pitt enjoyed a special relationship with the caricaturists and were seen as influential and divisive figures.

Nevertheless, a few caveats need to be taken into consideration. First, prior to becoming First Lord of the Treasury, Henry Addington was Mr Speaker Addington and as such was supposed to be a politically neutral figure and was therefore unlikely to attract the attention of the caricaturists. Second, his administration (1802–3) was relatively short and the Peace of Amiens brought about a period of relative calm. Third, Pitt died in January 1806 while Addington was a member of Lord Grenville's 'Ministry of All the Talents' from March. Fourth, there was a marked percentage increase in the number of prints in which Fox and Addington appear together during Addington's administration, with the percentage increasing to above 50 per cent after the renewal of hostilities

Table 2 Prints of Fox, Pitt and Addington 1800–1806

Year	Fox and Pitt	Fox and Addington	Fox Total	Pitt Total	Addington Total
1800	12	2	15	31	2
1801	12	0	20	30	7
1802	3	4	17	15	15
1803	3	5	11	17	13
1804	13	6	19	31	11
1805	18	11	28	38	13
1806	16	32	76	30	33

between Britain and France. In order to see the broader picture, the figures for Fox and Addington must be viewed alongside those for Fox and Lord North, in order to provide a proper context. Fox's relationship in caricature with Lord North prior to their coalition in 1783 was equally low and gives further credence to the idea of his enjoying a special relationship with Pitt the Younger. Indeed, it was not until 1782 that Fox and North began to appear together in any significant number of caricatures. It must be remembered, however, that 1782 saw them on opposite sides of the House until Fox's resignation in July, when they were both in opposition to Lord Shelburne's administration. A number of their associates (including North's son George, Lord John Townshend, William Adam and William Eden) were attempting to create a junction of parties, with Fox and North first meeting to discuss the idea of a coalition on 14 February 1783.[3] Similarly, Fox's early appearances with North can be explained by their being in government together.[4] When looking at the figures for Fox and North in caricature during this period, it is important to remember that Fox only entered Parliament in 1768 and did not come of age until 1770, a factor that must account for his relatively low appearance. It is important to note that after his break with North, Fox soon became one of the leading opposition spokesmen and by 1777 was effectively the unofficial leader of the Rockingham Connection in the House of Commons.[5]

This chapter will consider two topics that simmered along under the surface during the 1790s, that is religious and parliamentary reform, before going on to consider the death and legacy of Charles James Fox and William Pitt the Younger. These two topics of reform are considered separately from the earlier discussion of the French Revolution because they were matters more concerned with an individual's conscience. While the French Revolution would have had an impact on debates, political alignments differed and such measures were often proposed as private members bills, as opposed to government business.

Religious reform

Fox was unafraid to engage in debates on religious subjects and the policy differences between him and Pitt the Younger were frequently picked on by the caricaturists. His willingness to engage in religious debates appears on the face of it a little incongruous, given his own lack of strong religious convictions and church attendance.[6] However, it does tie in with two of the cardinal tenets of the Foxite creed: civil and religious liberty.[7] The nature of Fox's attitudes towards religious reforms was reflected in the enthusiastic welcome he and his colleagues gave the removal of religious tests for public office and the widening of religious toleration in France in the wake of the French Revolution.[8] Furthermore, J.C.D. Clark has argued that Grenville's support for Catholic Emancipation was essential to his alliance with Fox in the 'Ministry of All the Talents'.[9] Fox's avocation of greater religious freedoms ties in with the reformist nature of his politics more broadly, such as his championing of the widening of the franchise and the abolition of the slave trade. The link between religious non-conformity and electoral reform was a strong one, however, and might have prompted Fox to take up the fight. Indeed, Thomas Paine, Joseph Priestley and Dr Richard Price were frequently attacked for their reformist agenda and it was widely assumed that their aim was to bring down the church and constitution by violent means.[10]

The majority of the prints of Fox in connection with religion were produced during the 1790s. The main exception to this was John Boyne's 1784 print, *More Ways than One or the Patriot turn'd Preacher*.[11] This print, published on 2 November 1784, is not only interesting owing to its demonstration of the continued interest in the relationship of Charles James Fox and Lord North, but also due to the fact that, unusually for a plain print, it cost one shilling. The print clearly comments upon the subservient nature of Lord North's role within the Fox–North Coalition, as he is depicted as a clerk sitting beneath Fox's pulpit. Meanwhile, Edmund Burke is also present and is depicted as an old woman praying at the foot of the pulpit. The composition apes two of William Hogarth's 'religious prints', *Enthusiasm Delineated* and *The Sleeping Congregation*.[12] On the face of it the interior of a church seems an odd setting for a comment on the nature of politics; however, it should be remembered that the House of Commons met in St Stephen's Chapel in the Palace of Westminster. In *More Ways than One*, Boyne is providing comment not only on the relationship between Fox and North, but also on the presumed hypocrisy of the church, thus seeking to draw a parallel between the two. This would explain the parallel with the two Hogarth prints, which certainly points to discrepancies between what the church preached and how members of its congregation acted. With this analogy the artist also sought to accuse Fox of duplicity, in view of his constant attacks on Lord North and his ministers during the American War of Independence, immediately prior to becoming coalition partners in 1783.

The campaign around the removal of the Test Act[13] was another event that inspired negative prints of Fox in connection with religion. Interestingly, the caricaturists' comments on Fox and the attempts to repeal the Test Act once again saw him in the guise of Oliver Cromwell. John Derry has indicated that

Fox's opposition to the religious test for political office was not just limited to the removal of obstacles facing Catholics (as Edmund Burke advocated), but was more wide-ranging, wishing to remove the impediments facing non-conformists as well.[14] William Dent commented upon this fact in his print of 22 February 1790, *Meeting of Dissenters Religious and Political 1790*.[15] In this print, Fox stands in the centre of the foreground holding a paper, 'Motion to Repeal the Test and Corporation Acts'. He is dressed in a suit of armour in the style of Oliver Cromwell. This motif is enhanced by the presence of a sash round his waist bearing the words 'Spirit of Cromwell' and the presence of a pub on the extreme right of the print whose sign bears the name 'King's Head 1649' as well as an image of the severed head of Charles I. The idea that Fox is Cromwell returned from the past is backed up by the puff of smoke that surrounds him. The figure is clearly meant to be Fox, whose pronounced bovine jaw and five o'clock shadow, unkempt hair and bushy eyebrows are prominent aspects of the figure's features. Fox is flanked by Richard Brinsley Sheridan and Dr Joseph Towers, a Presbyterian minister. Also present is Dr Richard Price, whose presence is significant not only due to his prominence within the campaign for electoral reform and as a member of several reformist societies, but also due to his being a non-conformist minister. Another interesting addition to the gathering is a tall thin Jew, recognizable by a large proboscis nose, ringlets and a pointed beard. He is dressed soberly in black and is noticeably thinner than all the other characters within the piece. In the bottom right-hand corner, one of the non-conformist ministers is tearing up the 39 Articles of the Church of England, indicating that the assembled company were in favour of disestablishment, something that is backed up by the brushes on the church spires, indicating that they are for sale.

Fox calls on the crowd saying that 'I care not what's the established Religion – not I – heaven knows I trouble the Church very little – therefore I'll move the Repeal – in return – I have your interest at the General Election – and pray don't continue to preach against wenching and gaming – the Practice you know nothing about'. Fox's speech bubble reveals his uneasy relationship thus far with both the established church and dissenters, not only in terms of his lapsed attendance, but also owing to the fact that they both taught against his principal pastimes of drinking, gaming and wenching. Towers responds to Fox that 'We'll Preach and Pray for Nothing but the Constitution', a possible suggestion that his reformist ideas were designed to enhance and work alongside the constitution, but also serves to highlight his belief in both religious and political liberty.[16] Tower's statement indicates that he is willing to overlook some of Fox's vices and his lack of faith, seeing him as the best chance of gaining the religious reforms he desired.

While this print at first might appear to cast Fox in a positive light to modern viewers, owing to his association with moves for religious toleration, one only needs to look back to the Gordon Riots of 2–7 June 1780 to see how much suspicion there was about attempts to alter the country's religious settlement.[17] Religious reforms were not, therefore, always a positive thing with which to be associated. The fact that Fox is depicted as the spectre of Cromwell lends subversive undertones to the print and a suspicion that he wants to go further and disestablish the Church of England and remove the monarchy. This sentiment is reinforced by the presence of vipers overrunning a bishop's mitre and a crown. The presence of the Jew in the centre can also be seen as evidence that the artist saw the attempts to repeal the Test and Corporation Acts as the thin end of the wedge with regard to the expansion of religious freedoms and the opening up of civic responsibilities to non-Anglicans. The print is clearly designed to attack Fox and his embryonic alliance with the non-conformists, something that other prints of the time attempted to achieve.[18]

Other events that lent themselves to an attack upon Fox's religious principles, or lack of them, were the French Revolution and matters affecting Ireland. During the period of the French Revolution, Fox was constantly pilloried for his pro-revolutionary stance. It should be recalled at this stage that the revolutionaries were no friends of the Catholic Church, with its property in France being nationalized on 2 November 1789, before abolishing Christianity in October 1793.[19] Fox's perceived lack of religion, combined with his pro-revolutionary principles, led James Gillray, in May 1798, to depict him worshipping at the altar of revolution at St Ann's Hill in his print, *Shrine at St. Ann's Hill* (Plate 33).[20] There are certain parallels between this print and an earlier print of June 1780, *A Priest at his Private Devotion*,[21] which was also issued under the title *A Great Man at His Private Devotion*. Both impressions depict George III praying at an altar in front of 'icons' of Lord Sandwich and his prime minister, Lord North. The altar cloth bears the words 'The Holy Catholic Faith', suggesting that the King was a secret papist, a notion that is backed up by a framed portrait of the Pope above the entrance to his water closet and a torn unframed portrait of the religious reformer, Martin Luther, peeling from the wall. In contrast, Fox prays at the altar of the French Revolution, with a guillotine as reredos and a bonnet rouge on top of a skull and crossbones in place of a cross, flanked by small portrait busts of Maximilian Robespierre and Napoleon Bonaparte in place of candles behind are three stone tablets bearing the ten *Droit de l'homme* (Rights of Man). This is a clear attempt to show the Rights of Man as being analogous to the Ten Commandments of the Old Testament and to suggest that much as the Ten Commandments underpin Judaism and Christianity, so too the Rights of Man underpinned the French Revolution. The altar cloth has an emblem of crossed daggers on the front of it while in Fox's pocket is a book entitled 'New Constitut[ion]'. A thought bubble emanates from Fox's head with winged heads of several Foxites resplendent in *bonnets rouges*. These figures are the Duke of Norfolk, the Marquess of Lansdowne, the Duke of Bedford, George Tierney, Lord Lauderdale and John Nicholls.[22] The clear inference is that these six Foxites are 'angels of the Revolution', whereas to Fox the revolution and its principles have replaced Christianity and they are what he looks to for salvation.

Having been attacked by Gillray for believing more in the French Revolution than Christianity and worshipping at its altar, in 1805 Fox came under attack once more in connection with religion. On this occasion, it was due to the 'Fox–Grenville Coalition' raising the issue of Catholic Emancipation in relation to Ireland, with Lord Grenville petitioning the Lords and Fox presenting a petition to the Commons. Charles Williams, in his print *The Catholic Petitioners, Receiving the Papal Benediction*,[23] depicts Fox dressed in his traditional blue and buff, kneeling in front of the Pope and receiving a blessing. Behind him kneel the Duke of Norfolk and Richard Brinsley Sheridan, behind whom kneel Lord Derby and Lord Moira. Behind the kneeling Foxites stands Henry Grattan, thurible in hand, censing his colleagues. The notable thing is that, while this is ostensibly a 'Catholic scene', apart from the Pope and possibly Napoleon behind him, all the figures are Protestants, including the Irish Sheridan and Grattan and Moira.

The presence of Napoleon, dressed in imperial robes, complete with crown and sceptre, standing behind the Pope, hand on his shoulder and stepping on his robe, gives an impression of his being in control of the scene. This is enhanced by his instruction to the Pope, 'Thank them for pleading our case and particularly for their assertion that the rightoman Catholic Religion is totally altered, make the people believe that and we'll soon give them the second part of Fox's book of Martyrs'. Here the Pope is invoking memories of John Foxe's *Book of Martyrs*, which described the death of many of the Protestant martyrs who were killed for their beliefs during the reign of Queen Mary. However, in the context of this print, part one refers to the members of the Fox–North Coalition who lost their seats and were referred to as 'Fox's Martyrs',[24] while part two indicates that by supporting Catholic relief, politicians were risking their seats. The Pope, in response to Napoleon's prompt and Fox's apology 'Bad luck now, better next time please your Holiness', says, 'Bless you all my Children, for the great good you intended us, but it is not in Mortals, to command success, My Master here, will be very much disappointed'. The Pope's words of wisdom to the assembled

Foxites are curious for their ambiguity towards the end. While one might expect him to be referring to the Almighty when referring to his master, especially after a discussion of mortals, the reader is left with the overwhelming impression, especially through the use of the word 'here', that he is in fact referring to Napoleon.[25] Accordingly, the criticism of Fox in this print is not only levelled at him for being pro-Catholic and attempting religious reform, but also because he is pro-French and potentially a servant of Bonaparte.

Parliamentary reform

During the eighteenth century, the electoral borough franchise varied significantly from seat to seat; however, in all cases the proportion of inhabitants who had the vote as a proportion of the constituency's adult population was relatively small.[26] The political classes, therefore, were hugely privileged and candidates required a private income, especially in an age before the payment of MPs.[27] Consequently, many politicians were very conservative in nature when it came to electoral and parliamentary reform,[28] a position reflected in the fact that only two measures of this kind were passed in the House of Commons during Fox's political career.[29] MPs and peers who proposed and advocated parliamentary reform were often attacked within contemporary satirical prints.[30] Clive Emsley has argued that the Foxite Whigs and popular radicals did not have a monopoly of creating petitions for reform.[31] It is important to remember, however, that the Foxites, along with most people calling for parliamentary reform, were not demanding universal suffrage, with such people being dismissed as radicals. John Derry points out that Fox was neither a radical nor a democrat and while he supported household suffrage and triennial parliaments, he did not advocate manhood suffrage.[32] Meanwhile, Jennifer Mori has indicated that to the Foxites, parliamentary reform meant the 'reduction of ministerial influence in Treasury and Navy boroughs rather than an end to electoral corruption', while Fox, like Pitt, sought to repair rather than rebuild Parliament's reputation.[33] Parliamentary reform was not, however, the only controversial reform put before the House of Commons during this period. Reforms aimed at removing restrictions placed upon non-Anglicans had also proved controversial, as too had the discussions on the abolition of the slave trade.[34]

The question of parliamentary reform became a hot topic after the French Revolution of 1789, which polarized opinion.[35] During the French Revolution there were fears that 'British radicalism might metamorphose into violent Jacobinism'. Mori has argued it was for this reason that the Foxites remained in contact with metropolitan radicals during the 1790s.[36] Mori has also argued that the issue of reform was a major dividing line in 1792 between the conservative and radical Whigs.[37] Those who continued to favour reform, such as the Foxite Whigs, tended to point to the French Revolution as being akin to the Glorious Revolution of 1688 in its desire to establish a constitutional monarchy and so they supported the French Revolution.[38] Many of the supporters of reform after 1789 were, therefore, attacked within the satirical prints of the period for being supporters of the French Revolution who were seeking to destroy the constitution and Parliament and were supporting reforms based upon the worst excesses of the French Revolution. While this was not entirely the case, with most advocates of reform seeking only a modest increase in the franchise, support for the French Revolution was a useful propaganda tool for discrediting the advocates of reform, especially as two of the most notable parliamentary champions of reform, Charles James Fox and Charles Grey, had both greeted the French Revolution with enthusiasm. For his part, Fox was deeply saddened by the revolution from 1792 onwards, believing that their attempts at constitutional reform had descended into anarchy as a result of reactionary powers in Europe responding with force in an attempt to overthrow the revolution.[39] However, this did not prevent him from continuing to be attacked for his pro-reformist stance.

One of the most memorable prints attacking Fox in this vein is James Gillray's *Patriotic Regeneration, – viz. – Parliament Reform'd, a la Francoise, – that is – Honest Men (i.e.) – Opposition in the seat of Justice. Vide Carmagnol Expectations* (Colour Plate 16), published on 2 March 1795.[40] In this print, the House of Commons has been turned into a court room. Charles James Fox presides in the Speaker's chair and sports a blue jacket and a *bonnet rouge* over his hat. The royal coat of arms on the chair has been replaced with a French tricolour. This and the replacement motto, 'Vive la République', are an indication of the Francophile nature of this 'New House of Commons'. Thomas Erskine, in barrister's robes with a *bonnet rouge* on top of his legal wig, and Richard Brinsley Sheridan, also wearing a *bonnet rouge*, sit at the clerk's table. Erskine has a paper entitled 'Defence of Hardy' in his pocket, a reference to his successful defence of the radical shoemaker, Thomas Hardy, during his treason trial in October–November 1794.[41] He stands giving a speech from a paper headed 'guillotine', in his capacity of clerk to the court. It is probable that he is making his recommendation to the judge of the sentences available to the court if the defendant were found guilty. The invocation of the guillotine is deliberate and significant, aligning the court and the Foxites with French revolutionary principles and actions. The guillotine was the French revolutionaries' solution as to how to punish individuals for crimes against the state and the common people. In Britain, on the other hand, the punishment for high treason was to be hung, drawn and quartered.[42]

Sheridan meanwhile, also acting as clerk, makes notes on a paper entitled 'Value of the Guarde Meuble'. Arranged on the table are five volumes, *Rights of Man, Dr. Price, Dr. Priestley, Voltaire* and *Rousseau*. These works by prominent radical figures stand in for the legal volumes that one would expect to find on the clerk's table in a law court, or copies of the proceedings of the House in the Commons. The mace is just about visible at the foot of the table, peeking out, half covered by the tablecloth and a paper setting out the 'Decrees of the British Constitution'. To the side of the clerk's table on the government side are five money bags, 'Treasury Cash to be issued in ASSIGNATS'. Beyond the table is a pile of rolled papers with an open paper entitled 'Forfeited Estates of Loyalists' lying on top of them. Names of prominent noble members of Pitt's government can be seen on the scrolls, including 'Mansfield', 'Chatham' and 'Grenville'.[43] This invokes memories of the Reformation when Catholics were forced to forfeit their lands if they were unwilling to convert. Members of the lower orders and non-conformist clergy sit expectantly on the opposition benches, many of whom under the electoral system of the time would not have qualified to vote let alone become an MP, eagerly observing the unfolding case for the prosecution. In front of them sit two bags containing symbols of regal and clerical authority, destined to be sold in Duke's Place. This clearly signifies the perceived republican and anti-establishment ideas of both the Foxites and lower orders. This ties in also with the ideas of the French Revolution, where the monarchy was abolished and the church outlawed. The sack containing a chalice and bishop's mitre also helps to invoke images of the reformation and dissolution of the monasteries. Pitt the Younger stands in a makeshift dock, having had his jacket and breeches removed. He has been bound and has a rope around his neck, which is held by Lord Lauderdale, again in a *bonnet rouge*. In front of him stands Lord Stanhope as counsel for the prosecution, also sporting a *bonnet rouge* and who holds a list of charges and points at the defendant. The charges read:

> 1st. For opposing the Right of Subjects to dethrone their King. –
>
> 2d. For opposing the Right of Sans-Culottes [*sic*] to Equalize Property & to annihilate Nobility.
>
> 3d. For opposing the Right of Free Men to extirpate the farce of Religion. & to divide the Estates of the Church.

In front of the dock, Lord Lansdowne, again with a *bonnet rouge*, crouches before a set of scales, representing the scales of justice. He attempts to balance a crown with a bell labelled 'Libertas'. To the government side of the dock, the Dukes of Grafton and Norfolk and the Earl of Derby sit by a stove, all wearing *bonnets rouges*, burning the 'Magna Charta' and 'Holy Bible'. Interestingly, Charles Grey is conspicuous by his absence from the scene. In light of his support for the French Revolution and electoral reform, and as a founding member of the Society of the Friends of the People in 1792 and architect of the May 1793 Reform Bill, one might have expected him to be present.[44] In *Patriotic Regeneration*, therefore, Fox and his colleagues are clearly being attacked, not only for their reformist ideas, but also for their perceived alliance with the ideas of the French Revolution. The aim of the print is to discredit these reformist ideas and the individuals behind them for being foreign and totally alien to the British way of doing things. In doing so it also points the finger at Pitt's repressive legislation, suggesting that while unpopular they were for the public good. Accordingly, Pitt comes across as an arch-patriot standing up to foreign tyranny while at the same time standing accused for measures undertaken in order to ensure that the French Revolution did not spread to Britain.

Another theme that was invoked in prints attacking Charles James Fox's reformist credentials was that of Oliver Cromwell. The comparison between the two is interesting owing to Fox's ancestry and the comparison of their 'ideas of reform', which are invariably called to mind. Cromwell, as a regicide and puritanical tyrant who aimed at destroying the monarchy, dissolving the House of Lords and disestablishing the Church of England, has some interesting parallels with the French revolutionaries, who assassinated the monarch, executed aristocrats and disestablished the church. Accordingly, the invocation of the image of Cromwell is loaded with republican ideals and leads the viewer to question the loyalty of those associated with him. Fox himself was no fan of George III, especially after his removal from office in 1783 and because of the animosity the King felt towards him. The traditional Whig distrust of the prerogative powers of the monarch helped feed into this. The question of the Lords is, however, a difficult one to reconcile, given that the Whig party was extremely hierarchical and believed that its leaders should be drawn from men of rank. Accordingly, Fox, as the younger son of a baron, was ineligible in his party's eyes to become their candidate for First Lord of the Treasury, owing to his status as a commoner.[45] His position as the son of a baron,[46] however, did entitle him to expect a leading position within any government the party formed, unlike fellow commoners of lowlier birth, such as Edmund Burke and Richard Brinsley Sheridan, whose talents alone were insufficient to earn them cabinet rank.

William Dent's *Spirit of Democracy, or, The Rights of Man Maintained*,[47] while not an example of superior draftsmanship, does highlight this point. The fact that Dent has chosen to dress Fox in a suit of armour immediately conjures up images of Oliver Cromwell in the reader's mind.[48] The insertion of an individual into a suit of armour during this period was a common method of equating them with Cromwell, a trope that would not have been lost on an eighteenth-century reader. In the print, Fox as Cromwell, an axe at his side and flailing a whip above him, chases after George III and other monarchs of the allied nations into the sunset, down a path towards 'Equality or Annihilation'. While all of this is going on there is a native American standing in the background holding a glowing liberty bell on a pole. This is supposed to represent the noble savage and his inclusion seeks to cast a moral judgement on the other figures within the print. Fox is clearly being attacked for holding republican principles and the fact that he is attacking a number of the crown heads of Europe while in the guise of Oliver Cromwell is no coincidence. Indeed, the axe at Fox's side foretells the likely fate of the monarchs should he catch them.

Fox's association with leading English radicals and non-conformists also provided grist to his opponents' mill and provided another angle from which the caricaturists could attack his ideas of reform. William Dent was ready to seize this opportunity with his *Revolutionary Anniversary or, Patriotic Incantations*.[49] Fox is pictured with Dr Joseph Priestley, Dr Richard Price and Richard Brinsley Sheridan dancing round a steaming cauldron. Within the steam of 'French Spirits' is an inverted crown, which is evidently being carried off by the spirits. Dent is clearly attempting to highlight the pro-revolutionary stance of Fox, Price, Priestley and Sheridan, both by the image of a crown being spirited away, but also by the revolutionary cockades they are wearing. The print's central theme is the French Revolution; however, the presence of Price, a reformist agitator and the images of change hint at reform being part of the artist's inspiration. The presence of Wat Tyler[50] in the painting above Fox also contributes to the images of reform, which are represented in the old style through emblems. Emblems are once again present with the use of impish musicians to represent Satan, suggesting that Fox and his friends are in league with the Devil.

Shakespeare's *Macbeth* is also invoked, both in the image of the cauldron and through the prompt book held by Sheridan open at the cauldron scene from *Macbeth*.[51] This invocation of Shakespeare's *Macbeth* brings in menacing imagery, as well as a sense of foreboding/prophesy and regicide. There is something rather sinister about the way in which Dent has drawn on *Macbeth* to warn against the Francophile nature of the Foxite policies. This is in stark contrast to William Heath's use of the cauldron scene from *Macbeth* in his *The Last Resource or Supernatural Committee Employ'd*.[52]

The attacks on Fox over his sympathy for reform took many forms and invoked a lot of imagery both from the past and from literature. It is striking that while both he and Pitt the Younger advocated measures of parliamentary reform, it was only Fox who was vilified for these views in caricature. In many of the attacks, however, reform is only part of the equation, with events such as the French Revolution grabbing the headlines. It must be remembered that Fox's sympathy for reform was in part behind his embracing of the French Revolution of 1798, which he saw initially as reform along the lines of the Glorious Revolution of 1688. Accordingly, it was hard to consider Fox's reformist agenda, post-1789, without at least a passing consideration of his sympathetic view of the French Revolution. When this was linked with his distrust of royal despots and fear of the excesses of the royal prerogative, it is little wonder that caricaturists sought to align him with Oliver Cromwell, although for family reasons this coupling had a certain irony. The representation of reform through emblems also constituted a harkening back to the old style of caricature, prior to the 'Golden Age', to a time before the term 'revolution' acquired its modern bloody connotations. This practice can, in part, be seen as nostalgic, but can also be seen as the artists not being totally averse to the ideas of reform, but suggesting that the time was not right and that the advocates they were depicting espousing reformist ideas were not ones whose motives for doing so should be trusted. This continued use of emblems, however, is not entirely out of place if one remembers Nicholson's argument in favour of the tenacity and longevity of the emblem.[53]

Death and legacy

Charles James Fox and William Pitt the Younger both died in 1806, Pitt on 24 January and Fox on 13 September. Far from rejoicing at his expected change in fortunes following the death of his nemesis, Fox was devastated and reputedly exclaimed 'I think I shall pair off with Pitt'.[54] Indeed, Castalia, Countess Grenville, noted:

> When Mr. Fox heard it [the news of Pitt's death] he turn'd pale as ashes, and did not speak for some minutes, and then only in a low voice repeated several times: 'I am very sorry, very very sorry' and afterwards: 'This is not a time to lose talents like his'.[55]

The challenge of trying, and ultimate failure, of holding together a fragile pan-European coalition against Napoleon proved too much of a strain on Pitt the Younger's weak health, which declined through the latter half of 1805. His death did not mark an end of his appearances alongside Charles James Fox in caricature. Even after Pitt's death, his ghost continues to feature in prints with Fox during the remainder of the year. Indeed, in *Billy's Ghost; or, Seasonable Admonition*,[56] published by William Holland in February 1806, the ghost of William Pitt the Younger appears to Fox to offer him some advice on administration. Fox is portrayed as rotund and sits working at his desk. The artist has depicted him with a five o'clock shadow, which had been characteristic in earlier times, but after his return to office was frequently absent from images of him. The removal of Fox's five o'clock shadow appears to have been a general measure employed by the caricaturists as part of the rehabilitation of Fox and a renewal of his image as the 'Man of the People'.[57] This rehabilitation involved cleaning up Fox's image and attempting to make him more palatable. Shortly before the Fox–North Coalition's came to power, there were indications within the prints of attempts to clean up Fox's image by whitewashing him. This concept resurfaced during the 'Ministry of the Talents' in 1806.[58]

The death of his great rival acted as a belated catalyst to Fox's ministerial career, forcing the King to accept that a new ministry would require his presence. After Pitt the Younger's death, his fellow ministers did not believe they were able to continue and George III sent for Lord Grenville and eventually acceded to his forming a 'Ministry of All the Talents',[59] which would include Fox as foreign secretary. The 'Talents' were only able to struggle on for another six months after Fox's death before incurring the King's displeasure over their plans for Catholic relief.[60]

In contrast to Pitt the Younger, whose failing health was not considered a topic for jest in caricature, Fox's last illness was portrayed by the caricaturists in a number of prints. A good example is James Gillray's *Visiting the Sick* (Plate 34),[61] in which Fox can be seen sitting in a chair, his very swollen legs propped up on a large cushion. The belief that Fox's demise was imminent was indicated by the paper peeking out of Sheridan's pocket. It is entitled 'Plan for a New Administration' and combined with William Wyndham's question 'O Lord! what side can I tack round to Now?', indicating the potential loss one of his principal leaders. Lord Derby administers smelling salts to Mrs Fox[62] and says, 'My dear old Flame Bet, don't despare! If Charley is pop'd off – a'nt I left to comfort you?' creates the impression that it was perceived that Charles James Fox was not much longer for this world when the print was executed.

In *Billy's Ghost*, once again Fox's legs are visibly swollen by the dropsical disease that he was to surrender to in September 1806. It is clear, therefore, that it might be possible to trace the visible signs of his last illness through his portrayal in the satirical prints. The serious nature of Fox's illness began to raise concern among his friends and colleagues in June 1806. Such was the concern that on 26 June, the Marquess of Buckingham wrote to Earl Temple informing him that Fox was very seriously ill and was rightly influencing the questions of the day.[63] This sense of the serious nature of Fox's illness is reinforced by Thomas Grenville's letter to the Marquess of Buckingham on 28 June 1806 informing him that he had that morning met Lord Horwick, who assured him that while Fox's danger was not quite so immediate, there was no chance of Fox ever appearing in the Commons again.[64] This realization that Fox was unlikely ever again to enter the House of Commons was a bitter blow for the fledgling 'Ministry of All the Talents'. The contrast between Fox's build and Pitt's tall and lean frame in *Billy's Ghost; or, Seasonable Admonition* is accentuated by this illness. The white sheet in which Pitt the Younger is draped gives him the air of a spectre, as do the clouds of smoke behind him. The effect is emphasized by the fact that his appearance has caused Fox's hair to stand on end and has clearly distracted him from his work. This again is in stark contrast to the formerly dissolute images of Fox out of office,[65] and can be seen as another aspect of his rehabilitation within the prints.

In spite of Fox's rehabilitation and Pitt the Younger's death, Pitt was still considered a pitfall for Fox. In *The Lucky Hit or the Crafty Reynard – once more at Large*, published in April 1806, Fox, as a fox with human head, emerges from his den and squints at a number of branches that have been left in a pile across the ground in front of him. These branches are in front of a tombstone engraved 'Hic Jacet WP' and conceal a large hole in the ground. This hole is evidently the open grave of Pitt the Younger, something that Fox alludes to in his speech bubble 'Now the Pit is covered, I may venture out.' Indeed, Pitt's coffin is just visible beneath the branches. Fox's expression contains an hint of scepticism. It is unclear whether this is because he is checking that Pitt is indeed dead or whether he suspects that the branches are covering a trap. Fox's apparent suspicion and distrust could also relate to both his previous experiences of office, where he was turned out on a royal whim,[66] and the fact that the King had personally blocked his inclusion in Pitt the Younger's second administration when he attempted to construct a broad-based coalition amid renewed hostilities with France. Another possible explanation for his expression is his grief at the death of Pitt and his paying his last respects at his graveside.

The spectre of Fox and Pitt made numerous appearances after their deaths. As late as 1810, E. Walker published *The Last Resource or Supernatural Committee Employ'd*,[67] in which the then First Lord of the Treasury and Chancellor of the Exchequer, Spencer Perceval, appears with the ghosts of Edmund Burke, William Pitt the Younger and Charles James Fox. This portrayal demonstrates the fact that the three men continued to live on in the public memory sufficiently well that artists could still use them as a visual tool. There is also a sense of harkening back to the old days, while the print could also be viewed as an indictment on the present government and set of politicians that Perceval had to seek advice from three of the leading politicians of the previous generation who had all been dead for a number of years. The scene itself relates in part to William Shakespeare's play *Macbeth*, with Spencer Perceval in his Chancellor's robes addressing three witches who call the ghosts of Burke, Pitt and Fox up from their cauldron. The scene is reminiscent of James Gillray's earlier print (also based on a scene from Macbeth) *A Phantasmagoria – Scene – Conjuring up an Armed Skeleton*,[68] in which the First Lord of the Treasury, Henry Addington, Hawkesbury and Fox summon up from a cauldron the skeletal remains of Britannia at peace.

In *A Phantasmagoria – Scene – Conjuring up an Armed Skeleton*, Gillray is clearly attacking Addington, Hawkesbury and Fox, hinting at the sinister nature of their actions through their raising up of a skeleton of Britannia, which can also be seen as hinting at a lack of patriotism on their part. In *The Last Resource or Supernatural Committee Employ'd*, on the other hand, Fox, Pitt and Burke do not come out of the print as sinister and subversive figures, with Walker's scorn reserved for Spencer Perceval. Perceval is clearly standing in for Macbeth and it is significant that he is dressed in the Chancellor of the Exchequer's robes. The extract portrayed is from Scene 3 of Act 1 of *Macbeth* where Macbeth complains of the witches dressing him in borrowed robes.[69] It is probable that Walker was seeking to infer that Spencer Perceval was not up to the task to which he was appointed.

Conclusion

William Pitt the Younger and Charles James Fox clearly had a special relationship within caricature, which was most notable when they were prime minister and leader of the opposition, respectively. This special relationship between Fox and the prime minister did not extend to the North or Addington administrations in the same way, however, as neither were as long lasting as the rivalry with Pitt the Younger, which it should be remembered spilled over from their fathers into a second generation. Pitt invariably came out of their spates within caricature better. It is notable that his advocacy of granting Roman Catholics the vote as part of his 1801 Act for Anglo-Irish Union Parliamentary Reform and Parliamentary Reform received little or no comment, while Charles James Fox was attacked for supporting both religious and parliamentary reform.

The clear differences in the treatment by the caricaturists of Pitt the Younger and Fox was most apparent in their treatment of their final illnesses. Pitt's was not attacked, while the swelling of Fox's legs during his dropsical illness was clearly shown. Following his death, Pitt the Younger continued to feature in prints, particularly as a ghostly figure lurking in the background, a spectre that incoming administrations would have to deal with. This could reflect concern about the securing of his legacy, as well as forming a comment upon the untimely nature of his death, with Britain still at war with Napoleonic France. The fact that both Fox and Pitt were brought back by the caricaturists to either haunt, torment or advise their successors clearly demonstrates that they were considered the big political beasts of their day and shows how long lasting their legacies were.

In common with Charles James Fox and William Pitt the Younger, the stand-out political rivals of the nineteenth and twentieth centuries such as William Gladstone and Benjamin Disraeli and Margaret Thatcher and Neil Kinnock have not only differed over policy, but also contrasted starkly in appearance. While Fox's short and rotund frame contrasted perfectly with the tall and lean figure of William Pitt the Younger, the contrast between Disraeli and Gladstone can be seen in Carlo Pellegrini's depiction of the pair in *Vanity Fair* on 30 January 1869[70] and 6 February 1869,[71] respectively, while Harry Furniss also contrasts their appearance at the dispatch box.[72] This tradition dates from the eighteenth-century caricaturists of Charles James Fox and William Pitt the Younger. It is clear that through it the foundations had been laid for the rise of the modern political leader. However, it was not until after the Great Reform Act of 1832 that parties began to organize on a national level, with a clear central party management.[73]

Conclusion

Charles James Fox and William Pitt the Younger were the highest profile politicians of the late eighteenth century. They continued a rivalry begun by their fathers and ensured that the names Fox and Pitt would become synonymous with politics in the second half of the eighteenth century. Both Fox and Pitt the Younger came to lead and represent a political grouping not entirely based upon family ties or MPs representing seats in their family's influence. Both men were among the leading orators of their generation and had the ability to gather men to them and inspire loyalty. Their dominance of the political scene coincided with the 'Golden Age' of the English satirical print and led them to feature in over 370 prints together. They were the two most caricatured individuals in the late eighteenth century and increasingly became emblems for the government and opposition, in part owing to their respective positions of leader of the opposition and prime minister, and partly due to the visual contrast between them.

The relationship between Charles James Fox and William Pitt the Younger in caricature during the late eighteenth century fundamentally altered the image of the politician in caricature and how politics and politicians were viewed within the genre. Their pre-eminence was aided by the fact that they rose to prominence within the House of Commons during the 1780s, a period that coincided with the changing of the guard in terms of both artists and style. Indeed, the new style of accentuating an individual's prominent features was key to their success as a pairing. Not only were they politically opposed to one another, there was a strong physical contrast between the two men, which could not have been better designed for comic effect. This sense of contrast between the hirsute, corpulent and disreputable Fox with the aloof, rake-like and bottomless Pitt made interplay between the two figures visually funny before politics was added to the mix. The representation of individuals as themselves and not through emblems also helped give rise to the cult of the personality. The visual contrast between Fox and Pitt, along with the differences between their personalities when combined with their positions of leader of the opposition and First Lord of the Treasury, helped make them mainstays of political caricatures for the duration of their front-bench parliamentary careers. This, combined with the rise of the political party based upon ideological differences brought about by the French Revolution in 1789, helped cast them as the first 'Modern Party Leaders'.

The 1770s and 1780s witnessed both the rise of a new generation of artists and a marked change in the methods or representation used. Although a number of amateur artists continued to operate, this new generation of artists was increasingly professional with seven major artists working in the field of political prints: James Gillray, William Dent, Isaac Cruikshank, Charles Williams, Thomas Rowlandson, James Sayers and Richard Newton. These new artists drove the genre forward with innovations such as having their prints hand-coloured[1] and depicting their 'victim's' physical features as opposed to representing them emblematically as their predecessors had done. On the back of this change in style, the artists needed to arrive at new methods of making their subjects instantly recognizable. Politicians have always provided a rich seam of inspiration for caricaturists and the new style helped them to exploit this more fully. Alongside this change in style, the caricaturists also developed the idea of a 'stock image' in order to achieve their aim of rendering their characters more familiar. This development also played a leading role in the development of the cult of the personality, something that was instrumental in the development of the relationship of Charles James Fox and William Pitt the Younger in caricature. While the levels of text contained within a print continued to affect the ability of an illiterate or semi-literate person to fully understand the print, these 'stock images' helped to mitigate this by making figures identifiable without the need for textual explanation.

The study of satirical prints has long posed two major methodological issues in terms of production and access. This is in part owing to their ephemeral nature and the fact that many designs just have not survived, in part due to the lack of an archive for the majority of artists and printsellers. In addition to this, there are problems with measuring literacy and estimating the likelihood that a reader can fully understand a print they were viewing. Furthermore, it is impossible to estimate how many people would have consumed prints in shop windows as they went about their daily lives, in exhibitions or through being shown a friend's collection. In turn these points make it impossible to judge accurately the impact of a print. From evidence on the prints themselves, as well as through newspaper adverts, the likely cost of the prints at six pence plain or upwards of one shilling coloured is known. Accordingly, it is possible to make an educated guess as to who could afford to purchase them. Further to this, the inclusion of satirical prints as illustrations within contemporary magazines such as the *Town and Country Magazine*, the *Anti-Jacobin Review* and *Rambler's Magazine* would also have helped drive the consumption of these images out into the provinces and so help make caricatures accessible to a wider readership. There is a vibrant discussion of the reliability of prints depicting printshop window scenes, with two points in need of highlighting. First, such prints had an advertising function, prominently displaying the window and address of the shop in question. Second, they can also be viewed as a source of social comment providing an insight as to who might have paused to gaze longingly at a print-shop window as they passed by. Frequently, these crowd scenes contained individuals from all levels of society, including members of the lower orders, who were unlikely to have been able to afford to purchase prints in their own right. One should, however, be wary of accepting without question that such shops would always have a crowd of people around their window, as it is likely that such crowds would only have amassed when a new print by one of the principal artists had just been published. Even so the numbers passing the print-shops would only have been a tiny proportion of the London population.

One of the major challenges within the reporting of current affairs and politics is ensuring that your article or image is published in a timely fashion, so as to remain current. Caricature readily lent itself to this, as the prints were published individually as single sheets and they were relatively quick to produce. It was therefore important that the politicians depicted could be readily identifiable and so the 'stock image' rapidly became a useful tool within the caricaturists' arsenal. With key figures rising to prominence and disappearing from view on a regular basis, images based on appearance, rather than emblems or visual puns, became commonplace. In an age before 24-hour news coverage and when daily newspapers were the exception rather than the norm, satirical prints, owing to their rapid production, frequently found themselves at the forefront of political news reporting and were often the first source of comment on events. Accordingly, there was a need to modify and develop these images in response to the changing situation of the politician to which they were ascribed. Charles James Fox remained a constant figure in satirical prints after his fall from office, in part due to his position as leader of the main opposition 'party' and a leading spokesman in the House of Commons, and also in part because he provided a good visual foil to Pitt the Younger. With Pitt appearing as a constant as prime minister, for this to be effective, Fox's image needed to be subtly varied to suit, and he was developed into 'Fox the Jacobin' and 'Fox the Traitor' in order to help make his policies appear far worse than the government's position.

During the East India Bill crisis, Fox became an emblem for the coalition and its proposed policies towards India via the persona of Carlo Khan. While governments had long been represented through the person of the First Lord of the Treasury, this representation was unusual. For the first time, one image rather than an individual became the symbol and focal point for criticism of an entire administration and policy, having currency in both satirical prints and the press more widely. Part of the exceptional nature of the Carlo Khan trope was not only that it did not represent the First Lord of the Treasury, but also that in an administration with two principal figures, the full scorn of public anger was directed at only one. Equally, it was the first time when such an attack was made using a mythical alter ego, rather than through representing the 'victim' as themselves or likening them to a historical villain or despot. The trope of Carlo Khan was also significant, as it was one of the few images of Fox that rattled him so much that he complained about it.

From the 1790s, Fox's 'Man of the People' image was augmented by a *bonnet rouge* and immediately a new 'stock image' was born to reflect Fox's pro-revolutionary standpoint and perceived pro-French politics. The politically charged nature of the *bonnet rouge* instantly coloured the viewer's interpretation of Fox's actions and fostered suspicion and distrust in his motives. Following the death of William Pitt the Younger and Fox's return to government, his image underwent a rehabilitation with a return to the 'Man of the People' trope, thus indicating a renewed acceptance of his claims that he was a champion of the people, something that would also have been influenced in part by his work on the abolition of the slave trade.

In contrast, however, Pitt the Younger's stock image went virtually unchanged following his resignation in 1801. He was in government as his stock image was developed and so he became characterized by his being dressed in Windsor uniform. Other key features that never left his image was the superior and aloof look, occasioned by an elongated nose and his bean pole-like figure, frequently with no noticeable backside. Such an image contrasted with that of Fox and provided a wonderful visual counterbalance to Fox's excesses.

As caricature developed, its scope for use as propaganda also increased and this was pursued using a number of different methods. In part, this linked with the concept of the 'stock image' and the representation of an individual as being involved in treacherous activity. Some pre-'Golden Age' tropes, such as the invocation of Guy Fawkes or Oliver Cromwell to indicate treachery, were retained, as was a heavy use of emblems, while new methods were also employed. One of these was an adaptation of the high art genre of history painting though in a mirrored form with the main character being a villain rather than an hero of the past. The adaptation of this genre not only indicates that caricaturists had a knowledge and understanding of high art, but also displays a willingness to borrow ideas from other people and genres that would be popular with their likely customers. Portrait painters had long inserted the faces of their patrons into their representations of scenes from the classics or painted heroic death scenes for the nation's naval and military heroes, such as Admiral Nelson and General Wolfe, although artistic licence was often employed. Accordingly, these scenes frequently represented an ideal rather than reality. In the same way, caricaturists would depict scenes taken from the news – such as the attempt to shoot George III en route to the state opening of Parliament in 1795 and the stealing of the crown jewels in 1788 – and cast opposition politicians, whom they wished to cast in a less than favourable light and accuse of treason, in the lead roles. This practice provided an amusing means of casting politicians in a less than favourable light. The fact that these prints were borrowed from history painting makes it clear that they were apocryphal. Accordingly, their readers would realize that they were heavily imbued by artistic licence and therefore would not presume them to be literally true. This would not, however, have prevented their readers from teasing out the artist's message connecting the politicians cast in the lead role with other, unspecified, treachery.

Eighteenth-century satirical prints had a wider propaganda use than just indicating suspicions of treachery. They were widely used during election campaigns, with a number of different methods utilized to support or attack candidates. Rosettes, coloured or bearing a candidate's name, were particularly helpful for indicating the political allegiance of members of a crowd. Equally, by aligning an individual with a candidate, their actions would also be reflected back on the candidate they were supporting and so negative portrayals of supporters can also be viewed as attacks on the candidates even when the candidates themselves were not represented in person. Elections were not, however, the only areas where politicians were attacked in prints because of their associates. Indeed, Charles James Fox found himself the victim of the caricaturists' etching needle in connection with non-conformists and radical thinkers, because of his views on religious and political reform. Depicting politicians with individuals known for their radical views was a useful tool for the caricaturists when it came to producing negative images of an individual or politician and this method could be put to good use in the creation of propaganda. This method was utilized by James Gillray in his prints for the *Anti-Jacobin Review*, in which he attacked Charles James Fox and the Opposition Whigs for their perceived Jacobin and revolutionary views.

The 'Golden Age' of the English satirical print coincided with the development of the cult of the personality and celebrity. The stylistic changes of the 1780s, along with the production of colour plates, ushered forth by a new generation of artists such as James Gillray, Isaac Cruikshank and Thomas Rowlandson, added to the genre's sophistication and helped fuel the obsession with celebrated figures in politics and society. This led to the emergence of the 'Modern Party Leader', tying up the politics of an entire political grouping with the appearance and personality of an individual. The development of the image of the 'Modern Party Leader' was not only an important development for the representation of political leaders, it also altered the way that politicians were represented more generally, as it sought to group them visually around leaders, either by close physical association within the prints, or by association of dress. The development of the 'Windsor dress' by George III for his ministers and the emergence of the 'blue and buff' of Washington as the unofficial 'uniform' of the opposition and later Foxite Whigs provided the caricaturists with another invaluable tool for portraying politicians and representing their political alignment through image and colour, rather than through speech. After the development of the image of the 'Modern Party Leader', the leaders of the various political groupings found themselves becoming emblems within caricature for their respective groups and their policies. This became particularly effective when combined with John Bull as emblem of the English people or Britannia as emblem for the nation. When considering prints of this nature it is hard not to conclude that the majority of caricaturists were no friends of Fox, especially in the period of the French Revolution. No matter how tough the policy proposed by Pitt the Younger, the other option, Fox, invariably was portrayed as less palatable. The upshot of all these developments was that a new form of emblematic representation grew from the ashes of the old.

The careers of Charles James Fox and William Pitt the Younger saw huge strides forward both in the development of caricature and more specifically in the ways in which politicians were represented within it. The 'stock image' became an essential tool in representing the fast-changing world of politics. However, the arrival of the 'stock image' did not preclude deviation on occasions. The rise of the cult of personality is intrinsically linked to the development of both the 'stock image' and the rivalry of Charles James Fox and William Pitt the

Younger, and was fuelled and developed by the caricaturists during the 'Golden Age' of the English satirical print. It is little coincidence that 1806 and the deaths of Pitt and Fox marked the beginning of the decline of this 'Golden Age' for English caricature, losing its two main stars (or 'victims') in the space of a year. Equally significant to this was the decline in health of James Gillray in 1807. The declining mental powers of George III were also a contributory factor and there was a real sense that as the first decade of the nineteenth century drew to a close, Britain stood at the dawn of a new age, something that the Regency Act of February 1811 could only have re-enforced. The early nineteenth century saw a new generation of artists waiting in the wings to pick up the baton and develop caricature in a new direction. By 1806, much of the groundwork had been achieved for the representation of politics and politicians for years to come, with visual tools such as the 'stock image' proving their worth even today. The cult of the personality continues to go from strength to strength, while stock images of politicians retain their ability to cloud or equally clarify the public perception of them.[2]

Notes

Introduction

1   While caricature had its origins in Italy, British artists such as Hogarth, Gillray, Rowlandson and Isaac Cruikshank drove forward the transformation of this unfashionable genre becoming household names in the process and helped put London on the map as the premier centre of its production.

2   E.E.C. Nicholson has also argued for the continued importance of emblems during the 'Golden Age': E.E.C. Nicholson, 'Emblem v. Caricature: A Tenacious Conceptual Framework', in *Emblems and Art History*, ed. Alison Adams (Glasgow, 1996), 141–67; E.E.C. Nicholson, 'English Political Prints ca. 1640–ca. 1830: The Potential for Emblematic Research and the Failures of Prints Scholarship', in *Deviceful Settings: The English Renaissance Emblem and Its Contexts: Selected Papers from the Third International Emblem Conference*, ed. Michael Bath and Daniel Russell (New York, 1999), 139–66; Marcus Wood, *Radical Satire and Print Culture 1790–1822* (Oxford, 1994), 41; Frederick George Stephens and M. Dorothy George, eds, *Catalogue of Political and Personal Satires Preserved in the Department of Prints and Drawings in the British Museum*, 11 volumes (London, 1870–1954), volume 5, xii; and Charles Press, 'The Georgian Political Print and Democratic Institutions', *Comparative Studies in Society and History* 19, no. 2 (1977): 216.

3   Nicholson, 'Emblem v. Caricature', 142.

4   J.H. Plumb, *Georgian Delights* (London, 1980), 38.

5   Hannah Barker, *Newspapers, Politics and English Society 1695–1855* (Harlow, 2000), 63.

6   Shearer West, 'The De-formed Face of Democracy: Class, Comedy and Character in Eighteenth-century British Portraiture', in *Culture and Society in Britain 1660–1800*, ed. Jeremy Black (Manchester and New York, 1997), 172.

7   Diana Donald in her introduction to David Alexander, *Richard Newton and English Caricature in the 1790s* (Manchester, 1998), 1; see also Herbert M. Atherton, *Political Prints in the Age of Hogarth* (Oxford, 1974), vi; Judith Wechsler, 'The Issue of Caricature', *Art Journal* 43, no. 4 (1983): 317; P.D.G. Thomas, *The American Revolution* (Cambridge, 1986), 12; H.T. Dickinson, *Caricatures and the Constitution 1760–1832* (Cambridge, 1986), 12–13; Robert L. Patten, 'Conventions in Georgian Caricature', *Art Journal* 43, no. 4 (1983): 331; Kenneth Baker, *George IV: A Life in Caricature* (London, 2005), 18; and E.E.C. Nicholson, 'English Political Prints and Pictorial Political Argument ca. 1640–ca. 1832: A Study in

Historiography and Methodology', 3 volumes (University of Edinburgh, PhD. thesis, 1994), volume 1, 63.

8   Todd Porterfield, 'The Efflorescence of Caricature', in *The Efflorescence of Caricature, 1759–1838*, ed. Todd Porterfield (Farnham and Burlington, 2011).

9   Michael, J. Turner, *Pitt the Younger: A Life* (London and New York, 2003), 89.

10 Nicholas K. Robinson, *Edmund Burke: A Life in Caricature* (New Haven and London, 1996), 194–5.

11 Edward Lascelles, *The Life of Charles James Fox* (Oxford, 1936), 4.

12 Anon., *Memoirs of Nine Illustrious Living Characters* (Dublin, 1799), 71.

13 The Lennox's were related to the royal family by virtue of the fact that the first Duke of Richmond was the illegitimate son of Charles II and Louise de Kéroualle, later the Duchess of Portsmouth.

14 On 14 February, the printer Woodfall was summoned to the House to answer for his part in publishing a pamphlet by John Horne (later known as John Horne Tooke (1736–1812)), which questioned the impartiality of the Speaker of the House of Commons. Woodfall apologized to the House for his conduct. This might have been the end of the matter, but Fox insisted that the printer should be committed to Newgate, having got Lord North's agreement that he would vote with him prior to Woodfall's appearance at the Bar of the House of Commons. North later was impressed by Woodfall's defence of his actions and penitence, and sensed that the mood of the House was for a more moderate approach. North begged release from Fox of his earlier promise, which Fox refused to grant him, leaving North in the embarrassing situation of voting in favour of Fox's motion while at the same time advising colleagues to oppose it: L.G. Mitchell, *Charles James Fox* (London, 1992), 22–3; and Sir John Fortescue, ed., *The Correspondence of King George the Third from 1760 to December 1783*, 6 volumes (London, 1927), volume 3, 68–70.

15 John Derry, *Charles James Fox* (London, 1972), 47.

16 L.G. Mitchell, *Charles James Fox and the Disintegration of the Whig Party 1782–1794* (Oxford, 1971), 7.

17 John Derry, 'The Opposition Whigs and the French Revolution 1789–1815', in *Britain and the French Revolution, 1789–1815*, ed. H.T. Dickinson (Basingstoke, 1989), 53.

18 Mary 'Perditia' Robinson (1756/1758?–1800) and Mrs Elizabeth Armistead (1750–1842), whom he was later to marry on 28 September 1795.

19 J.H. Plumb, *England in the Eighteenth Century* (Harmondsworth, 1960), 187.

20 Ibid., 187.

21 John Ehrman, *The Younger Pitt*, 3 volumes (London, 1969–96), volume 1, 5 and 7.

22 John Brooke, 'Pitt, Hon. William (1759–1806)', in *The House of Commons 1754–1790*, ed. Sir Lewis Namier and John Brooke, 3 volumes (London, 1985), volume 3, 299–301, 301.

23 Ehrman, *The Younger Pitt*, 52.

24 William Hague, *William Pitt the Younger* (London, 2004), 66.

25 Brooke, 'Pitt, Hon. William', 299.

26 Ibid., 299.

27 Ibid., 300.

28 Ibid.

29 Ibid.

30 Turner, *Pitt the Younger*, 89.

31 Ibid and Diana Donald, *The Age of Caricature: Satirical Prints in the Reign of George III* (New Haven and London, 1996), 26.

32 David Johnson, 'Britannia Roused: Political Caricature and the Fall of the Fox-North Coalition', *History Today* (June 2006): 22–8, 27.

33 For example, BM 8683.

34 S.A. Hunn, 'Negative Perceptions of Whiggery 1760–1807' (Oxford, PhD. thesis, 1997), 39 and 63; John Ehrman, 'Pitt the Younger, William (1759–1806)', in *Who's Who in British History*, ed. Juliet Gardiner (London: Collins and Brown, 2000), 654–6.

35 Turner, *Pitt the Younger*, 89.

36 Ibid. and Mitchell, *Fox*, 95.

37 Brooke, 'Pitt, Hon. William', 299.

38 Sir Lewis Namier argued that by the mid-eighteenth century, Britain ceased to be a two-party state as the old Tory party, discredited by its Jacobite associations, dwindled and faded away. See Sir L.B. Namier, *The Structure of Politics at the Accession of George III* (London, 1929), viii, 6–7; Sir L.B. Namier, *Crossroads of Power: Essays on Eighteenth Century England* (London, 1970), 231–2.

39 Mitchell, *Fox*, 7.

40 Richard E. Willis, '"An Handful of Violent People": The Nature of the Foxite Opposition 1794 Mitchell 1801', *Albion* 8, no. 3 (1976): 236–7.

41 Paul Langford, *Walpole and the Robinocracy* (Cambridge, 1986); John Miller, *Religion in the Popular Prints, 1600–1832* (Cambridge, 1986); J.A. Sharpe, *Crime and the Law in English Satirical Prints, 1600–1832* (Cambridge, 1986); John Brewer, *The Common People and Politics, 1750–1790s* (Cambridge, 1986); Dickinson, Caricatures and the Constitution; Thomas, American Revolution; and Michael Duffy, *The Englishman and the Foreigner* (Cambridge, 1986).

42 Roy Porter, 'Review Article: Seeing the Past', *Past and Present* 118 (1988): 186.

43 Ibid., 188.

44 E.E.C. Nicholson has also argued for the continued importance of emblems during the 'Golden Age': Nicholson, 'Emblem v. Caricature', 141–67; Nicholson, 'English Political Prints', 139–66.

45 E.E.C. Nicholson, 'Consumers and Spectators: The Public of the Political Print in Eighteenth-century England', *History* 81, no. 216 (1996): 5–21.

46 Ibid., 10.

47 Ibid., 18–19.

48 Ibid., 15–18.

49 Robinson, *Edmund Burke*; Baker, *George IV*; Kenneth Baker, *George III: A Life in Caricature* (London, 2007).

50 Roy Porter, *Bodies Politic: Disease, Death and Doctors in Britain, 1650–1900* (New York, 2001), 247.

51 Brewer, *Common People and Politics*, 16.

52 Nicholson, 'English Periodical Prints', volume 1, 73.

53 Draper Hill, *Mr. Gillray The Caricaturist* (London, 1965).

54 There is evidence that Gillray, Rowlandson and Sayers all had some formal education.

55 British Library, London – Gillray Papers, British Library Additional Manuscripts 27337 ff. 39–40, 96–7 and 106–7 – Letters.

56 BM 10560.

57 British Library, London – Gillray Papers, Additional Manuscripts 27337, ff. 106–7, Letter – Anon. to Mrs Humphreys (1806).

58 *Morning Chronicle*, 28 April (1806).

59 British Library, London – Gillray Papers, BM Additional Manuscripts 27337, ff. 96–7, Letter – G.G.S. to James Gillray (29 November 1803).

60 L.H. Cust, 'Sayers, James (1748–1823)', in *ODNB*, ed. rev. E.A. Smith (Oxford University Press, 2004). Available online: http://www.oxforddnb.com/view/article/24771 (accessed 19 February 2008).

61 See BM 6286; BM 8624; and BM 8990.

62 Robert L. Patten, 'Isaac Cruikshank', *ODNB*, volume 14, 529. Available online: http://www.oxforddnb.com/abstract/10.1093/ref:odnb/9780198614128.001.0001/odnb-9780198614128-e-6844

63 James Gillray, Isaac Cruikshank, Thomas Rowlandson, Richard Newton and George Cruikshank.

64 The sample used Cruikshank is based on images held in the British Museum, Derbyshire Record Office, the National Portrait Gallery and images accessed online at the Library of Congress and Lewis Walpole Library.

65 Hill, *Mr. Gillray The Caricaturist*, 30–1 and 38.

66 Alexander, *Richard Newton*, 36–41.

67 Ibid., 55.

68 Timothy Clayton, 'Humphrey, William (b. 1742?, d. in or before 1814)', in *ODNB*, ed. H.C.G. Matthew and Brian Harrison, 61 volumes (Oxford, 2004), volume 28, 801–2.

69 The reference provided (BL. Add. MS. 27337) is in fact the call number for the Gillray Papers and points to correspondence between Hannah Humphrey and James Gillray.

70 Anthony Griffiths, 'A Checklist of Catalogues of British Print Publishers *c.* 1650–1830', *Print Quarterly* 1, no. 1 (1984): 13–15.

71 See *Anti-Jacobin Magazine*, volume 1, July–December, 1798. In the back of the volume, it contains instructions to the binder, detailing where the accompanying prints should be inserted.

72 *Oracle and Public Advertiser*, 26 January 1796, and *Whitehall Evening Post*, 23 January 1796. Reports in the *Star, Morning Chronicle* and *E. Johnson's British Gazette and Sunday Monitor* suggest Fores was in fact in front of the bench on 22 January 1796.

73 BM 8779.

74 *Morning Chronicle*, 25 January 1796.

75 N.G. Howe, 'The Politician in Caricature: The Case of Charles James Fox' (University of Nottingham, unpublished PhD. thesis, 2011), 75. This figure largely ignores prints published by multiple printsellers, prints by unknown printsellers and prints published in magazines.

76 S.W. Fores, Hannah Humphrey, William Holland, William Humphrey, William Dent, Thomas Cornell, James Aitken, Elizabeth D'Archery, J. Brown, Edward Hedges, Richard Newton, William Wells, J. Barrow, William Moore, George Humphrey, John Wallis, J. (or W.) Dickie, Aaron Martinet, Piercy Roberts, J. Cattermoul, Robert Dighton and William Richardson.

77 S.W. Fores, Hannah Humphrey, William Holland, William Humphrey, William Dent, Thomas Cornell, James Aitken, Elizabeth D'Archery, J. Brown, Edward Hedges, Richard Newton, William Wells, J. Barrow, William Moore, George Humphrey and John Wallis.

78 S.W. Fores, Hannah Humphrey, William Holland, William Humphrey and William Dent.

79 *c.* 1780–1820.

80 *Morning Chronicle*, 28 January 1793, Issue 7379 and *Oracle*, 8 December 1792, Issue 1104.

81 British Museum, London – 1876,0510.764.

82 British Museum, London – Heal 100.7.

83 J.A. Simpson and E.S.C. Weiner, eds, *The Oxford English Dictionary*, 2nd edition, 20 volumes (Oxford, 1989), volume 13, 655.

84 Cindy McCreery, 'Prints and Politics in the East India Bill crisis, 1783–4' (Oxford, MPhil. thesis, 1991), 14; Cindy McCreery, 'Satiric Images of Fox, Pitt and George III: The East India Bill Crisis 1783–4', *Word and Image* 9 (1993): 163–4; John Wardroper, *The Caricatures of George* Cruikshank (London, 1977), 23; Stana Nenadic, 'Print Collecting and Popular Culture in Eighteenth-century Scotland', *History* 82, no. 266 (1997): 220; L.G. Mitchell, *The Whig World 1760–1837* (London and New York, 2005), 22.

85 Sheila O'Connell, *The Popular Print in England 1550–1850* (London, 1999), 167.

86 Draper Hill, *Fashionable Contrasts: Caricatures by James Gillray* (London, 1966), 22; Richard Godfrey, 'Introduction', in *James Gillray: The Art of Caricature*, ed. Mark Hallet (London, 2001), 234–5.

87 Godfrey, 'Introduction', 234–5.

88 BM 9180.

89 Godfrey, 'Introduction', 234–5.

90 Sheffield City Council, Libraries, Archives and Information Services: Sheffield Archives, WWM/H/130.

91 *Daily Advertiser*, 11 February 1772, Issue 12835 – BM 4692; BM 4693; *Public Advertiser*, 10 December 1776, Issue 13155 – BM 5375; *Morning Herald and Daily Advertiser*, 1 January 1783, Issue 679; *Morning Chronicle and London Advertiser*, 11 March 1783, Issue 4310 – BM 6321; *Oracle*, 22 June 1790, Issue 332 – BM 7728; *Sun*, 16 August 1800, Issue 2466; *Morning Chronicle*, 24 October 1806, Issue 11681; https://www.bl.uk/collection-guides/burney-collection https://www.gale.com/uk/c/british-library-newspapers-part-i.

92 *Morning Chronicle and London Advertiser*, 18 June 1782 – BM 6001, BM 5996, BM 6006, BM 5992, BM 5987, BM 5979, 1943,1209.2 (British Museum, London); BM 5659 and BM 5980.

93 *Morning Herald and Daily Advertiser*, 21 February 1783 – BM 6176; *World*, 25 February 1790, Issue 984 – BM 7629.

94 There are 2,979 political prints and 2,475 social prints listed in the *BM Catalogue* for the period 1771–1806.

95 P.D.G. Thomas, *The House of Commons in the Eighteenth Century* (Oxford, 1971), 89.

96 Johnson, 'Britannia Roused', 23; see also Nicholson, 'English Political Prints', 1, 337.

97 Vic Gatrell, *City of Laughter* (London, 2007), 14.

98 Ibid., 233.

99 Ibid., 235; Wood, *Radical Satire and Print Culture*, 41.

100 Nicholson, 'English Political Prints', volume 1, 237.

101 E.P. Thompson, *The Making of the English Working Class* (Harmondsworth, 1968), 810.

102 BM 3758, BM 4701 and BM 11100.

103 British Museum, London – 1861,1012.246.

104 BM 4701.

105 BM 11100.

106 BM 6352.

107 BM 9167.

108 BM 9160.

109 Diana Donald, *Followers of Fashion: Graphic Satire from the Georgian Period* (London, 2002), 7.

110 Mark Bills, *The Art of Satire: London in Caricature* (London, 2006), 12.

111 Donald, *The Age of Caricature*, 20.

112 BM 9167.

113 Rab Houston, *Literacy in Early Modern Europe: Culture and Education, 1500–1800* (London and New York, 1988), 140; Peter Burke, *Popular Culture in Early Modern Europe*, revised edition (Aldershot, 1994), 251.

114 Mitchell, *Fox*, 95.

Chapter 1

1 Richard Godfrey, 'Introduction', in *James Gillray: The Art of Caricature*, ed. Mark Hallet (London, 2001), 16.

2 BM 3860 and BM 3977.

3 Other examples of individuals characterized through 'stock images' include Lord North who was invariably depicted wearing the blue riband of a knight of the garter; Edmund Burke, with his steel-rimmed spectacles and long sharp nose, who frequently dressed in clerical garb as a Jesuit or with a rosary indicating a suspicion of latent Catholic tendencies; Richard Brinsley Sheridan who was always depicted with a red bulbous nose and red pock-marked cheeks indicating his heavy drinking; and Pitt the Younger who invariably had an upturned nose and black ribbon in his hair.

4 BM 5223.

5 For the difficulties in defining John Bull, see Tamara L. Hunt, *Defining John Bull: Political Caricature and National Identity in Late Georgian England* (Aldershot and Burlington, 2003), and Reva Wolf, 'John Bull, Liberty, and Wit: How England Became Caricature', in *Efflorescence of Caricature*, ed. T. Porterfield, 49–60.

6 Gwyn A. Williams, *Artisans and Sans-Culottes*, 2nd edition (London, 1989), xviii.

7 Miles Taylor, 'John Bull and the Iconography of Public Opinion in England c. 1712–1929', *Past and Present* 134 (1992): 108.

8 BM4892.

9 Upon returning from his Grand Tour in August 1768, Charles cut quite a figure in the world of fashion, sporting red-heeled shoes and an odd little French hat. Aileen Ribeiro has argued that from 1772 to 1773 Fox and his friends were among the leaders of the 'macaroni' fashion, something that is backed up by his appearance in two prints, *The Macaroni Cauldron* (BM 4829) and *The Original Macaroni* (BM 5010), published by Matthew Darly on 9 March 1772 and 20 May 1772, respectively, as part of his *Macaroni Series*. Strikingly, these two prints account for two-fifths of the prints listed by the *BM Catalogue* as representing Charles James Fox in 1772. Two others (BM 4943 and BM 4944) depict Fox as a member of the government in his role as a Junior Lord of the Admiralty; Aileen Ribiero, 'The Macaronis', *History Today* 28, no. 7 (1978): 466.

10 Such prints were included as loose leaves rather than being pre-bound into the magazines.

11 BM 4859.

12 Later in his career North would be portrayed as a badger, especially during the Fox–North Coalition or *Boreas*, the north wind. See BM 5231, BM 6093, BM 6176 and BM 6186.

13 Lord John Russell, *Memorials and Correspondence of Charles James Fox*, 4 volumes (London, 1853).

14   BM 5010 and BM 4829.

15   BM 4829.

16   BM 5010.

17   BM 4892.

18   During his early parliamentary career, Fox was a supporter of Lord North's
     administration. Neither Fox nor Lord North were in fact Tories.

19   The Massacre of the Pelhamite Innocents occurred in the early 1760s following
     the resignation of the Duke of Newcastle as First Lord of the Treasury. After
     his resignation, his friends and dependants were purged from office, while 'old
     servants, who had retired and been preferred to very small places, were rigorously
     hunted out and deprived of their livelihood'. Henry Parris, 'The Origins of the
     Permanent Civil Service, 1780–1830', *Public Administration* 46, no. 2 (1968): 150;
     L.G. Mitchell, *Charles James Fox and the Disintegration of the Whig Party 1782–1794*
     (Oxford, 1971), 16.

20   BM 5964.

21   Stanley Ayling, *Fox: The Life of Charles James Fox* (London, 1991), 86.

22   For Fox's rise within and influence upon the Rockingham Whigs, see Frank
     O'Gorman, *The Rise of Party in England: The Rockingham Whigs 1760–82* (London,
     1975).

23   William Cobbett, ed., *The Parliamentary History of England: From the Earliest
     Period to the Year 1803*, 36 volumes (London, 1806–1820), volume 22, columns
     1150–70.

24   Earl Chatham's second administration is another notable exception, when he led
     the government as Lord Privy Seal; however, it was very much his government.

25   BM 6176.

26   For the text of these debates, see Cobbett, *Parliamentary History*, 23, columns
     374–435; 438–98.

27   BM 10555.

28   For further examples, see George III, BM 8106; Lord North, NPG D12345; and
     William Pitt the Younger, BM 8070.

29   Derbyshire Record Office, Matlock – D5459/1/55.

30   The preliminary pen, ink and watercolour over graphite sketches are held at
     the Yale Centre for British Art, New Haven, and form part of the Paul Mellon
     Collection; the resultant engravings are held by the Guild Hall Art Gallery, London.

31   The only notable deviation away from this came during the East India Bill crisis of
     1783–4, when he was portrayed as an Eastern despot; see below, pp. 67–71.

32   Windsor uniform had a blue coat with red facings and cuffs. See E.A. Smith, *George
     IV* (New Haven and London, 1999), 4.

33   See BM 5575, BM 5625 and BM 5966.

34   See BM 6215, BM 6188 and British Museum, London – 1943,1209.2.

35   BM 5755.

36 BM 5707.

37 For the debate on Fox's Motion for an Enquiry into the Causes of the Want of Success of the British Navy, see Cobbett, *Parliamentary History*, 22, columns 878–946. For a discussion of the causes of the American War of Independence, see P.D.G. Thomas, *British Politics and the Stamp Act Crisis: The First Phase of the American Revolution, 1763–1767* (Oxford, 1975); P.D.G. Thomas, *The Townshend Duties Crisis: The Second Phase of the American Revolution, 1767–1773* (Oxford, 1987); P.D.G. Thomas, *Tea Party to Independence: The Third Phase of the American Revolution, 1773–1776* (Oxford, 1991). For a discussion of the war, see Jeremy Black, *War for America* (Stroud, 1991).

38 P.D.G. Thomas, *Lord North* (London, 1976), 113.

39 BM 6117.

40 A term in use at the time to mean a formally recognized gallant.

41 W.S. Lewis, ed., *Horace Walpole's Correspondence*, 48 volumes (Oxford, 1937–1983), volume 35, p. 523; B.C. Walpole, *Days of the Dandies: Charles James Fox* (Edinburgh, N.D.), 90; Lord Palmerston's anecdote book cited by Brian Cornell, *Portrait of a Whig Peer* (London, 1957), 137.

42 Amanda Foreman, *Georgiana, Duchess of Devonshire* (London, 1999), 158.

43 The future George IV.

44 I.M. Davis, *The Harlot and the Statesman: The Story of Elizabeth Armistead and Charles James Fox* (Abbotsbrooke, 1986), 47.

45 Derbyshire Record Office, Matlock – D5459/1/36.

46 Ayling, *Fox*, 50.

47 J.R. Dinwiddy, 'Charles James Fox and the People', *History* 55, no. 185 (1970): 342.

48 BM 9042, BM 9171 and BM 9411.

49 British Museum, London – 1985,0119.190.

50 From 1793, cropped hair became fashionable as a political gesture indicating support for the French Revolution: M. Dorothy George, *Hogarth to Cruikshank: Social Change in Graphic Satire* (London, 1967), 136.

51 For a discussion of the 'Ministry of All the Talents' taxation policies, see A.D. Harvey, 'The Ministry of All the Talents: The Whigs in Office, February 1806 to March 1807', *The Historical Journal* 15, no. 4 (1972): 640–3.

52 Aileen Ribeiro, *Fashion in the French Revolution* (New York, 1988), 85; James Epstein, *Radical Expression: Political Language, Ritual, and Symbol in England, 1790–1850* (New York and Oxford, 1994), 72; Richard Wrigley, 'Transformations of a Revolutionary Emblem: The Liberty Cap in the French Revolution', *French History* 11, no. 2 (1997): 131–69.

53 Wrigley, 'Transformations of a Revolutionary Emblem', 131.

54 Ibid., 147.

55 Edmund Burke had been the leading intellectual thinker in the party prior to the death of the Marquess of Rockingham. After Rockingham's death, Fox became a

serious rival for directing the party's policies and between them they are credited with drawing up the Fox–North Coalition's India Bill, which was introduced in the House of Commons by Fox. Paul Langford, 'Edmund Burke (1729/30–1797)', in *ODNB*, 8 (Oxford University Press, 2004), 832.

56 Henry Offley Wakeman, *The Life of Charles James Fox* (London, 1890), 154.

57 Ibid., 179.

58 BM 8310.

59 Thomas Wright, ed., *The Works of James Gillray, The Caricaturist* (Amsterdam, 1970), 13.

60 Curator's comment – see http://www.britishmuseum.org/research/search_the_collection_database/search_object_details.aspx?objectId=1477717&partId=1 (accessed 17 November 2010).

61 Nicholas K. Robinson, *Edmund Burke: A Life in Caricature* (New Haven and London, 1996), 1.

62 BM 8142.

63 BM 8291.

64 Charles Fox and his brother, Stephen, 'borrowed great sums of [*sic*] Jews at exorbitant premiums. Charles James Fox called his outward room, where those Jews waited till he rose, the *Jerusalem Chamber*'. A. Francis Steuart, ed., *The Last Journals of Horace Walpole* (London and New York, 1910), 7.

65 BM 9258.

66 BM 7526.

67 For further information of the Foxite failure at the 1784 general election, see W.T. Laprade, 'Public Opinion and the General Election of 1784', *The English Historical Review* 31, no. 122 (1916); C.E. Freyer, 'Historical Revisions: The General Election of 1784', *History* 9 (1924/5): 221–3; M. Dorothy George, 'Fox's Martyrs: The General Election of 1784', *Transactions of the Royal Historical Society*, 4th series, 21 (1939): 133–68; Ian Christie, 'The Anatomy of the Opposition in the Parliament of 1784', *Parliamentary History* 9, no. 1 (1990): 50–7.

68 Frank O'Gorman, *The Whig Party and the French Revolution* (London, 1967), 33.

69 For further discussion, see O'Gorman, *Whig Party*, and Mitchell, *Disintegration of the Whig Party*.

70 Fox, Moira and Sheridan were all called as witnesses by O'Connor, and their involvement in his trial was represented by James Gillray in his *Evidence to Character*. For discussion of this print, see below, pp. 137–8.

71 For a discussion of the treason trials of 1798, see F.K. Prochaska, 'English State Trials in the 1790s: A Case Study', *The Journal of British Studies* 13, no. 1 (1973): 64–70.

72 *Mirror of the Times* (London), 27 January 1798, Issue 96.

73 BM 8995, BM 9217 and BM 9261.

74 Fintan Cullen, *Visual Politics: The Representation of Ireland 1750–1930* (Cork, 1997), 50.

75 Guilhem Scherf, 'The History Portrait', in *Citizens and Kings*, ed. Royal Academy of Arts (London, 2007), 112.

76 See BM 6389, BM 7862 and James Barry, *Ulysses and a Companion Fleeing from the Cave of Polyphemus* – Crawford Municipal Art Gallery.

77 Scherf, 'History Portrait', 113.

78 Byron W. Gassman, 'Smollett's *Britain* and the Art of Political Cartooning', *Studies in Eighteenth-century Culture* 14 (1985): 251.

79 Alarik Rynell, 'Some Political Nicknames in Caricatures under George III', *Studia Neophilologica* 14 (1942): 348.

80 BM 6389.

81 John Cannon, *The Fox–North Coalition: Crisis of the Constitution* (Cambridge, 1969), 111.

82 BM 7862.

83 John Derry, *Charles James Fox* (London, 1972), 311.

84 Francis Tresham wrote to his cousin, Lord Monteagle, to warn him not to go to Parliament on the day of the plot and thus effectively betrayed the conspiracy.

85 By the debate on the Quebec Bill (6 May 1791) relations between Fox and Burke were stretched to breaking point. They eventually snapped during the debate and Fox reportedly broke down into tears in the Commons chamber over his loss of friendship with Burke. Cobbett, *Parliamentary History*, volume 29, columns 361–430, for Fox weeping, see column 388.

86 Charles Grey (1764–1845), Richard Brinsley Sheridan and Edmund Burke. By December 1789, Burke had become estranged from Sheridan and Fox over the impeachment of Warren Hastings, the Regency Crisis and later the French Revolution. F.P. Lock, *Edmund Burke*, 2 volumes (Oxford, 2006), volume 2, pp. 205–22, 265–6. For a discussion of the Whigs' response to the Regency Crisis, see John Derry, *The Regency Crisis and the Whigs, 1788–9* (Cambridge, 1963).

87 BM 8681.

88 William Petty (formerly Fitzmaurice) had, as Lord Shelburne, served with Fox in the Marquess of Rockingham's second administration in 1782. As First Lord of the Treasury, after Rockingham's death he gave William Pitt the Younger his first political office but was not included in Pitt the Younger's administration following the fall of the Fox–North Coalition in 1783.

89 BM 9035.

90 BM 5961.

91 BM 5984.

92 BM 6032.

93 BM 6044.

94 BM 8599.

95   Nicholson, 'English political prints ca. 1640–ca. 1830: The potential for emblematic
     research and the failures of prints scholarship', in *Deviceful Settings: The English
     Renaissance Emblem and Its Contexts: Selected Papers from the Third International
     Emblem Conference*, ed. Michael Bath and Daniel Russell (New York, 1999), 163.
96   BM 6380.
97   Epstein, *Radical Expression*, 72 and 78.
98   See Hunt, *Defining John Bull*; Taylor, 'John Bull'; and Wolf, 'John Bull'.
99   For a discussion on the *bonnet rouge*'s association with the French Revolution, see
     Epstein, *Radical Expression*, 70–99; Wrigley, 'Transformations of a Revolutionary
     Emblem', 131–69.

Chapter 2

1   Numerous biographies have been written of both Charles James Fox and William
     Pitt the Younger, for example, John Ehrman, 'Pitt the Younger, William (1759–1806)',
     in *Who's Who in British History*, ed. Juliet Gardiner (London: Collins and Brown,
     2000); Michael Duffy, *The Younger Pitt* (Harlow, 2000); L.G. Mitchell, *Charles James
     Fox and the Disintegration of the Whig Party 1782–1794* (Oxford, 1971); Loren Reid,
     Charles James Fox: A Man for the People (London and Harlow, 1969); and *House
     Magazine*, Autumn (2006) – Special edition for the House of Commons exhibition
     Pitt and Fox: The Great Rivals. Equally for the nineteenth century there have
     been numerous biographies written about Benjamin Disraeli and William Ewart
     Gladstone, for example, D.C. Somervell, *Disraeli and Gladstone: A Duo-Biographical
     Sketch* (London, 1938); Robert Blake, *Disraeli* (London, 1969). Such prominent
     personalities have also lent their names to political studies of the period, for
     example, John W. Derry, *Politics in the Age of Fox, Pitt and Liverpool* (London, 1990)
     and Paul Adelman, *Gladstone, Disraeli and Later Victorian Politics* (Harlow, 1970).
     Also, see John Campbell, *Pistols at Dawn: Two Hundred Years of Political Rivalry
     From Pitt and Fox to Blair and Brown* (London, 2009), 9–56 and 90–140.
2   G.H. Powell, ed., *The Table Talk of Samuel Rogers* (London, 1903), 139.
3   Michael Wynn Jones, *The Cartoon History of Britain* (New York, 1971), 62.
4   Incidentally, both Lord Chatham and Lord Holland were themselves second sons.
5   Lord John Russell, *Memorials and Correspondence of Charles James Fox*, 4 volumes
     (London, 1853), volume 1, p. 25.
6   Formerly William Pitt the Elder.
7   Amateur dramatics were a popular pastime for the élite during the eighteenth
     century. As well as providing entertainment, they also offered an ideal platform for
     the aspiring public figure to refine their oratorical skills; John Derry, *Charles James
     Fox* (London, 1972), 14.

8 Anon., *Memoirs of Nine Illustrious Living Characters* (Dublin, 1799), 71, see also W.S. Lewis, ed., *Horace Walpole's Correspondence*, 48 volumes (Oxford, 1937–1983), volume 23, pp. 187–8; volume 25, pp. 406 and 449; volume 39, p. 380.

9 Powell, *Table Talk*, 48.

10 Lewis, *Walpole's Correspondence*, volume 25, p. 449.

11 Alexander Wedderburn was Solicitor General in Lord North's Administration. He later became Baron Loughborough (1780) and first Earl Rosslyn (1801).

12 Derek Jarrett, ed., *Horace Walpole Memoirs of the Reign of George III*, 4 volumes (New Haven and London, 2000), volume 4, p. 136.

13 Figures taken from *BM Catalogue*.

14 Michael, J. Turner, *Pitt the Younger: A Life* (London and New York, 2003), 89 and L.G. Mitchell, *Charles James Fox* (London, 1992), 95.

15 For further information on the importance of fashion during the French Revolution, see discussion above, p. 37. See also Aileen Ribiero, *Fashion in the French Revolution* (New York, 1988). Frank O'Gorman has also written about the importance of party colours and hat ribbons during elections. See Frank O'Gorman, 'Campaign Rituals and Ceremonies: The Social Meaning of Elections in England 1780–1860', *Past and Present* 135 (1992): 79–115 and Frank O'Gorman, *Voters, Patrons and Parties: The Unreformed Electoral System of Hanoverian England 1734–1832* (Oxford, 1989).

16 Tim Clayton, *Caricatures of the Peoples of the British Isles* (London, 2007), 14–37; BM 5624.

17 BM 8458.

18 BM 9270.

19 This might have purely been posturing by the young Pitt, however, as Lord Shelburne, one of his father's key supporters, did agree to join the government. Indeed, George III offered him the post of First Lord of the Treasury before offering it to Rockingham. Shelburne declined due to his inability to command a superior majority in the House of Commons – John Ehrman, *The Younger Pitt* (London, 1969–96), volume 1, pp. 79–80.

20 BM 8599.

21 BM 8600.

22 BM 8601.

23 BM 8602.

24 BM 8603.

25 BM 8604.

26 BM 8605.

27 BM 8606.

28 http://www.britishmuseum.org/research/collection_online/collection_object_details.aspx?objectId=1632239&partId=1&searchText=ministerial+eloquence&page=1 and http://www.britishmuseum.org/research/collection_online/collection_object_details. aspx?objectId=1632242&partId=1&searchText=opposition+eloquence&page=1

29 *BM Catalogue*, volume VII.

30 http://www.britishmuseum.org/research/collection_online/collection_object_details.aspx?objectId=1632210&partId=1&searchText=naval+eloquence&page=1

31 For example, *Britannia between Death and the Doctors* BM 10244 and *Opening the Budget; – or – John Bull Giving His Breeches to Save His Bacon* BM 8836.

32 BM 6044.

33 Stanley Ayling, *Fox: The Life of Charles James Fox* (London, 1991), 38–9.

34 Marcus Wood, *Radical Satire and Print Culture 1790–1822* (Oxford, 1994), 226.

35 BM 6775.

36 Sir Nathanial William Wraxall, Bart., *Historical Memoirs of My Own Time* (London, 1904), 377.

37 BM 6398.

38 In office, Fox abandoned the tables of Brooks and the lure of the turf, devoting himself to the rigours and routines of office. B.C. Walpole, *Days of the Dandies: Charles James Fox* (Edinburgh, ND), 95; and Edward Lascelles, *The Life of Charles James Fox* (Oxford, 1936), 100.

39 Boyd Hilton, *A Mad, Bad and Dangerous People?: England 1783–1846* (Oxford, 2006), 54.

40 Patronage was an overt demonstration of the King's confidence in his ministers. It was often key in accruing support from unattached members of the House and in prizing people away from other political groupings.

41 BM 3923.

42 BM 3909.

43 BM 6201.

44 Mitchell, *Fox*, 58–9.

45 Mitchell, *Disintegration of the Whig Party*, 47–91.

46 John Cannon, *The Fox–North Coalition: Crisis of the Constitution* (Cambridge, 1969), 142.

47 Ibid., 118 and 221, citing M. Dorothy George in Stephens and George, *BM Catalogue*.

48 Cindy McCreery, 'Prints and Politics in the East India Bill Crisis, 1783–4' (Oxford, MPhil. thesis, 1991), 2.

49 Sir John Fortescue, ed., *The Correspondence of King George the Third from 1760 to December 1783*, 6 volumes (London, 1927), volume 6, p. 476.

50 L.G. Mitchell, *Holland House* (London, 1980), 61.

51 Sir John Fortescue, ed., *The Correspondence of King George the Third from 1760 to December 1783*, 6 volumes (London, 1927), 477.

52 Lewis, *Walpole's Correspondence*, volume 24, p. 460.

53 Russell, *Memorials and Correspondence*, volume 2, p. 28.

54 Donald E. Ginter, *Voting Records of the House of Commons 1761–1820*, 6 volumes (London and Rio Grande, 1995).

55 George III had previously sounded out Pitt the Younger in 1783 after the collapse of the Shelburne administration. Ehrman, *The Younger Pitt*, volume 1, pp. 102–4.

56 It was the custom that the King would have a hand in selecting his ministers and the post of Lord Chancellor was by convention solely in the gift of the King, and was supposed to be his eyes and ears within the cabinet. The tension between King and coalition is best summed up by the fact that they did not have a Lord Chancellor as both Fox and North refused to accommodate the King's choice of Lord Thurlow, and the King refused to countenance their nominee, Lord Loughborough; Cannon, *The Fox–North Coalition*, 84.

57 Lewis, *Walpole's Correspondence*, volume 24, p. 460.

58 J. Wright, ed., *The Speeches of the Right Honourable Charles James Fox, in the House of Commons*, 6 volumes (London, 1815), volume 2, p. 268.

59 See Great Britain, Parliament, *The Parliamentary History of England: From the Earliest Period to the Year 1803*, 36 volumes (London, 1806–1820), volume 24, columns 154–5, 196, 203 and 225, and J. Wright, ed., *The Speeches of the Right Honourable Charles James Fox, in the House of Commons*, 6 volumes (London, 1815), 264–5, 267 and 268.

60 Lord Herbert, ed., *The Pembroke Papers*, 2 volumes (London, 1942–1950), volume 2, p. 248.

61 Lewis, *Walpole's Correspondence*, volume 36, p. 209; William Hadley, *The Letters of Horace Walpole* (London and New York, 1926), 47.

62 BM 6286. John Ehrman has suggested that this print was the work of James Gillray (Ehrman, *The Younger Pitt*, volume 1, p. 143).

63 Stephens and George: *BM Catalogue*, volume 5, p. 474.

64 http://www.britishmuseum.org/research/collection_online/collection_object_details.aspx?objectId=1457655&partId=1&searchText=the+fall+of+carlo+khan&page=1

65 Cannon, *Fox–North Coalition*, 118.

66 M. Dorothy George, *English Political Caricature to 1792: A Study in Opinion and Propaganda* (Oxford, 1959), 169.

67 David Powell, *Charles James Fox: Man of the People* (London, 1989), 146.

68 Lewis, *Walpole's Correspondence*, volume 25, pp. 490–1.

69 A. Aspinall, ed., *The Later Correspondence of George III*, 5 volumes (Cambridge, 1962–1970), volume 1, p. 8.

70 BM 6588.

71 BM 6497, *Carlo Khan*, published anonymously in 1784.

72 BM 6395.A, *Carlo Khan*, published by Edward Hedges, 1 February 1784.

73 BM 6448.

74 BM 10575, *Carlo the Great Running Away with the East Indies*, published by William Holland June 1806.

75 BM 6395, published by Edward Hedges, 1 February 1784.

76 Lewis, *Walpole's Correspondence*, volume 23, p. 530.

77 Reid, *Fox*, 188.

78 See Anon., *A Collection of Odes, Songs and Epigrams against the Whigs Alias the Blue and Buff; in which are included Mr. Hewerdine's Political Songs* (London, 1790), 33–6; Anon., *A Collection of Odes, Songs and Epigrams against the Whigs Alias the Blue and Buff; in which are included Mr. Hewerdine's Political Songs* (London and Dublin, 1790), 31–3; Anon., *The Amours of Carlo Khan: Interspersed with Curious Anecdotes and Bon Mots of Many Distinguished Personages* (London, 1789); and Anon, *The Coalitional Rencontre Anticipated; A Poetical Dialogue* (London, 1785), *passim*.

79 See discussion of 'stock images' above starting on p. 25.

80 Horace Twiss, *The Public and Private Life of Lord Chancellor Eldon*, 3 volumes (London, 1844), volume 1, p. 162.

81 Ibid., 4.

82 David Johnson, 'Britannia Roused: Political Caricature and the Fall of the Fox–North Coalition', *History Today* (June 2006): 27 and Stephens and George, *BM Catalogue*, volume 7, p. xiv.

83 McCreery, 'Prints and Politics', 53.

84 Stephens and M. Dorothy George, *BM Catalogue*, volume 7, p. xiii; Richard Godfrey, 'Introduction', in *English Caricature: 1760 to the Present*, ed. Victoria and Albert Museum (London, 1984), 18; and Wynn Jones, *Cartoon History*, 63.

85 Derry, *James Fox*, 206.

86 Published 24 December 1783.

87 The Duke of Richmond was an uncle of Charles James Fox and a former member of the Rockingham connection. He broke with the group after the death of the Marquess of Rockingham, remaining in post as Master General of the Ordnance when other leading Rockingham Whigs resigned over the appointment of Lord Shelburne as First Lord of the Treasury; Mitchell, *Fox*, 52–3.

88 See Ehrman, *The Younger Pitt*, volume 1, p. 457.

89 Mitchell, *Disintegration of the Whig Party*, 67.

90 BM 6462.

91 For the terms of Pitt's Bill see Ehrman, *The Younger Pitt*, volume 1, p. 658.

92 Lewis, *Walpole's Correspondence*, volume 36, p. 219.

93 BM 6400.

94 BM 9389.

95 BM 6406.

Chapter 3

1   M. Dorothy George, 'Fox's Martyrs: The General Election of 1784', *Transactions of the Royal Historical Society*, 4th series, 21 (1939); W.T. Laprade, 'Public Opinion and the General Election of 1784', *The English Historical Review* 31, no. 122 (1916); W.T. Laprade, 'William Pitt and Westminster elections', *The American Historical Review* 18, no. 2 (1913), and C.E. Fryer, 'Historical Revisions: The General Election of 1784', *History* 9 (1924/1925): 221–3.

2   W.T. Laprade, *The Parliamentary Papers of John Robinson, 1774–1784* (London, 1922).

3   George, 'Fox's Martyrs', 133–4.

4   Ibid., 136–7.

5   BM 6544.

6   Anne Stott, '"Female Patriotism": Georgiana, Duchess of Devonshire, and the Westminster election of 1784', *Eighteenth-century Life* 17, no. 3 (2003): 60–84.

7   Phyllis Deutsch, 'Moral Trespass in Georgian London: Gaming, Gender and Electoral Politics in the Age of George III', *The Historical Journal* 39, no. 3 (1996), *passim.*

8   Renata Lana, 'Women and Foxite Strategy in the Westminster election of 1784', *Eighteenth-century Life* 26, no. 1 (2002): 46–69 and Amelia Rauser, 'The Butcher-Kissing Duchess of Devonshire: Between Caricature and Allegory in 1784', *Eighteenth-century Studies* 36, no. 1 (2002): 23–46.

9   Lana, 'Women and Foxite Strategy', 63–4.

10 John Brooke, 'Pitt, Hon. William (1759–1806)' in *The House of Commons 1754–1790*, 3 volumes, ed. Sir Lewis Namier and John Brooke (London, 1985), volume 1, *passim*; Frank O'Gorman, *Voters, Patrons and Parties: The Unreformed Electoral System of Hanoverian England 1734–1832* (Oxford, 1989), 13 and John W. Derry, *Politics in the Age of Fox, Pitt and Liverpool* (London, 1990), 18.

11 P.D.G. Thomas, 'Party Politics in Eighteenth-century Britain: Some Myths and a Touch of Reality', *British Journal for Eighteenth Century Studies* 10 (1987): 205; Frank O'Gorman, 'Campaign Rituals and Ceremonies: The Social Meaning of Elections in England 1780–1860', *Past and Present* 135 (1992): 80–1, 84, 87, 102–3 and 115.

12 Lana, 'Women and Foxite Strategy', *passim.*

13 The scot-and-lot franchise entitled any adult male poor rate payer to vote; Sean Lang, *Parliamentary Reform 1785–1928* (London, 1999), 173.

14 Namier and Brooke, eds, *House of Commons*, volume 1, pp. 335–6.

15 Penelope Corfield, Edmund M. Green, and Charles Harvey, 'Westminster Man: Charles James Fox and His Electorate', *Parliamentary History* 20, no. 2 (2001): 160–1, 177 and 182.

16 BM 6558.

17 W.S. Lewis, ed., *Horace Walpole's Correspondence*, 48 volumes (Oxford, 1937–1983), volume 23, p. 530, Horace Walpole to Sir Horace Mann – 28 November 1773.

18 It was common practice for politicians to 'treat' voters during eighteenth-century elections with food and ale at inns and taverns. During these 'treats' the candidate and their supporters would sometimes wait at table upon the voters.

19 O'Gorman, 'Campaign Rituals', 81 and 85.

20 BM 6527, BM 6547, BM 6564 and BM 6625.

21 E.E.C. Nicholson, 'Emblem v. Caricature: A Tenacious Conceptual Framework', in *Emblems and Art History*, ed. Alison Adams (Glasgow, 1996), 141–67.

22 Stott, '"Female Patriotism"', 60.

23 Lewis Walpole Library – 784.04.24.01+.

24 See BM 6530, BM 6548 and BM 6633.

25 See BM 6555, BM 6560, BM 6611 and BM 6625.

26 BM 6560.

27 BM 6611.

28 BM. 6577.

29 Linda Colley, *Britons: Forging the Nation 1707–1837*, 2nd edition (New Haven and London, 2005), 244.

30 Ibid., 244.

31 Elaine Chalus, *Elite Women in English Political Life, c. 1754–1790* (Oxford, 2005), 13.

32 Amanda Foreman, *Georgiana, Duchess of Devonshire* (London, 1999), 29–30.

33 Rauser, 'The Butcher-Kissing Duchess', 23.

34 Colley, *Britons*, 244.

35 William Hague, *William Pitt the Younger* (London, 2004), 60.

36 S.A. Hunn, 'Negative Perceptions of Whiggery 1760–1807' (Oxford, PhD. thesis, 1997), 45–6.

37 Foreman, *Georgiana*, 130.

38 BM 6625.

39 'David Wilkinson, Wray, Sir Cecil, Thirteenth Baronet (1734–1805)', in *ODNB*, volume 60, ed. Matthew and Harrison (Oxford: Oxford University Press, 2004), 398–9.

40 Foreman, *Georgiana*, 80.

41 BM 6494 (additional), BM 6530, BM 6546, BM 6551 and BM 6559.

42 Lana, 'Women and Foxite Strategy', 54.

43 Ibid., 55.

44 BM 6494, BM 6493 and BM 6524.

45 BM 6559.

46 Lewis Walpole Library, 784.05.24.01+.

47 BM 6551.

48 BM 6546.

49 BM 6494 (after).

50 BM 6530.

51 BM 6527.

52 BM 6612.

53 BM 6621.

54 BM 6619.

55 Pitt the Younger's dearest wish at the 1784 election was to prevent Fox's return for Westminster; Marjorie Villiers, *The Grand Whiggery* (London, 1939), 68.

56 Brooke, 'Pitt, Hon. William (1759–1806)', volume 1, pp. 335–7 and 510–12.

57 BM 6550, BM 6589 and BM 6596.

58 BM 6589.

59 BM 6596.

60 See: http://www.britishmuseum.org/research/search_the_collection_database/search_object_details.aspx?objectId=1458518&partId=1 (accessed 13 February 2013).

61 Loren Reid, *Charles James Fox: A Man for the People* (London and Harlow, 1969), 30.

62 BM 6624.

63 For example, BM 5845, 6215 and 6261.

64 Namier, Sir Lewis and John Brooke, eds, *The House of Commons 1754–1790*, 3 volumes (London, 1964), 511.

65 At the end of the 1784 Westminster election the defeated candidate, Sir Cecil Wray, called for a scrutiny of the result. In many cases, eighteenth-century elections were only decided after parliamentary scrutiny of the result and election process. During the 1784 Westminster election, there was a suspicion that Fox had secretly polled votes from Catholics, who were ineligible to vote. See Paul Kelly, 'Pitt versus Fox: The Westminster Scrutiny, 1784–85', *Studies in Burke and His Time* 14, no. 46 (1972–3): 156.

66 Derbyshire Record Office, Matlock – D5459/1/14.

67 Pitt the Younger's dearest wish at the 1784 election was to prevent Fox's return for Westminster. Villiers, *Grand Whiggery*, 68.

68 The candidates in the 1784 Westminster election were Admiral Hood, Charles James Fox and Sir Cecil Wray.

69 Namier and Brooke, *The House of Commons 1754–1790*, 3 volumes, 335–7 and 510–12.

70 Questions were raised about his eligibility to be a burgess of Kirkwall by the defeated candidate, Sir John Sinclair, who petitioned against Fox's return claiming that the delegation from Kirkwall that swore him in as a burgess was irregular. His petition was unsuccessful. Namier and Brooke, *House of Commons 1754–1790*, volume 1, p. 511.

71 BM 6635.

72 BM 6553.

73 Corfield, Green and Harvey, 'Westminster Man', 165.

74 BM 6577.

75 BM 6612 and BM 6621.

76 BM 6625.

77 Lewis Walpole Library, 784.05.24.01+ and BM 6551.

78 BM 6560.

79 BM 6611.

80 See BM 2702, 6110; BM 8112 and BM 9838.

Chapter 4

1 These divisions were on: 'Parliamentary Reform' (18 April 1785); 'Irish Commercial Propositions' (12 May 1785); 'Dockyard Fortifications Plan' (27 February 1786); 'Repeal of Test and Corporation Acts' (28 March 1787); 'Impeachment of Sir Elijah Impey' (9 May 1788); Donald E. Ginter, *Voting Records of the House of Commons 1761–1820*, 6 volumes (London and Rio Grande, 1995), volume 5, 281–311.

2 Michael Duffy, *The Younger Pitt* (Harlow, 2000), 23 and 79.

3 Stanley Ayling, *Fox: The Life of Charles James Fox* (London, 1991), 147–8.

4 L.G. Mitchell, *Charles James Fox and the Disintegration of the Whig Party 1782–94* (Oxford, 1971), 105.

5 Ginter, *Voting Records*, volume 5, 281–3.

6 BM 6770.

7 See: http://www.britishmuseum.org/research/collection_online/collection_object_details.aspx?objectId=1646238&partId=1&searchText=BM+6770&page=1 (accessed 15 November 2016).

8 Ibid.

9 BM 7139.

10 BM 7312.

11 BM 7320.

12 L.G. Mitchell, *Charles James Fox* (London, 1992), 80–91; Ayling, *Fox*, 160–5. For a fuller discussion of the role of the Whigs during the regency crisis, see John Derry, *The Regency Crisis and the Whigs, 1788–89* (Cambridge, 1963).

13 S.A. Hunn, 'Negative Perceptions of Whiggery 1760–1807' (Oxford, PhD. thesis, 1997), 16.

14 John Derry, *Charles James Fox* (London, 1972), 208.

15 British Library, London – (Fox Papers) BL. Add. Mss. 47560 f.1, George, Prince of Wales to Charles James Fox, Wednesday Evening, *c.* 1782–83.

16 Cecil Price, ed., *The Letters of Richard Brinsley Sheridan*, 3 volumes (Oxford, 1966), volume 1, 202.

17 Hunn, 'Negative Perceptions', 125.

18 John Brooke, 'Pitt, Hon. William (1759–1806)', in *The House of Commons 1754–1790*, ed. Sir Lewis Namier and John Brooke, 3 volumes (London, 1985), volume 2, 457.

19 Thomas Wright, *Caricature History of the Georges* (London, 1898), 430.

20 Countess of Granville Castilia, ed., *Lord Granville Leveson Gower (First Earl Granville) Private Correspondence 1781 to 1782*, 2 volumes (London, 1917), 11; British Library, London – (Fox Papers) Bl Add. Mss. 47561 ff 108–9; 47560 ff 28–9; Wentworth Woodhouse Muniments: Sheffield Archives, Sheffield – (Burke Papers) WWWM/BkP/15/44, WWWM/BkP/15/57, (Fitzwilliam Papers) WWWM/F/32/75 and J.H. Plumb, *England in the Eighteenth Century* (Harmondsworth, 1960), 192–3.

21 British Museum, London – 1991,0720.19.

22 BM 7476.

23 Mitchell, *Fox*, 81.

24 Gospel of St. John Chapter 19 verse 5.

25 'Related by Admiral B' in *The Festival of Wit or the Small Talker*, ed. King George (Dublin, 1783), 138–39.

26 W.S. Lewis, ed., *Horace Walpole's Correspondence*, 48 volumes (Oxford, 1937–83), volume 32, 166.

27 William Cobbett, ed., *The Parliamentary History of England: From the Earliest Period to the Year 1803*, 36 volumes (London, 1806–20), volume 21, columns 367–68 and volume 22, columns 1220–22.

28 BM 7381.

29 BM 7526.

30 For discussion of Ireland and the regency crisis see Nicholas K. Robinson, 'Caricature and the Regency Crisis: An Irish Perspective', *Eighteenth-century Ireland* 1 (1986): 157–76.

31 Fox and Grattan had met during Fox's visit to Ireland in 1779 and had seen him in action while he sat in the body of the Irish House of Commons. Martyn J. Powell, 'Charles James Fox and Ireland', *Irish Historical Studies* 33, no. 130 (2002): 170.

32 Sheffield Archives – Sheffield Wentworth Woodhouse Muniments (Burke Papers): WWM/BkP/15/57, (Fitzwilliam Papers): WWM/F/32/75.

33 This occurred when he declared in the House of Commons that the Prince of Wales had a natural right to the regency in the event of the King's incapacity, in the same way he did to succeeding to the throne upon the death of his father. This statement was widely seen as a move away from Fox's traditional line of attacking royal power and prerogative, and showed him as power hungry, as the argument was made as a way of trying to avoid prolonging the crisis by establishing a committee to examine precedents, when it was widely believed that the Prince of Wales would install him in government, soon after becoming regent – Mitchell, *Fox*, 80–8.

34 Mitchell, *Fox*, 89.

35 Lord John Russell, *Memorials and Correspondence of Charles James Fox*, 4 volumes (London, 1853), 278–83.

36 Ibid., 279.

37 Ibid.

38 Alan Palmer, *George IV* (London, 1975), 22.

39 BM 6932.

40 Loren Reid, *Charles James Fox: A Man for the People* (London and Harlow, 1969), 226.

41 Lord Thurlow was one of George III's longest serving advisers. He dispensed with his services as Lord Chancellor in 1792 after he openly spoke out against the policies of Pitt the Younger in the House of Lords. After Thurlow's scheming during the regency crisis this became the straw which broke the camel's back and Pitt presented George III with an ultimatum; either Lord Thurlow went or he would resign. G.M. Ditchfield, 'Thurlow, Edward, First Baron Thurlow (1731–1806)', in *ODNB*, ed. Matthew and Harrison, volume 54, 715–20.

42 For a detailed discussion of Pitt's strategy during the regency crisis, see John Ehrman, 'Pitt the Younger, William (1759–1806)', in *Who's Who in British History*, ed. Juliet Gardiner, volume 1 (London: Collins and Brown, 2000), 644–66.

43 BM 7377.

44 Granville, Castalia Countess of Granville, ed., *Lord Granville Leveson Gower (First Earl Granville) Private Correspondence 1781–1821*, 2 volumes (London, 1917), 11.

45 BM 7497.

46 For terms of Pitt the Younger's Regency Bill see Ehrman, *Pitt*, volume 1, 658.

47 Library of Congress, Washington DC, USA – PC 3–1789 – Tories and the Whigs.

48 Nicholas K. Robinson, *Edmund Burke: A Life in Caricature* (New Haven and London, 1996), 16, 40 and 47; (BM 6026, BM 6205 and BM 8316).

49 Fox refused to countenance Lord Thurlow's presence as Lord Chancellor in the Fox–North Coalition over a deep distrust of the fact that he was very much George III's man, a personal distrust of Lord Thurlow and a remembrance of the duplicity of Lord Shelburne, who had been George III's man in the cabinet of the second Rockingham administration – Mitchell, *Fox*, 60.

50 E.A. Smith, *George IV* (New Haven and London, 1999), 51–52.

51 Ehrman, *Pitt*, volume 1, 647–63.

52 Kenneth Garlick and Angus Macintyre, eds, *The Diary of Joseph Farington*, 16 volumes (New Haven and London, 1978–98), volume 3, 837.

Chapter 5

1 Fintan Cullen, *The Irish Face: Redefining the Irish Portrait* (London, 2004), 153.

2 Frank O'Gorman, *The Whig Party and the French Revolution* (London, 1967), 33 and 70–90; and L.G. Mitchell, *Charles James Fox and the Disintegration of the Whig Party 1782–1794* (Oxford, 1971), 239.

3   Henry Offley Wakeman, *The Life of Charles James Fox* (London, 1890), 154.

4   Herbert Butterfield, 'Charles James Fox and the Whig Opposition in 1792', *Cambridge Historical Journal* 9, no. 3 (1949): 324.

5   John Derry, *Charles James Fox* (London, 1972), 293.

6   E.A. Smith, *Whig Principles and Party Politics: Earl Fitzwilliam and the Whig Party 1748–1833* (Manchester, 1975), 118.

7   British Library, London – (Fox Papers) BL Add. Mss. 47580 f. 139, Charles James Fox to Right Honourable Colonel Richard Fitzpatrick, 30 July 1789.

8   Mitchell, *Disintegration of the Whig Party*, 194.

9   BM 8310.

10   Thomas Wright, ed., *The Works of James Gillray, The Caricaturist* (Amsterdam, 1970), 13.

11   Curator's comment – see: http://www.britishmuseum.org/research/search_the_collection_database/search_object_details.aspx?objectId=1477717&partId=1 (accessed 17 November 2010).

12   BM 8142.

13   BM 8291.

14   Charles Fox and his brother Stephen 'borrowed great sums of [*sic*] Jews at exorbitant premiums. Charles James Fox called his outward room, where those Jews waited till he rose, the *Jerusalem Chamber*.' A. Francis Steuart, ed., *The Last Journals of Horace Walpole* (London and New York, 1910), 7.

15   Michael, J. Turner, *Pitt the Younger: A Life* (London and New York, 2003), 89 and Cullen, *The Irish Face*, 153.

16   Turner, *Pitt*, 89.

17   Wakeman, *Charles James Fox*, 179.

18   Ibid., 179.

19   British Library, London – (Fox Papers) BL Add. Mss. 47580 f. 139, Charles James Fox to Right Honorable Colonel Richard Fitzpatrick, 30 July 1789.

20   J. Wright, ed., *The Speeches of the Right Honourable Charles James Fox, in the House of Commons*, 6 volumes (London, 1815), volume 4, 199–200.

21   Derry, *Fox*, 10.

22   Ibid., 296.

23   L.G. Mitchell, *Charles James Fox* (London, 1992), 36 and 109.

24   BM 7892.

25   BM 6380.

26   Diana Donald, *The Age of Caricature: Satirical Prints in the Reign of George III* (New Haven and London, 1996), 167.

27   *Book of Common Prayer 1662 Version*, Everyman's Library Edition (London, 1999), 95.

28   Ibid., 95–6.

29   Donald, *Age of Caricature*, 167.

30 Mitchel, *Fox*, 5–6; Derry, *Fox*, 11–12.

31 The Crown and Anchor Tavern was a loyalist club established on 20 November 1792 by John Reeves and was a key meeting place for both loyalists and loyalist organizations, such as the Reeves' Association.

32 Richard Brinsley Sheridan, 'School for Scandal 1777' Act III, Scene III, in *The Meridian Anthology of Eighteenth- and Nineteenth-century Drama*, ed. Katherine M. Rogers (Harmondsworth, 1996), 356.

33 BM 8699.

34 John Reeves was the founder of the Association for Preserving Liberty and Property against Republicans and Levellers (the Association), and also established the Crown and Anchor Tavern Association in 1792. Reeves is seen as a key loyalist figure and the Association played an important role in the suppression of republican and revolutionary ideas in Britain during the 1790s. Philip Schofield, 'John Reeves (1752–1829)', in *ODNB*, ed. Matthew and Harrison, volume 46 (Oxford: Oxford University Press, 2004), 351–2.

35 For further information on 'Pitt's Terror' see Clive Emsley, '"An Aspect of Pitt's Terror": Prosecutions for Sedition during the 1790s', *Social History* 6, no. 2 (1981): 155–84.

36 BM 8836.

37 BM 9986.

38 BM 11054.

39 Addington's father, Dr Anthony Addington (1713–90), was one of George III's physicians and as such acquired the nickname the Doctor. Claire L. Nutt, 'Addington, Anthony (1713–1790)', in *ODNB*, ed. Matthew and Harrison, volume 1 (Oxford: Oxford University Press, 2004), 302.

40 The fate of Malta was a controversial aspect of the Treaty of Amiens – Philip Ziegler, *Addington: A Life of Henry Addington, First Viscount Sidmouth* (London, 1965), 145. The articles of the Treaty of Amiens did not restrain French colonial expansion and the British were deceived by the French about the size of the force they sent to the West Indies to re-conquer San Domingo. During the war, Britain had secured Trinidad and Ceylon, but they had to give up Malta in order to conciliate Tsar Alexander and lost the Cape of Good Hope. Piers Mackesy, *War without Victory: The Downfall of Pitt 1799–1802* (Oxford, 1984), 216, 218 and 223. For a wider discussion of the war with Napoleonic France and the Peace of Amiens.

41 Lord John Russell, *Memorials and Correspondence of Charles James Fox*, volume 2 (London, 1853), 361.

42 Upon the resignation of William Pitt the Younger as First Lord of the Treasury in March 1801, Mr Speaker Addington was invited by George III to form a government. Addington resigned in May 1804 and was succeeded by Pitt the

Younger on 10 May 1804. J.E. Cookson, 'Addington, Henry, First Viscount Sidmouth (1757–1844)', in *ODNB*, ed. Matthew and Harrison, volume 1 (Oxford: Oxford University Press, 2004), 303–11.

43 His father William Pitt, First Earl Chatham, made his name as First Lord of the Treasury during the Seven Years' War (1756–63).

44 During this period, Fox believed that opposition was pointless owing to the arithmetic within the House of Commons. Opposition was instead symbolic. Fox also believed that with the Peace of Amiens Napoleon's triumph was complete and that as there was no political liberty in the world then Napoleon was the fittest person to be its master. Mitchell, *Fox*, 195; and Stanley Ayling, *Fox: The Life of Charles James Fox* (London, 1991), 209. With the Peace of Amiens looking increasingly shaky, Addington looked to Pitt as he sought to strengthen his administration in early 1803. Initially he refused, eventually stating that he would only return as head of the administration. This was turned down, however, when Addington's majority started to crumble in 1804 after the renewal of hostilities with France; Addington resigned on 29 April 1804 and the King had little alternative than to send for Pitt. Michael Duffy, *The Younger Pitt* (Harlow, 2000), 215–17. During the debate on the renewal of hostilities with France on 23 and 24 May 1803, Addington was uninspiring and demonstrated his inability to lead the House of Commons. Ziegler, *Addington*, 185–6. For a wider discussion of the war see Mackesy, *War without Victory*.

45 Ehrman, *Pitt*, volume 3, 566–75.

46 Gwyn A. Williams *When Was Wales?* p. 170.

47 Gwyn A. Williams, *Artisans and Sans-Culottes*, 2nd edition (London, 1989), 65.

48 R.G. Hawtrey, 'The 1797 Banking Crisis', *The Economic Journal* 28, no. 109 (1918): 52.

49 Ibid., 52–65.

50 Ian R. Christie, *Wars and Revolutions: Britain, 1760–1815* (London, Melbourne and Auckland, 1991), 237.

51 Philip Jenkins, *A History of Modern Wales, 1536–1990* (London and New York, 1992), 183.

52 Williams, *Artisans and Sans-Culottes*, 65.

53 BM 8990.

54 Sheridan's indebtedness began when he borrowed heavily to purchase a share in the Drury Lane Theatre in 1776, thus beginning a 'long sequence of increasingly tangled financial arrangements'. After he ceased to be an MP in 1812, Sheridan was arrested as a debtor and relied on the benevolence of his friends to keep his creditors at bay. Arnold Hare, *Richard Brinsley Sheridan* (Windsor, 1981), 8 and 12.

55 BM 8998.

56 BM 8994.

57 BM 8980.

58   Donald E. Ginter, *Voting Records of the House of Commons 1761–1820*, 6 volumes (London and Rio Grande, 1995), 400–2.

59   BM 7497.

60   BM 8995.

61   The legend of King Midas is from book 11 of Ovid's *Metamorphosis*; see David Raeburn, trans., *Ovid: Metamorphoses* (London, 2004), 426–31.

62   Ibid., 427.

63   Apollo was the Roman god of the sun.

64   Raeburn, *Ovid*, 431.

65   Erskine, Sheridan, Grey and Taylor remained loyal to Fox after the defection of the Duke of Portland, Earl Fitzwilliam and other Whig grandees in 1794 and with Fox were the leading Whig spokesmen in the House of Commons.

66   BM 8318, BM 8612 and BM 8979.

67   For further discussion on the nature of Foxite opposition from 1790 to the end of the Foxite secession, see Donald E. Ginter, 'The Financing of the Whig Party Organization, 1783–1793', *The American Historical Review* 71, no. 2 (1966): 421–40; Butterfield, 'Whig opposition', 293–330; Richard E. Willis, '"An Handful of Violent People": The Nature of the Foxite Opposition 1794 Mitchell 1801', *Albion* 8, no. 3 (1976): 236–54; Richard E. Willis, 'Fox, Grenville, and the Recovery of Opposition, 1801–1804', *The Journal of British Studies* 11, no. 2 (1972): 24–43; and Mitchell, *Disintegration of the Whig Party*, 194–239.

68   BM 8992, BM 8683, BM 8145, BM 8149 and BM 8284.

69   BM 8683.

70   S.A. Hunn, 'Negative Perceptions of Whiggery 1760–1807' (Oxford, PhD. thesis, 1997), 63.

71   Ibid., 39.

72   BM 8992.

73   For a contemporary account of the invasion see J. Baker, *A Brief Narrative of the French Invasion Near Fishguard Bay: Including Perfect Description of that Part of the Coast of Pembrokeshire on Which Was Effected the Landing of the French Forces on 22nd of February 1797, and of Their Surrender to the Welch Provincial Troops, Headed by Lord Cawdor* (Worcester, 1797). For further discussion of the invasion see Margaret Ellen James, *The Fishguard Invasion by the French in 1797* (London, 1892).

74   BM 5424.

75   BM 6012.

76   BM 6027.

77   BM 6220.

78   BM 6220A.

79   *Phaeton Alarm'd* draws strongly on iconography used by Gillray in an earlier print entitled *Light Expelling Darkness* (BM 8644) with the First Lord of the

Treasury cast as Apollo, riding in a chariot with the sun behind him. Both images also have the First Lord of the Treasury as the saviour fighting Jacobin and revolutionary forces.

80   The *Anti-Jacobin Review* sold around 2,500 copies each week. H.T. Dickinson, *British Radicalism and the French Revolution 1789–1815* (Oxford, 1985), 30.

81   Jennifer Mori, *Britain in the Age of the French Revolution* (Harlow, 2000), 80.

82   Ibid., 165.

83   Whose name appears twice on the list of subscribers.

84   British Library, London – (Gillray Papers) BL Add. MS. 27337, ff. 59–68.

85   British Library, London – (Gillray Papers) BL Add. MS. 27337, f. 69.

86   Emily Lorraine de Montluzin, *The Anti-Jacobins, 1798–1800: The Early Contributors to the Anti-Jacobin Review* (New York, 1988), 21.

87   Ibid., 21–7.

88   BM 9270.

89   BM 9240.

90   BM 9245.

91   BM 9261.

92   This is demonstrated within the copy of volume one held by the University of Nottingham; *Anti-Jacobin Review and Magazine* (London, 1798–1810).

93   Frank MacDermot, 'Arthur O'Connor', *Irish Historical Studies* 5, no. 57 (1966): 55–6.

94   BM 9245.

95   For a discussion of O'Connor's trial for treason see MacDermot, 'Arthur O'Connor', 55–6 and 59–60; and F.K. Prochaska, 'English State Trials in the 1790s: A Case Study', *The Journal of British Studies* 13, no. 1 (1973): 66–9.

96   Ehrman, *Pitt*, volume 2, 398; and Alan Wharam, *The Treason Trials, 1794* (London, 1992), 213–15.

97   David Bindman, *From Ape to Apollo: Aesthetics and the Idea of Race in the Eighteenth-century* (London, 2002), 120–1.

98   Ibid., 108.

99   H.T. Dickinson, *The Politics of the People in Eighteenth-century Britain* (Basingstoke: 1994), 272.

100 For further information on the political meaning of the cap of liberty or *bonnet rouge* see James Epstein, *Radical Expression: Political Language, Ritual, and Symbol in England, 1790–1850* (New York and Oxford, 1994), 70–99; and Richard Wrigley, 'Transformations of a Revolutionary Emblem: The Liberty Cap in the French Revolution', *French History* 11, no. 2 (1997): 131–69.

101 Although he gained some followers afterwards while in office.

102 For example, David Cameron and Nick Clegg, see *Private Eye*, numbers 1264–74 and *The Times*, 13 May 2010, 29.

Chapter 6

1   Richard E. Willis, "'An Handful of Violent People": The Nature of the Foxite Opposition 1794 Mitchell 1801', *Albion* 8, no. 3 (1976): 243.

2   *London und Paris*, volumes 1–6, 1801–6; *Anti-Jacobin Review*, volume 1, 1798.

3   John Derry, *Charles James Fox* (London, 1972), 162–3.

4   BM 4859, BM 4864, BM 4962, BM 5098 and BM 5109.

5   Derry, *Fox*, 52–3 and Frank O'Gorman, *The Rise of Party in England: The Rockingham Whigs 1760–82* (London, 1975), 431.

6   L.G. Mitchell, *Charles James Fox and the Disintegration of the Whig Party 1782–1794* (Oxford, 1971), 242.

7   John Derry, 'The Opposition Whigs and the French Revolution 1789–1815', in *Britain and the French Revolution, 1789–1815*, ed. H.T. Dickinson (Basingstoke, 1989), 53.

8   John W. Derry, *Politics in the Age of Fox, Pitt and Liverpool* (London, 1990), 72.

9   J.C.D. Clark, *English Society 1660–1832*, 2nd edition (Cambridge, 2000), 507.

10 H.T. Dickinson, *British Radicalism and the French Revolution 1789–1815* (Oxford, 1985), 31. For a discussion of Joseph Priestley in caricature, see Martin Fitzpatrick, 'Priestley Caricatured', in *Motion towards Perfection: The Achievement of Joseph Priestley*, ed. A. Truman Schwartz and John G. McEvoy (London, 1990), 161–218.

11 BM 6661.

12 BM 2425 and BM 2285.

13 The Test Act debarred all non-Anglicans from holding civil or military office.

14 Derry, *Fox*, 242.

15 BM 7630.

16 Alexander Gordon, 'Towers, Joseph (1737–1799)', rev. M.J. Mercer, in *ODNB*, ed. Matthew and Harrison, volume 55, 101–2.

17 For further information see George Rudé, 'The Gordon Riots: A Study of the Rioters and Their Victims', *Transactions of the Royal Historical Society*, 5th series, volume 6 (1956), and J. Paul de Castro, *The Gordon Riots* (London, 1926).

18 BM 7628, BM 7629 and BM 9240.

19 Colin Jones, *The Longman Companion to the French Revolution* (London and New York, 1988), 13, 243–4.

20 BM 9217.

21 BM 5680.

22 Charles Howard, 11th Duke of Norfolk, was born and educated a Roman Catholic, but by the time of the Gordon Riots in 1780 he had conformed to the Church of England. Very little is known about John Nicholls, MP for Tregony. The fact that the other figures were all Oxbridge educated, Lansdowne (Christ Church College, Oxford), Bedford (Trinity College, Cambridge), Tierney (Peterhouse College,

Cambridge), Lauderdale (Trinity College, Oxford), indicates that they at least conformed to the Church of England.

23 BM 10405.

24 Anon., *Fox's Martyrs; or A New Book of the Sufferings of the Faithful* (London, 1784).

25 Gillray's reference to Napoleon as Pope Pius VI's master could itself be a reference to Napoleon's coronation, as the Pope accepted Napoleon's proposal that he assist at his coronation at Notre Dame on 2 December 1804 and the Pope's agreeing that after he anointed Napoleon, Napoleon should crown himself. Felix Markham, *Napoleon* (London, 1963), 100. Equally it could be a reference to the concordat between Napoleon's government and the Pope, which was signed on 15 July 1801. J.M. Thompson, *Napoleon Bonaparte: His Rise and Fall* (Oxford, 1952), 173.

26 Frank O'Gorman, 'Campaign Rituals and Ceremonies: The Social Meaning of Elections in England 1780–1860', *Past and Present* 135 (1992): 92, and John Brooke, 'Pitt, Hon. William (1759–1806)' in *The House of Commons 1754–1790*, ed. Sir Lewis Namier and John Brooke, 3 volumes (London, 1985), 205–512.

27 MPs were not to gain an annual salary until 1911.

28 For votes on Bills on aspects of parliamentary reform see Donald E. Ginter, *Voting Records of the House of Commons 1761–1820*, 6 volumes (London and Rio Grande, 1995), volume 5, 89, 101–15, 131–42, 159–79, 199–205, 271–4, 283–7, 347–9, 360–1, 405–6, 408–11, 430–3 and 440–2.

29 These were the votes to make Grenville's Election Act permanent (25 February 1774),which was carried by 252 votes to 124 and the passing of Anglo Irish Union in 1800.

30 BM 8087, BM 8289, BM 9878 and BM 9108; also Dickinson, *British Radicalism*, 30–1.

31 Clive Emsley, *Britain and the French Revolution* (Harlow, 2000), 34.

32 Derry, *Politics in the Age of Fox*, 31.

33 Jennifer Mori, *Britain in the Age of the French Revolution* (Harlow, 2000), 5 and 8.

34 For votes on Bills on aspects of religious toleration see Ginter, *Voting Records*, volume 5, 297–9, 332–4 and 529–31. For votes on abolishing the slave trade see Ginter, *Voting Records*, volume 5, 339–40 and 391–4.

35 Derry, *Politics in the Age of Fox*, 58 and 80, and Mori, *French Revolution*, 31.

36 Mori, *French Revolution*, 9.

37 Ibid., 8.

38 H.T. Dickinson, 'Themes: Revolution or Reaction', *Modern History Review* 6, no. 4 (1995): 10, and H.T. Dickinson, 'Introduction: The Impact on Britain of the French Revolution and the French Wars 1789–1815', in *Britain and the French Revolution*, ed. H.T. Dickinson (Basingstoke, 1989), 6.

39 Mori, *French Revolution*, 8.

40 BM 8624.

41 For a transcript of the trial, see John Barrell and Jon Mee, eds, *Trials for Treason and Sedition 792–4*, 5 volumes (London, 2006), volumes 2–5. For a discussion of the trials, see Alan Wharam, *The Treason Trials, 1794* (London, 1992),and John Barrell, *Imagining the King's Death: Figurative Treason, Fantasies of Regicide 1793–1796* (Oxford, 2000), 318–65.

42 F.K. Prochaska, 'English State Trials in the 1790s: A Case Study', *The Journal of British Studies* 13, no. 1 (1973): 67.

43 William Murray, first Earl of Mansfield (1705–1793), William Pitt, first Earl of Chatham and William Wyndham Grenville, first Baron Grenville.

44 Mori, *French Revolution*, 8; and E.A. Smith, *Lord Grey 1764–1845* (Oxford, 1990), 36, 38, 40–1, 47.

45 Members of the House of Commons were, however, entitled by law to serve as First Lord of the Treasury and a number of occupants of the post during the eighteenth century did, including Sir Robert Walpole, Henry Pelham, Lord North and William Pitt the Younger. Meanwhile, the head of the government was not always the First Lord of the Treasury, for example, Lords Chatham and Bute.

46 Fox's father became a Baron in 1763, fourteen years after Charles James Fox's birth.

47 British Museum, London – 1988,1001.6.

48 BM 6380.

49 BM 7890.

50 Wat Tyler was the leader of the 1381 Peasants' Revolt.

51 Nicholas Brooke, ed., *William Shakespeare: The Tragedy of Macbeth* (Oxford, 2008), Act 1, Scene 3.

52 BM 11555.

53 E.E.C. Nicholson, 'Emblem v. Caricature: A Tenacious Conceptual Framework', in *Emblems and Art History*, ed. Alison Adams (Glasgow, 1996), 141–67.

54 Katie Hickman, *Courtesans* (London, 2003), 138.

55 Granville, Castalia Countess of Granville, ed., *Lord Granville Leveson Gower (First Earl Granville) Private Correspondence 1781–1821*, 2 volumes (London, 1917), 162.

56 BM 10534.

57 See British Museum – 1851,0901.1191 and 1985,0119.190.

58 BM 6192 and British Museum, London – 1948,0214.727.

59 John Ehrman, 'Pitt the Younger, William (1759–1806)', in *Who's Who in British History*, ed. Juliet Gardiner, volume 3, 838–9.

60 For a discussion of the Ministry of All the Talents see A.D. Harvey, 'The Ministry of All the Talents: The Whigs in Office, February 1806 to March 1807', *The Historical Journal* 15, no. 4 (1972): 619–48, and Peter Jupp, *Lord Grenville: 1759–1834* (Oxford, 1985), 345–412.

61 BM 10589 and BM 10589.A.

62 Fox married his long-term mistress, Mrs Elizabeth Bridget Armistead, secretly in August 1795. The marriage was not announced until 1802 ahead of their visit to the Continent during the Peace of Amiens. Her previous lovers included the Prince of Wales and Lord Derby. I.M. Davies, *The Harlot and the Statesman: The Story of Elizabeth Armistead & Charles James Fox* (Abbotsbrooke: 1986), 31–3, 42–3 and 121; British Library, London (Fox Papers) – BL. Add. Mss. 47564 ff. 151–2.

63 Duke of Buckingham and Chandos, eds, *Memoirs of the Court and Cabinet of George the Third*, 4 volumes (London, 1855), volume 4, 37.

64 Ibid., 40.

65 BM 6012, BM 6500 and BM 6207.

66 The Fox–North Coalition, which George III had been reluctant to appoint, was dismissed in December 1784, once a more acceptable candidate, Pitt the Younger, could be prevailed to take the government on. Meanwhile the King had ordered his dismissal a decade earlier, following his obliging Lord North to fulfil a promise made before the facts of the printer's case had become clear.

67 BM 11555.

68 BM 9962.

69 Brooke, *Macbeth*, 105.

70 NPG 6659.

71 NPG 1978.

72 NPG 3341 (Benjamin Disraeli) and NPG 3360 (William Ewart Gladstone).

73 For a discussion of the development of Conservative and Whig electoral organization in the wake of the Great Reform Act of 1832, see Philip Salmon, *Electoral Reform At Work: Local Politics and National Parties, 1832–1841* (Woodbridge, 2002), 43–86.

Conclusion

1 James Sayers is alone among this group to have never published coloured prints.

2 Sir Menzies Campbell resigned the leadership of the Liberal Democrats (aged 66) on 15 October 2007 due to constant questions over his age, in part resulting from his constant portrayal in caricature as a decrepit old man who could only walk with the aid of a Zimmer frame after his election to the leadership of the Liberal Democrats in 2006.

Select Bibliography

Printed Primary

Anon., *The Amours of Carlo Khan: Interspersed with Curious Anecdotes and Bon Mots of Many Distinguished Personages* (London, 1789).

Anon., *The Coalitional Rencontre Anticipated; A Poetical Dialogue* (London, 1785).

Anon., *A Collection of Odes, Songs and Epigrams against the Whigs Alias the Blue and Buff; in which are included Mr. Hewerdine's Political Songs* (London, 1790).

Anon., *Fox's Martyrs; or A New Book of the Sufferings of the Faithful* (London, 1784).

Anon., *Memoirs of Nine Illustrious Living Characters* (Dublin, 1799).

Aspinall, A. (ed.), *The Later Correspondence of George III*, 5 volumes (Cambridge, 1962–1970).

Baker, J., *A Brief Narrative of the French Invasion Near Fishguard Bay: Including Perfect Description of That Part of the Coast of Pembrokeshire on Which Was Effected the Landing of the French Forces on 22nd of February 1797, and of Their Surrender to the Welch Provincial Troops, Headed by Lord Cawdor* (Worcester, 1797).

Book of Common Prayer, 1662 version, Everyman's Library Edition (London, 1999).

Buckingham and Chandos, Duke of (ed.), *Memoirs of the Court and Cabinet of George the Third*, 4 volumes (London, 1855).

Cobbett, William (ed.), *The Parliamentary History of England: From the Earliest Period to the Year 1803*, 36 volumes (London, 1806–1820).

Fortescue, Sir John (ed.), *The Correspondence of King George the Third from 1760 to December 1783*, 6 volumes (London, 1927).

G.K., *The Festival of Wit or the Small Talker* (Dublin, 1783).

Garlick, Kenneth and Angus Macintyre (eds), *The Diary of Joseph Farington*, 16 volumes (New Haven and London, 1978–1998).

Ginter, Donald E., *Voting Records of the House of Commons 1761–1820*, 6 volumes (London and Rio Grande, 1995).

Granville, Castilia, Countess of (ed.), *Lord Granville Leveson Gower (First Earl Granville) Private Correspondence 1781 to 1782*, 2 volumes (London, 1917).

Hadley, William, *The Letters of Horace Walpole* (London and New York, 1926).

Herbert, Lord (ed.), *The Pembroke Papers*, 2 volumes (London, 1942–1950).

Jarrett, Derek (ed.), *Horace Walpole Memoirs of the Reign of George III*, 4 volumes (New Haven and London, 2000).

Laprade, W.T., *The Parliamentary Papers of John Robinson, 1774–1784* (London, 1922).

Lewis, W.S. (ed.), *Horace Walpole's Correspondence*, 48 volumes (Oxford, 1937–1983).

Powell, G.H. (ed.), *The Table Talk of Samuel Rogers* (London, 1903).

Price, Cecil (ed.), *The Letters of Richard Brinsley Sheridan*, 3 volumes (Oxford, 1966).

Russell, Lord John, *Memorials and Correspondence of Charles James Fox*, 4 volumes (London, 1853).

Steuart, A. Francis (ed.), *The Last Journals of Horace Walpole* (London and New York, 1910).

Twiss, Horace, *The Public and Private Life of Lord Chancellor Eldon*, 3 volumes (London, 1844).

Wraxall, Sir Nathanial William Bart, *Historical Memoirs of My Own Time* (London, 1904).

Wright, J. (ed.), *The Speeches of the Right Honourable Charles James Fox, in the House of Commons*, 6 volumes (London, 1815).

Unpublished Theses

Hunn, S.A., 'Negative perceptions of Whiggery 1760–1807' (Oxford, PhD. thesis, 1997).

McCreery, Cindy, 'Prints and politics in the East India Bill Crisis, 1783–4' (Oxford, MPhil. thesis, 1991).

Nicholson, E.E.C., 'English political prints and pictorial political argument *c.* 1640–*c.* 1832: A study in historiography and methodology', 3 volumes (University of Edinburgh, PhD. thesis, 1994).

Secondary Sources

Adams, Alison, *Emblems and Art History* (Glasgow, 1996).

Adelman, Paul, *Gladstone, Disraeli and Later Victorian Politics* (Harlow, 1970).

Alexander, David, *Richard Newton and English Caricature in the 1790s* (Manchester, 1998).

Atherton, Herbert M., *Political Prints in the Age of Hogarth* (Oxford, 1974).

Ayling, Stanley, *Fox: The Life of Charles James Fox* (London, 1991).

Baker, Lord Kenneth, *George IV: A Life in Caricature* (London, 2005).

Baker, Lord Kenneth, *George III: A Life in Caricature* (London, 2007).

Barrell, John, *Imagining the King's Death: Figurative Treason, Fantasies of Regicide 1793–1796* (Oxford, 2000).

Barrell, John and Jon Mee (eds), *Trials for Treason and Sedition 792–4*, 5 volumes (London, 2006).

Bath, Michael and Daniel Russell (eds), *Deviceful Settings: The English Renaissance Emblem and Its Contexts: Selected Papers from the Third International Emblem Conference* (New York, 1999).

Bills, Mark, *The Art of Satire: London in Caricature* (London, 2006).

Bindman, David, *From Ape to Apollo: Aesthetics and the Idea of Race in the Eighteenth-Century* (London, 2002).

Black, Jeremy, *War for America* (Stroud, 1991).

Black, Jeremy (ed.), *Culture and Society in Britain 1660–1800* (Manchester and New York, 1997).

Blake, Lord Robert, *Disraeli* (London, 1969).

Brewer, John, *The Common People and Politics, 1750–1790s* (Cambridge, 1986).

Brooke, Nicholas (ed.), *William Shakespeare: The Tragedy of Macbeth* (Oxford, 2008).

Burke, Peter, *Popular Culture in Early Modern Europe*, revised edition (Aldershot, 1994).

Campbell, John, *Pistols at Dawn: Two Hundred Years of Political Rivalry from Pitt and Fox to Blair and Brown* (London, 2009).

Cannon, John, *The Fox–North Coalition: Crisis of the Constitution* (Cambridge, 1969).

Chalus, Elaine, *Elite Women in English Political Life, c. 1754–1790* (Oxford, 2005).

Christie, Ian R., *Wars and Revolutions: Britain, 1760–1815* (London, Melbourne and Aukland, 1991).

Clark, J.C.D., *English Society 1660–1832*, 2nd edition (Cambridge, 2000).

Clayton, Tim, *Caricatures of the Peoples of the British Isles* (London, 2007).

Colley, Linda, *Britons: Forging the Nation 1707–1837*, 2nd edition (New Haven and London, 2005).

Cornell, Brian, *Portrait of a Whig Peer* (London, 1957).

Cullen, Fintan, *Visual Politics: The Representation of Ireland 1750–1930* (Cork, 1997).

Cullen, Fintan, *The Irish Face: Redefining the Irish Portrait* (London, 2004).

Davis, I.M., *The Harlot and the Statesman: The Story of Elizabeth Armistead and Charles James Fox* (Abbotsbrooke, 1986).

de Castro, J. Paul, *The Gordon Riots* (London, 1926).

de Montluzin, Emily Lorraine, *The Anti-Jacobins, 1798–1800: The Early Contributors to the Anti-Jacobin Review* (New York, 1988).

Derry, John, *The Regency Crisis and the Whigs, 1788–9* (Cambridge, 1963).

Derry, John, *Charles James Fox* (London, 1972).

Derry, John W., *Politics in the Age of Fox, Pitt and Liverpool* (London, 1990).

Dickinson, H.T., *British Radicalism and the French Revolution 1789–1815* (Oxford, 1985).

Dickinson, H.T., *Caricatures and the Constitution 1760–1832* (Cambridge, 1986).

Dickinson, H.T. (ed.), *Britain and the French Revolution, 1789–1815* (Basingstoke, 1989).

Donald, Diana, *The Age of Caricature: Satirical Prints in the Reign of George III* (New Haven and London, 1996).

Donald, Diana, *Followers of Fashion: Graphic Satire from the Georgian Period* (London, 2002).

Duffy, Michael, *The Englishman and the Foreigner* (Cambridge, 1986).

Duffy, Michael, *The Younger Pitt* (Harlow, 2000).

Ehrman, John, *The Younger Pitt*, 3 volumes (London, 1969–1996).

Emsley, Clive, *Britain and the French Revolution* (Harlow, 2000).

Epstein, James, *Radical Expression: Political Language, Ritual, and Symbol in England, 1790–1850* (New York and Oxford, 1994).

Foreman, Amanda, *Georgiana, Duchess of Devonshire* (London, 1999).

Gatrell, Vic, *City of Laughter* (London, 2007).

George, M. Dorothy, *English Political Caricature to 1792: A Study in Opinion and Propaganda* (Oxford, 1959).

George, M. Dorothy, *Hogarth to Cruikshank: Social Change in Graphic Satire* (London, 1967).

Hague, William, *William Pitt the Younger* (London, 2004).

Halett, Mark (ed.), *James Gillray: The Art of Caricature* (London, 2001).

Hare, Arnold, *Richard Brinsley Sheridan* (Windsor, 1981).

Hickman, Katie, *Courtesans* (London, 2003).

Hill, Draper, *Mr. Gillray The Caricaturist* (London, 1965).

Hill, Draper, *Fashionable Contrasts: Caricatures by James Gillray* (London, 1966).

Hilton, Boyd, *A Mad, Bad and Dangerous People?: England 1783–1846* (Oxford, 2006).

Houston, Rab, *Literacy in Early Modern Europe: Culture and Education, 1500–1800* (London and New York, 1988).

Hunt, Tamara L., *Defining John Bull: Political Caricature and National Identity in Late Georgian England* (Aldershot and Burlington, 2003).

James, Margaret Ellen, *The Fishguard Invasion by the French in 1797* (London, 1892).

Jenkins, Philip, *A History of Modern Wales, 1536–1990* (London and New York, 1992).

Jones, Colin, *The Longman Companion to the French Revolution* (London and New York, 1988).

Jupp, Peter, *Lord Grenville: 1759–1834* (Oxford, 1985).

Langford, Paul, *Walpole and the Robinocracy* (Cambridge, 1986).

Lascelles, Edward, *The Life of Charles James Fox* (Oxford, 1936).

Lock, F.P., *Edmund Burke*, 2 volumes (Oxford, 2006).

Mackesy, Piers, *War without Victory: The Downfall of Pitt 1799–1802* (Oxford, 1984).

Markham, Felix, *Napoleon* (London, 1963).

Matthew, H.C.G. and Brian Harrison (eds), *Oxford Dictionary of National Biography*, 61 volumes (Oxford, 2004).

Miller, John, *Religion in the Popular Prints, 1600–1832* (Cambridge, 1986).

Mitchell, L.G., *Charles James Fox and the Disintegration of the Whig Party 1782–1794* (Oxford, 1971).

Mitchell, L.G., *Holland House* (London, 1980).

Mitchell, L.G., *Charles James Fox* (London, 1992).

Mitchell, L.G., *The Whig World 1760–1837* (London and New York, 2005).

Mori, Jennifer, *Britain in the Age of the French Revolution* (Harlow, 2000).

Namier, Sir L.B., *The Structure of Politics at the Accession of George III* (London, 1929).

Namier, Sir L.B., *Crossroads of Power: Essays on Eighteenth-Century England* (London, 1970).

Namier, Sir Lewis and John Brooke (eds), *The House of Commons 1754–1790*, 3 volumes (London, 1985).

O'Connell, Sheila, *The Popular Print in England 1550–1850* (London, 1999).

O'Gorman, Frank, *The Whig Party and the French Revolution* (London, 1967).

O'Gorman, Frank, *The Rise of Party in England: The Rockingham Whigs 1760–82* (London, 1975).

O'Gorman, Frank, *Voters, Patrons and Parties: The Unreformed Electoral System of Hanoverian England 1734–1832* (Oxford, 1989).

Palmer, Alan, *George IV* (London, 1975).

Plumb, J.H., *England in the Eighteenth Century* (Harmondsworth, 1960).

Plumb, J.H., *Georgian Delights* (London, 1980).

Porter, Roy, *Bodies Politic: Disease, Death and Doctors in Britain, 1650–1900* (New York, 2001).

Porterfield, Todd (ed.), *The Efflorescence of Caricature, 1759–1838* (Farnham and Burlington, 2011).

Powell, David, *Charles James Fox: Man of the People* (London, 1989).

Raeburn, David (trans.), *Ovid: Metamorphoses* (London, 2004).

Reid, Loren, *Charles James Fox: A Man for the People* (London and Harlow, 1969).

Ribeiro, Aileen, *Fashion in the French Revolution* (New York, 1988).

Robinson, Nicholas K., *Edmund Burke: A Life in Caricature* (New Haven and London, 1996).

Royal Academy of Arts, *Citizens and Kings* (London, 2007).

Salmon, Philip, *Electoral Reform at Work: Local Politics and National Parties, 1832–1841* (Woodbridge, 2002).

Schwartz, A. Truman and John G. McEvoy (eds), *Motion towards Perfection: The Achievement of Joseph Priestley* (London, 1990).

Sharpe, J.A., *Crime and the Law in English Satirical Prints, 1600–1832* (Cambridge, 1986).

Smith, E.A., *Whig Principles and Party Politics: Earl Fitzwilliam and the Whig Party 1748–1833* (Manchester, 1975).

Smith, E.A., *Lord Grey 1764–1845* (Oxford, 1990).

Smith, E.A., *George IV* (New Haven and London, 1999).

Somervell, D.C., *Disraeli and Gladstone: A Duo-Biographical Sketch* (London, 1938).

Stephens, Frederick George and M. Dorothy George (eds), *Catalogue of Political and Personal Satires Preserved in the Department of Prints and Drawings in the British Museum*, 11 volumes (London, 1870–1954).

Thomas, P.D.G., *The House of Commons in the Eighteenth Century* (Oxford, 1971).

Thomas, P.D.G., *British Politics and the Stamp Act Crisis: The First Phase of the American Revolution, 1763–1767* (Oxford, 1975).

Thomas, P.D.G., *Lord North* (London, 1976).

Thomas, P.D.G., *The American Revolution* (Cambridge, 1986).

Thomas, P.D.G., *The Townshend Duties Crisis: The Second Phase of the American Revolution, 1767–1773* (Oxford, 1987).

Thomas, P.D.G., *Tea Party to Independence: The Third Phase of the American Revolution, 1773–1776* (Oxford, 1991).

Thompson, E.P., *The Making of the English Working Class* (Harmondsworth, 1968).

Thompson, J.M., *Napoleon Bonaparte: His Rise and Fall* (Oxford, 1952).

Turner, Michael, J., *Pitt the Younger: A Life* (London and New York, 2003).

Victoria and Albert Museum, *English Caricature: 1760 to the Present* (London, 1984).

Villiers, Marjorie, *The Grand Whiggery* (London, 1939).

Wakeman, Henry Offley, *The Life of Charles James Fox* (London, 1890).

Walpole, B.C., *Days of the Dandies: Charles James Fox* (Edinburgh, ND).

Wardroper, John, *The Caricatures of George Cruikshank* (London, 1977).

Wharam, Alan, *The Treason Trials, 1794* (London, 1992).

Williams, Gwyn A., *Artisans and Sans-Culottes*, 2nd edition (London, 1989).

Wood, Marcus, *Radical Satire and Print Culture 1790–1822* (Oxford, 1994).

Wright, Thomas, *Caricature History of the Georges* (London, 1898).

Wright, Thomas (ed.), *The Works of James Gillray, The Caricaturist* (Amsterdam, 1970).

Wynn Jones, Michael, *The Cartoon History of Britain* (New York, 1971).

Ziegler, Philip, *Addington: A Life of Henry Addington, First Viscount Sidmouth* (London, 1965).

Articles

Butterfield, Herbert, 'Charles James Fox and the Whig Opposition in 1792', *Cambridge Historical Journal* 9/3 (1949), pp. 93–330.

Christie, Ian, 'The anatomy of the opposition in the Parliament of 1784', *Parliamentary History* 9/1 (1990), pp. 50–77.

Corfield, Penelope, Edmund M. Green and Charles Harvey, 'Westminster man: Charles James Fox and his electorate', *Parliamentary History* 20/2 (2001), pp. 157–85.

Deutsch, Phyllis, 'Moral trespass in Georgian London: Gaming, gender and electoral politics in the age of George III', *The Historical Journal* 39/3 (1996), pp. 637–56.

Dickinson, H.T., 'Themes: Revolution or reaction', *Modern History Review* 6/4 (1995), pp. 8–10.

Dinwiddy, J.R., 'Charles James Fox and the people', *History* 55/185 (1970), pp. 342–59.

Emsley, Clive, 'An aspect of Pitt's Terror': Prosecutions for sedition during the 1790s', *Social History* 6/2 (1981), pp. 155–84.

Freyer, C.E., 'Historical revisions: The General Election of 1784', *History* 9 (1924/5), pp. 221–3.

Gassman, Byron W., 'Smollett's Britain and the art of political cartooning', *Studies in Eighteenth-Century Culture* 14 (1985), pp. 243–58.

George, M. Dorothy, 'Fox's martyrs: The General Election of 1784', *Transactions of the Royal Historical Society*, 4th series, volume 21 (1939), pp. 133–68.

Ginter, Donald E., 'The financing of the Whig party organization, 1783–1793', *The American Historical Review* 71/2 (1966), pp. 421–40.

Griffiths, Anthony, 'A checklist of catalogues of British print publishers *c.* 1650–1830', *Print Quarterly* 1/1 (1984), pp. 4–22.

Harvey, A.D., 'The Ministry of All the Talents: The Whigs in office, February 1806 to March 1807', *The Historical Journal* 15/4 (1972), pp. 619–48.

Hawtrey, R.G., 'The 1797 Banking Crisis', *The Economic Journal* 28/109 (1918), pp. 52–65.

Johnson, David, 'Britannia roused: Political caricature and the fall of the Fox–North Coalition', *History Today* (June 2006), pp. 22–8.

Kelly, Paul, 'Pitt versus Fox: The Westminster Scrutiny, 1784–85', *Studies in Burke and His Time* 14/46 (1972–3), pp. 155–62.

Lana, Renata, 'Women and Foxite Strategy in the Westminster election of 1784', *Eighteenth-Century Life* 26/1 (2002), pp. 46–69.

Laprade, W.T., 'William Pitt and Westminster Elections', *The American Historical Review* 18/2 (1913), pp. 253–74.

Laprade, W.T., 'Public opinion and the General Election of 1784', *The English Historical Review* 31/122 (1916), pp. 224–37.

MacDermot, Frank, 'Arthur O'Connor', *Irish Historical Studies* 5/57 (1966), pp. 48–69.

McCreery, Cindy, 'Satiric images of Fox, Pitt and George III: The East India Bill Crisis 1783–4', *Word and Image* 9 (1993), pp. 163–85.

Nenadic, Stana, 'Print collecting and popular culture in eighteenth-century Scotland', *History* 82/266 (1997), pp. 203–22.

Nicholson, E.E.C., 'Consumers and spectators: The public of the political print in eighteenth-century England', *History* 81/216 (1996), pp. 540–65.

O'Gorman, Frank, 'Campaign rituals and ceremonies: The social meaning of elections in England 1780–1860', *Past and Present* 135 (1992), pp. 79–115.

Parris, Henry, 'The origins of the permanent civil service, 1780–1830', *Public Administration* 46/2 (1968), pp. 143–66.

Patten, Robert L., 'Conventions in Georgian caricature', *Art Journal* 43/4 (1983), pp. 331–8.

Porter, Roy, 'Review article: Seeing the past', *Past and Present* 118 (1988), pp. 186–205.

Powell, Martyn J., 'Charles James Fox and Ireland', *Irish Historical Studies* 33/130 (2002), pp. 325–50.

Press, Charles, 'The Georgian political print and democratic institutions', *Comparative Studies in Society and History* 19/2 (1977), pp. 216–38.

Prochaska, F.K., 'English state trials in the 1790s: A case study', *The Journal of British Studies* 13/1 (1973), pp. 63–82.

Rauser, Amelia, 'The butcher-kissing Duchess of Devonshire: Between caricature and allegory in 1784', *Eighteenth-Century Studies* 36/1 (2002), pp. 23–46.

Ribiero, Aileen, 'The Macaronis', *History Today* 28/7 (1978), pp. 463–8.

Robinson, Nicholas K., 'Caricature and the Regency Crisis: An Irish perspective', *Eighteenth-Century Ireland* 1 (1986), pp. 157–76.

Rudé, George, 'The Gordon Riots: A study of the rioters and their victims', *Transactions of the Royal Historical Society*, 5th series, volume 6 (1956), pp. 93–114.

Rynell, Alarik, 'Some political nicknames in caricatures under George III', *Studia Neophilologica* 14 (1942), pp. 343–56.

Stott, Anne, '"Female Patriotism": Georgiana, Duchess of Devonshire, and the Westminster Election of 1784', *Eighteenth-Century Life* 17/3 (2003), pp. 60–84.

Taylor, Miles, 'John Bull and the iconography of public opinion in England *c.* 1712–1929', *Past and Present* 134 (1992), pp. 93–128.

Thomas, P.D.G., 'Party politics in eighteenth-century Britain: Some myths and a touch of reality', *British Journal for Eighteenth-Century Studies* 10 (1987), pp. 201–10.

Wechsler, Judith, 'The issue of caricature', *Art Journal* 43/4 (1983), pp. 317–18.

Willis, Richard E., 'Fox, Grenville, and the recovery of opposition, 1801–1804', *The Journal of British Studies* 11/2 (1972), pp. 24–43.

Willis, Richard E., '"An handful of violent people": The nature of the Foxite Opposition 1794–1801', *Albion* 8/3 (1976), pp. 236–54.

Wrigley, Richard, 'Transformations of a revolutionary emblem: The liberty cap in the French Revolution', *French History* 11/2 (1997), pp. 131–69.

Index

Plate 1 James Gillray, *The Presentation – or – the Wise Men's Offering*, hand-coloured etching, 9 January 1796, 248 mm × 348 mm (NPG D12553).

Plate 2 James Gillray, *Very Slippy-Weather*, hand-coloured etching, 10 February 1808, 260 mm × 204 mm (NPG D13700).

Plate 3 Anon., *The Young Politician*, hand-coloured etching, 1771, 253 mm × 206 mm (LWL 771.00.00.07).

Plate 4 James Gillray, *Changing Places; – Alias; Fox Stinking the Badger out of His Nest*, hand-coloured etching, 22 March 1782, 250 mm × 358 mm (NPG D12982).

Plate 5 G.M. Woodward, *Reynard the Fox*, N.D., hand-coloured drawing, 285 mm × 224 mm (D5459/1/55).

Plate 6 G.M. Woodward, *The Black Man of the People* (reverse), N.D., *c.* 1784, hand-coloured drawing (D5459/1/36).

Plate 7 Isaac Cruikshank, *A Right Honourable alias A Sans Culotte*, hand-coloured etching, 20 December 1792, 375 mm × 323 mm (LWL 792.12.20.01.1+).

Plate 8 James Gillray, *Guy Vaux Discovered in His Attempt to Destroy the King and House of Lords – His Companions Attempting to Escape – NB – His Associates Were All Afterwards Executed*, hand-coloured etching, 14 May 1791, 354 mm × 500 mm (NPG D13072).

Plate 9 James Gillray, *The Republican Attack*, hand-coloured etching, 1 November 1795, 250 mm × 352 mm (NPG D12543).

Plate 10 James Gillray, *Jove in His Chair*, hand-coloured etching, 11 September 1782, 252 mm × 348 mm (NPG D12315).

Plate 11 James Gillray, *Aside He Turn'd for Envy, yet with Jealous Leer Maligne, Eyed Them Askance*, etching, 12 December 1782, 211 mm × 249 mm (NPG D12302).

Plate 12 James Gillray, *Ministerial Eloquence*, etching, 6 January 1795, 123 mm × 80 mm (NPG D12507).

Plate 13 James Gillray, '*Two Pair of Portraits: Presented to All the Unbiassed Electors of Great Britain*' by John Horne Tooke, etching, 1 December 1798, 208 mm × 275 mm (NPG D13687).

Plate 14 James Gillray, *Opposition Eloquence*, etching, 6 January 1795, 122 mm × 82 mm (NPG D12511).

Plate 15 James Gillray, *Westminster School or – Dr. Busby Settling Accounts with Master-Billy and His Playmates*, hand-coloured etching, 4 February 1785, 354 mm × 256 mm (NPG D12993).

Plate 16 Anon., *The Rival Quacks*, etching, 2 February 1784, 196 mm × 285 mm (LWL 784.02.02.02+).

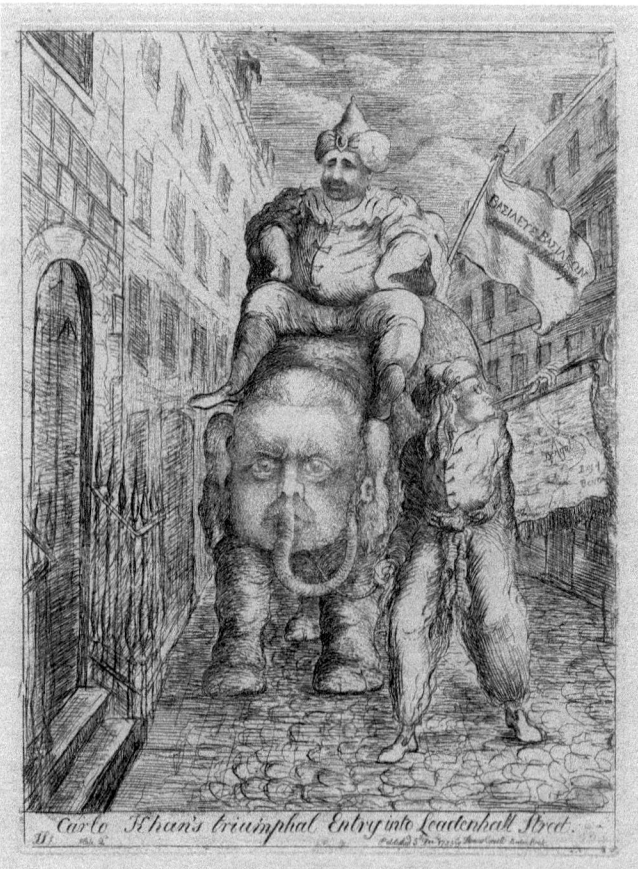

Plate 17 James Sayers, *Carlo Khan's Triumphal Entry into Leadenhall Street*, etching, 5 December 1783, 336 mm × 236 mm (NPG D16765).

Plate 18 Anon., *Carlo Khan Dethron'd or Billy's Triumph*, etching, 24 March 1784, 230 mm × 291 mm (LWL 784.03.24.01+).

Plate 19 Thomas Rowlandson, *Dark Lanthern Business, or, Mrs. Hob and Nob on a Night Canvass with a Bosom Friend*, etching, 24 April 1784, 270 mm × 340 mm (LWL 784.04.24.01+).

Plate 20 Anon., *The Devonshire Amusement*, hand-coloured etching, 5 May 1784, 310 mm × 410 mm (LWL 784.05.05.01+).

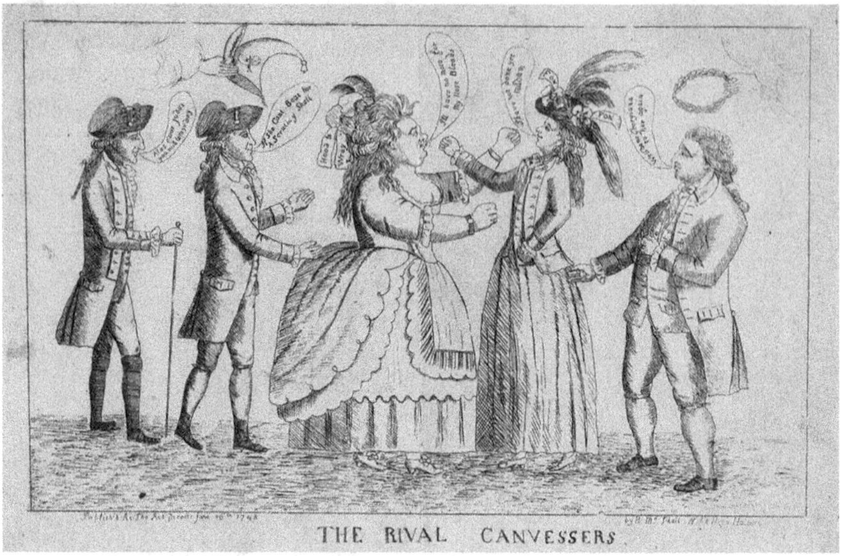

Plate 21 Anon., *The Rival Canvassers*, etching, 16 June 1784, 225 mm × 329 mm (LWL 784.06.16.02+).

Plate 22 Isaac Cruikshank, *Westminster Races*, etching, 19 May 1784, 215 mm × 352 mm (BM 6589).

In the drawing, text reads:

J.M.W. Delt.

A View of the Orkney Isles, with one of Mr. Fox's New Constituents

July 1784

Plate 23 G.M. Woodward, *A View of the Orkney Isles with One of Mr. Fo-x's New Constituents*, July 1784, hand-coloured drawing, 230 mm × 172 mm (D5459/1/14).

Plate 24 Anon., *The Scrutiny, or, Examination of the Filth*, etching, 24 April 1784, 187 mm × 260 mm (BM 6553).

Plate 25 James Gillray, *State-Jugglers*, hand-coloured etching, 16 May 1788, 349 mm × 248 mm (NPG D12381).

FARMER GEORGE'S WONDERFUL MONKEY

The Naturalist's of this Country is at a Loss how to give an Account of this Extraordinary Animal, therefore we may Suppose it to be an Offspring of the Devil's, & that he = Shit it Flying.

Pub'd by I Aitken Castle Street Leicester Fields, 1795

July 2d

Plate 26 William O'Keefe, *Farmer George's Wonderful Monkey*, hand-coloured etching, 2 July 1795, 343 mm × 240 mm (Yale B1981.25.1510).

Plate 27 James Gillray, *WIFE & No WIFE _ or _ A Trip to the Continent*, hand-coloured etching, 27 March 1786, 377 mm × 482 mm (NPG D13066).

Plate 28 James Gillray, *The Crown & Anchor Libel Burnt by the Public Hangman*, hand-coloured etching, 28 November 1795, 246 mm × 347 mm (NPG D12550).

Plate 29 James Gillray, *Doctor Sangrado Curing John Bull of Repletion – with the Kind Offices of Young Clysterpipe & Little Boney – with a Hint from Gil Blas*, hand-coloured etching, 2 May 1803, 257 mm × 360 mm (NPG D12807).

Plate 30 James Gillray, *Hanging: Drowning (The Fatal Effects of the French Defeat)*, hand-coloured etching, 9 November 1795, 247 mm × 347 mm (LWL 795.11.09.02+).

Plate 31 James Gillray, *The Tables Turn'd*, hand-coloured etching, 4 March 1797, 255 mm × 358 mm (Yale B1981.25.901).

Plate 32 James Gillray, *Doublûres of Characters; – or – Striking Resemblances in Physiognomy*, hand-coloured etching, 1 November 1798, 262 mm × 362 mm (NPG D12663).

Plate 33 James Gillray, *Shrine at St. Anne's Hill*, hand-coloured etching, 26 May 1798, 340 mm × 251 mm (B1981.25.898).

Plate 34 James Gillray, *Visiting the Sick*, hand-coloured etching, 28 July 1806, 263 mm × 363 mm (NPG D12871).

Plate 1 G.M. Woodward, *The Black Man of the People*, N.D. *c.* 1784, hand-coloured drawing, 198 mm × 160 mm (D5459/1/36).

Plate 2 James Gillray, *A Democrat or Reason & Philosophy*, hand-coloured etching, 1 March 1793, 346 mm × 248 mm (NPG D12472).

Plate 3 Anon., *Political Game of Shuttlecock or Fluctuation of Indian Stock*, hand-coloured etching, 3 February 1784, 230 mm × 340 mm (LWL 784.02.03.02+).

Plate 4 Anon., *The Political Shaver*, hand-coloured etching, 10 May 1784, 250 mm × 330 mm (LWL 784.05.10.01+).

Plate 5 Anon., *The Devonshire Method to Restore a Lost Member*, hand-coloured etching, 14 April 1784, 245 mm × 351 mm (LWL 784.04.14.01.1).

Plate 6 James Gillray, *The Bow to the Throne, – alias – the Begging Bow*, hand-coloured etching, 6th May, 1788, 221 mm × 282 mm (NPG D12378).

Plate 7 James Gillray, *The Funeral Procession of Miss Regency*, hand-coloured etching, 29 April 1789, 225 mm × 705 mm (NPG D13053).

Plate 8 Henry Kingsbury, *Dead, Positively Dead*, hand-coloured etching, 16 November 1788, 250 mm × 343 mm (LWL 788.11.16.01+).

Plate 9 Thomas Rowlandson, *Suitable Restrictions*, hand-coloured etching, 28 January 1789, 232 mm × 346 mm (LWL 789.01.28.01+).

Plate 10 James Gillray, *The Hopes of the Party, Prior to July 14th _ 'From Such Wicked Crown and Anchor-Dreams, Good Lord Deliver Us'*, hand-coloured etching, 19 July 1791, 359 mm × 507 mm (NPG D13074).

Plate 11 James Gillray, *Opening of the Budget – or John Bull Giving His Breeches to Save His Bacon*, hand-coloured etching, 17 November 1796, 263 mm × 369 mm (NPG D12583).

Plate 12 James Gillray, *Britannia between Death and the Doctor's*, hand-coloured etching, 20 May 1804, 254 mm × 378 mm (NPG D12830).

Plate 13 Isaac Cruikshank, *Billy a Cock-Horse or the Modern Colossus Amusing Himself*, hand-coloured etching, 8 March 1797, 278 mm × 235 mm (LWL 797.03.08.01).

The GIANT-FACTOTUM amusing himself.

Plate 14 James Gillray, *The Giant-Factotum Amusing Himself*, hand-coloured etching, 21 January 1797, 366 mm × 264 mm (NPG D12593).

Plate 15 James Gillray, *Evidence to Character; – Being a Portrait of a Traitor, by His Friends & by Himself*, hand-coloured etching, 1 October 1798, 193 mm × 261 mm (NPG D12674).

Plate 16 James Gillray, *Patriotic Regeneration, – viz. – Parliament Reform'd, a la Francoise, – that is – Honest Men (i.e.) – Opposition in the Seat of Justice. Vide Carmagnol Expectations*, hand-coloured etching and aquatint, 2 March 1795, 316 mm × 425 mm (NPG D12519).

www.ingramcontent.com/pod-product-compliance
Lightning Source LLC
Chambersburg PA
CBHW050420280326
41932CB00013BA/1936